THEATRE IN REVOLUTION
Russian Avant-Garde Stage Design
1913–1935

THEATRE IN REVOLUTION
Russian Avant-Garde Stage Design
1913–1935

Nancy Van Norman Baer

with contributions by

John E. Bowlt

Mel Gordon

Valerii Gubin

Simon Karlinsky

Mikhail Kolesnikov

Georgii Kovalenko

Nicoletta Misler

Steven A. Nash

Elizabeth Souritz

 Thames and Hudson

The Fine Arts Museums of San Francisco

Theatre in Revolution
Russian Avant-Garde Stage Design
1913–1935

The Fine Arts Museums of San Francisco
California Palace of the Legion of Honor
9 November 1991 through
16 February 1992

IBM Gallery of Science and Art
New York, New York
14 April 1992 through
13 June 1992

The Armand Hammer Museum of Art
and Cultural Center
Los Angeles, California
25 August 1992 through
2 November 1992

The exhibition is organized by The Fine
Arts Museums of San Francisco. The
majority of the works are graciously
lent by the Bakhrushin State Central
Theatrical Museum, Moscow.

Front cover:
Konstantin Vialov
Costume design for a Bandit
in *The Camorra of Seville* (detail),
1923, cat. no. 203

Frontispiece:
Alexandra Exter
Costume design for a man in an
unidentified production, 1920, cat. no. 69

Pages 3, 23, 175, 208:
Boris Erdman
Dance sketch for an unidentified
production, ca. 1923, cat. no. 35
Costume sketch for *Spanish Dances*,
cat. no. 40
Dance sketch for *Famira Kifared*,
cat. no. 33
Dance sketch for *Machine Dances*,
cat. no. 34

First published in Great Britain in 1991
by Thames and Hudson Ltd, London

Printed and bound in Hong Kong

Contents

Preface

With the cooperation of the Bakhrushin State Central Theatrical Museum in Moscow, The Fine Arts Museums of San Francisco is pleased to present the first major museum survey in America devoted exclusively to the Russian avant-garde theatre. *Theatre in Revolution: Russian Avant-Garde Stage Design 1913–1935* brings attention to the experimental and creative achievement of Russian theatre between the years 1913 and 1935, and to the visual artists who used the theatrical stage as a testing ground for the development of their innovative approaches to art. In the process they revolutionized existing concepts of scenic design and left a remarkable legacy that is only now appreciated in the context of twentieth-century modern art.

An exhibition of this scale, requiring the support of many institutions and individuals in the USSR, had its origins in the cultural agreement signed by the Soviet Union and the United States at the 1985 Geneva summit meeting that initiated an era of unprecedented cooperation between our two countries. The ensuing mutual enthusiasm for cultural sharing facilitated the unique Accord signed between The Fine Arts Museums and the Bakhrushin Museum in December 1989. Fostering an exchange of research and exhibitions over a five-year period, the Accord has made possible this impressive showing of Russian avant-garde stage designs, the majority of which have never been seen in the United States.

The achievement of this ambitious project involved many individuals, but above all we wish to acknowledge Nancy Van Norman Baer, Curator of the Museums' theatre and dance department, who organized both the exhibition and the catalogue. Through her exemplary dedication and scholarship, she has established The Fine Arts Museums as a forerunner in the field of interdisciplinary exhibitions with the success of *Pavlova!* in 1981, *Dance in Art* in 1983, *Bronislava Nijinska: A Dancer's Legacy* in 1986, and *The Art of Enchantment: Diaghilev's Ballets Russes* in 1989. We wish also to thank Steven A. Nash, Associate Director and Chief Curator at The Fine Arts Museums, who offered support for the idea of this exhibition from the beginning and who helped to negotiate the Accord that made it possible. We are also deeply indebted to John E. Bowlt, consulting curator for the project and noted authority on the Russian avant-garde, who generously lent his expertise to this endeavor.

We are most grateful to our fellow professionals at the Bakhrushin

Museum, in particular Valerii Gubin, Director, whose cooperation and generosity enabled the unprecedented loan of objects from the Bakhrushin Museum's extraordinary collection. We also owe much gratitude to the other institutions and individuals in the Soviet Union who generously lent us works of art, including the State Tretiakov Gallery, Moscow; the Leningrad State Museum of Theatrical and Musical Arts; the State Museum of Theatre, Music, and Film Art of the Ukraine, Kiev; the Central State Archive of Literature and Art (TsGALI), Moscow; the Central Cinema Museum, Moscow; the Rodchenko-Stepanova Archives, Moscow; and Igor Dychenko, Natalia Galadzheva, the Kasian Goleizovsky family, Alexander Lavrentiev, Anatolii A. Petritsky, Dmitrii Sarabianov, and Brigitta Vetrova.

Generous support for the exhibition has been provided by grants from the National Endowment for the Arts, a Federal agency; the Trust for Mutual Understanding; The Golden Grain Company; and Louisa Stude Sarofim. We deeply appreciate their assistance and encouragement.

We are pleased to be able to share this exhibition with two participating institutions, the IBM Gallery of Science and Art in New York and The Armand Hammer Museum of Art and Cultural Center in Los Angeles. Their recognition of the show's significance will enable visitors from coast to coast to recognize the remarkable achievement of the avant-garde theatre in Russia and its influence on twentieth-century modern art.

The expected next step in the Accord between The Fine Arts Museums of San Francisco and the Bakhrushin State Central Theatrical Museum will be a reciprocal exhibition drawn from the holdings of the Alma de Bretteville Spreckels collection of theatre and dance material. We are hopeful that these first two exhibitions will lead to a lasting and ongoing exchange of research and scholarship between our two countries and museums.

Harry S. Parker III
Director of Museums
The Fine Arts Museums of San Francisco

Acknowledgments

An exhibition is a collaborative endeavor that depends on the cooperation and interaction of many individuals. I would first like to convey my gratitude to John E. Bowlt, consulting curator, who originally suggested that we undertake this project and who has provided ongoing support and advice. I also wish to thank the Bakhrushin State Central Theatrical Museum, Moscow, and Valerii Gubin, Director, for having made available their remarkable collection of Russian avant-garde stage design for research and exhibition. I am most grateful to Mr. Gubin and my colleagues at the Bakhrushin Museum, in particular Tatiana Klim, Deputy Director for Academic Affairs; Galina Daruze, Head of Exhibitions Department; Mikhail Kolesnikov, Senior Curator; and Nina Vydrina, Chief Curator. Their sustained commitment to the project and their professionalism have been essential to its success, and the opportunity to work with them has given me great personal pleasure.

Support of the exhibition and recognition of its significance have been gratifying and I would like to express my thanks for major grants from the National Endowment for the Arts, a Federal agency; the Trust for Mutual Understanding; The Golden Grain Company; and Louisa Stude Sarofim. I would also like to thank the following participating museums who have shared the organizational responsibility of the show: Early enthusiasm for the exhibition on the part of Richard Berglund, Director of Cultural Programs, IBM Corporation, and Robert Murdock, Program Director, IBM Gallery of Science and Art, New York, gave me added resolve, as did the encouragement of Alla T. Hall, Director of Fine Arts, The Armand Hammer Museum of Art and Cultural Center, Los Angeles.

Among the catalogue authors, I particularly wish to thank Simon Karlinsky for his ready and detailed answers to all inquiries, and I extend my appreciation and admiration to John E. Bowlt, Mel Gordon, Valerii Gubin, Mikhail Kolesnikov, Georgii Kovalenko, Nicoletta Misler, Steven A. Nash, and Elizabeth Souritz. Enormous appreciation is due my colleagues who assisted in the production of the catalogue, in particular Desne Border, who created the outstanding design; Elena Bridgman, who translated the Soviet essays and manifestos and provided invaluable personal insights; Derrick Cartwright, who indexed the book; and Ann Karlstrom, Director of Publications, and Karen Kevorkian, Editor, The Fine Arts Museums of San Francisco. Ms. Kevorkian deserves special thanks for many helpful suggestions that made this book more complete, and for her skilled editing and synthesis of diverse manuscript material.

I am extremely grateful to members of the staff of The Fine Arts Museums of San Francisco for their effort and professionalism in realizing this project. Deep appreciation is extended to Harry S. Parker III, Director, and Steven A. Nash, Associate Director and Chief Curator, who have given their wholehearted support to the show and lent invaluable expertise to the surrounding diplomatic negotiations. Debra Pughe, Exhibitions Support Department Manager, and William White, Chief Technician and Exhibition Designer, also assumed crucial roles in the organization and presentation of the exhibition. Of course a show of this scale requires the support of the entire museum staff, to whom I am infinitely grateful. I would particularly like to call attention to the efforts of the many responsible for the exhibition's graphic design, lighting design, and installation, as well as to the departments of development, education, information services, interpretation, public information, public programs, registration, and *Triptych*. I also wish to express my appreciation to the board of trustees, especially Alexandra Phillips, President of the Board, and to the Docent Council and the Volunteer Council of the Museums.

A number of others were also helpful in advancing the cause of this exhibition and I especially wish to thank Norma Schlesinger for her research assistance and ongoing moral support, and Lynn Garafola for having shared thoughts, ideas, and research materials. My deep appreciation is extended to Valentin Kamenev, former Consul General, and Gennady Zolotov, Deputy Consul General, the Union of Soviet Socialist Republics, San Francisco. I also wish to acknowledge Stella Ogonkova Duff, William Eddelman, Doug Engmann, Dorothy Globus, Steven A. Jones, Susan Katz, Edith Kramer, Richard Lanier, Martin Muller, Tjasa Owen, Irina Nijinska Raetz, Steve Seid, Stephen Steinberg, Helgi Tomasson, Rouben Ter-Arutunian, Andrew Wachtel, Julie Wolfe, and Stephanie Zimmerman as well as the Cooper-Hewitt Museum, the Smithsonian Institution's National Museum of Design, New York; the Department of Dramatic Art, University of California, Berkeley; the Institute of Modern Russian Culture, Los Angeles; Modernism Gallery, San Francisco; Pacific Film Archives, University Art Museum, Berkeley; and the Performing Arts Library and Museum, San Francisco.

The effort to organize an exhibition of this complexity and scale requires the continuous support of a confidant and I extend my heartfelt thanks to Alan Baer. Lastly, I wish to dedicate this catalogue to the memory of my mother, Grace Ann Hamill Van Norman, and to my father, Allen Van Norman.

NVNB

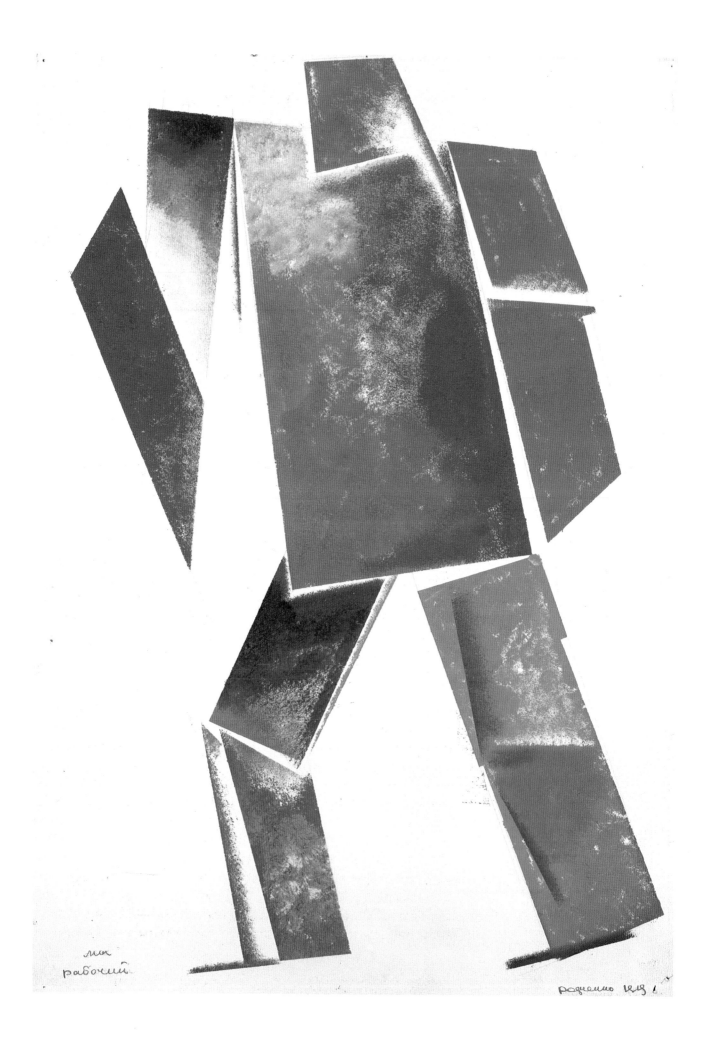

лик
рабочий

родченко 1913 г.

Introduction to Alexei Bakhrushin and His Theatrical Museum

On Lenin Square in Moscow, near Paveletsky railroad station, stands a modest-sized mansion, whose pointed roof and elaborate red-and-white exterior could be a stage set for a fairy tale. It is the house of Alexei Alexandrovich Bakhrushin (1865–1929), a place sacred to all who love the theatre. "It is an old adage that an actor's fame is smoke," wrote the great Russian actress Maria Yermolova to Bakhrushin at the end of the previous century. "Yet you, through will and energy, accomplished a great feat: you immortalized the actor. . . . I bow to you deeply for your great deed."* The Bakhrushin house is permeated with mystery and the slightly melancholy air of the theatre of yesterday. The atmosphere suggests long-departed conjurers of the stage, scenes from glorious plays, and the voices and music of bygone performances. The museum is a repository of all the genres and varieties of the art of the stage from its inception to this day.

Bakhrushin was born into a family of Moscow merchants and manufacturers. By means of hard labor, commercial shrewdness, the mechanization of production, and the efficient organization of labor at their factories, they rapidly built a fortune and became one of Moscow's wealthiest families and leading citizens. In the last century they excited the old capital with their largesse: They built a free hospital, a shelter for the terminally ill, an orphanage, rent-free lodging for indigent widows, housing for female students, a shelter for homeless children, a building for popular education courses, and a shelter for aged actors, for whom they also established pensions. Numerous members of the Bakhrushin family were attracted to the arts. Bakhrushin's uncle, Alexei Petrovich Bakhrushin, bequeathed his collection of old prints and rare books to the Rumiantsev Museum in Moscow.

Alexei Alexandrovich Bakhrushin (fig. 1) owned tanneries, woolen mills, country estates, and real estate. From morning until afternoon he energetically managed his financial and industrial affairs, and the rest of the time he devoted to his beloved theatre as an organizer, patron, historian, and educator. Because of his enthusiasm and dedication, Bakhrushin soon joined the ranks of those Muscovite merchants who contributed enormously to the development of Russian culture such as the brothers Tretiakov, who founded the State Tretiakov Gallery,

Cat. no. 152

Alexander Rodchenko

Costume for a Worker, *We*, 1920

*All quotations are taken from the personal papers of Alexei Bakhrushin in the archives of the Bakhrushin State Central Theatrical Museum.

Fig. 1
Alexei Alexandrovich Bakhrushin

Konstantin Stanislavsky, who founded the Moscow Art Theatre, Savva Morozov, who founded the People's House Theatre in Tver and was the financial supporter of the Moscow Art Theatre, and Savva Mamontov, founder of the Abramtsevo workshop and the Moscow Private Opera.

Prompted by his passion for the theatre, Bakhrushin began to collect souvenirs of the stage. "Sukhariovka [the old Moscow flea-market] was the main source of supply," he recalled. "There, theatrical memorabilia was regarded as rubbish. I remember my first purchase—twenty-two dirty, dusty portraits, for which, as it turned out, serf actors of Count Sheremetiev's theatre had posed. I paid fifty rubles for the whole lot." Later, having developed an impressive instinct for theatrical arts and a solid knowledge of theatrical history, Bakhrushin determined that those portraits were actually preliminary costume sketches executed by Marianne Kürtsinger, a costume designer with the Paris Opera, which was later confirmed by one of Count Sheremetiev's descendants.

Bakhrushin procured objects and works of art from artists, antiquarians, second-hand book dealers, collectors, and actors—sketches and maquettes of stage sets, costumes, ballet shoes, annotated texts of plays, correspondence by persons associated with the theatre, state mementos, props, directors' outlines of productions, theatrical literature, portraits and sculptures of artists, playwrights, and composers, and anything that could serve as a record of a play or an actor's performance. Gradually Bakhrushin accumulated a large and interesting collection.

Many viewed Bakhrushin's preoccupation with the theatre as peculiar. Museum sections may have existed at certain well-known theatres, and displays of theatre-related objects may have begun to appear at international exhibitions, but a single museum of theatrical art was unique, and, at the same time, an unlikely possibility. Nasty witticisms at the expense of the collector appeared in the newspapers, with malicious references to Bakhrushin's collection of "stockings, shoes, and snuffboxes." It was claimed that the eccentric moneybags exhibited a button from the actor Mochalov's trousers, the actor Shchepkin's suspenders, a burned match of the actor Yuriev, and a dried core from an apple eaten by the singer Feodor Chaliapin.

On 11 June 1894 Bakhrushin for the first time allowed his collection of theatrical arts to be viewed by friends and acquaintances. But he always regarded 29 October 1894, which was a typically damp, cold autumn day, as the actual date of the museum's opening, when anyone interested could view its first exhibition. On that day a large, curious crowd of actors, literati, teachers, students, common folk, and passersby gathered at his house. And the twenty-nine-year-old owner, squinting behind a *pince-nez*, bearded, tall, and lean—a Chekhovian character—invited his first visitors into the museum. "Posterity will value this collection highly and with gratitude," was one of the first inscriptions in the guest book, made by Ivan Gorbunov, a well-known actor of the Alexandrinsky Theatre in St. Petersburg, who was also a writer and theatrical historian.

In Moscow's Zatsep district, on Luzhnikovskaya Street, Bakhrushin later purchased the orchards of the former mayor Koroliov. There in 1896 he built an estate, reserving space for a museum alongside the living quarters; this is the building we now know as the Bakhrushin Museum

(fig. 2). Visitors referred to Bakhrushin's house as a "palace of theatrical arts," whose lavishly decorated interior integrated Russian modernist style, gothic motifs, and Empire neoclassicism. Bakhrushin's house, according to a 1903 account in the influential *St. Petersburg Gazette*, quickly became a vital theatrical and artistic center in Moscow.

Everyone who mattered in Moscow's theatrical world gathered at the famous artistic Saturdays at Bakhrushin's. "It was the day," reminisced Yurii Bakhrushin, Alexei's son,

> when we kept an open table for anyone in the arts. Both the invited and the uninvited came, acquaintances and strangers. The Saturdays began at about 10 p.m., and guests then wandered through the museum or simply chatted. At 2 a.m. a simple home-style supper was served, after which guests often improvised theatrical performances, wrote and drew in the family album. . . . The artistic worlds of Moscow and St. Petersburg flashed in kaleidoscopic fashion through our Saturday evenings and Sunday breakfasts in the winter, and in the spring, at Lent, a mighty wave rolled in from the provinces. . . .

To expand the collection, Bakhrushin traveled many times around the country and several times to Europe. In Italy he found materials related to the history of the commedia dell'arte and from France he carried home a selection of French theatrical memorabilia. In Moscow, especially, he strove to cultivate friendly relations with eminent theatrical figures.

All his life he revered the talent of the actress Yermolova. For her thirtieth stage jubilee Bakhrushin published an album, presenting the actress with the first copy. It is said that when Bakhrushin learned, in the middle of his wedding, that her benefit performance was occurring at the same time at the Maly Theatre, he quickly looked around and chose a beautiful bouquet for hand delivery to Yermolova. To the consternation of his bride, Vera, the bouquet turned out to be the same one the groom had just presented to her. Yermolova repaid Bakhrushin by highly valuing his museum, giving him documents from her archives throughout her career.

Legends circulated about Bakhrushin's enterprising spirit. When the actor Alexander Lensky of the Maly Theatre, who was famous for his transformations onstage, died in 1908, Bakhrushin headed for the theatre and sealed the artist's dressing room. The next day, having secured the relatives' permission, he requisitioned all of the actor's possessions for his museum. Bakhrushin had anticipated finding elaborate aids to disguise and a quantity of makeup, for Lensky had been unrecognizable in his roles. However he found nothing more than burned cork, mascara, and rouge in the actor's makeup case. Thus the Bakhrushin collection often helped not only to document theatrical activity but also made it possible to understand, to some degree, the mundane concerns underlying creativity.

At times Bakhrushin resorted to well-intentioned guile. When the famous Russian actress Glikeria Fedotova visited the museum after her retirement, she found herself in front of a display dedicated to the founder of Russian stage realism Mikhail Shchepkin, where she remained for an especially long time. And Bakhrushin, who quietly followed at a distance, noticed her tears. Bakhrushin always kept an empty display case for such occasions. Having beforehand placed in it a couple of programs from Fedotova's performances, he said, "And this part of the exhibition I wanted to dedicate to you, but there is such a dearth of materials, an extreme scarcity, completely at odds with your enormous contribution to Russia's theatrical arts." According to Yurii Bakhrushin, "Such maneuvers invariably met with success. They appealed to the visitor's artistic vanity, and soon a valuable and generous donation of memorabilia followed."

At the end of the nineteenth century, Bakhrushin came to the decision that the museum needed to be made public. Offered as a gift to Moscow, a city he had always deeply loved, the museum was refused by the city fathers. However, in the end Bakhrushin's wish was fulfilled because Vladimir Ryshkov, the secretary of the Russian language and philology section of the Russian Academy of Sciences in St. Petersburg, was a great supporter of the museum. So, too, was Grand Duke Konstantin Konstantinovich Romanov, an educated and influential member of the czar's family and the president of the Russian Academy of Sciences, who was a poet.

The museum was transferred to the state in the care of the Academy of Sciences on 25 November 1913. Attending the transfer ceremony were famous academicians and luminaries of the theatre, including Fedotova, Yermolova, Alexander Yuzhin, Alexandra Yablochkina, Stanislavsky, Grand Duke Konstantin, Vladimir Nemirovich-Danchenko, and the great writer Ivan Bunin. Thus the world's first theatrical museum became established in Moscow, a precursor of musical and theatrical museums of our time and the mainspring of the present Bakhrushin Museum.

When it was suggested that the collection be moved to St. Petersburg, the home of the Academy of Sciences, Bakhrushin insisted that it remain in Moscow, as a Moscow affiliate of the Academy. According to Yurii Bakhrushin, Czar Nicholas II extended a special

Cat. no. 154
Alexander Rodchenko
Costume design for a Clown, *We*, 1920

invitation to Bakhrushin for an audience at Tsarskoe Selo (now the town of Pushkin), his summer residence, in order to thank him for his generous gift to the state. The czar presented the art patron with the medal of the order of St. Vladimir, IV Degree, which elevated its holder into the nobility.

In 1917, the great October Revolution abolished capitalism, private property, and the old order. Unlike many wealthy Russians, Bakhrushin did not flee the country. As the first Commissar of Enlightenment Anatolii Lunacharsky recalled, Bakhrushin remained in his museum, having been awarded a salary of forty-three rubles a month, becoming a sincere supporter of the new educational effort. Although he was just over fifty years old, in the new republic he was known as "the grandfather of the theatre" and as "a most lovable figure"; he was invited to take part in the activities of the theatre department of Narkompros (the People's Commissariat for Enlightenment), where he headed the theatrical history section.

Bakhrushin continued his work on the board of directors of the Russian Theatrical Society, headed the theatrical history subsection at the State Academy of Arts and Sciences, and was elected an honorary member of that academy. Lunacharsky wrote:

> There was not one theatrical event in which Alexei Alexandrovich [Bakhrushin] did not take part. We saw him, with a face full of joy, at jubilee celebrations of various theatres, at festivities occasioned by high awards bestowed on this or that actor, at premieres; and in wishing to congratulate those who were the cause of the celebrations one also wanted to congratulate [him], for it was always his celebration. He almost seemed to be the soul of the theatre, which he loved so deeply and served so devoutly.

Lunacharsky informed Lenin about Bakhrushin's work, and by Lenin's decree the Moscow Theatrical Museum was named after its founder in 1919 and Bakhrushin appointed its director.

Five years later, in 1924, at the very beginning of the "witch hunt" and by the demand of the workers of the factory the Red Spindle, the Zamoskvorechie Control Commission found Bakhrushin to be "a class enemy of the worst kind" and decreed that the museum did not justify "its purpose of serving the industry" (minutes of the commission, 24 November 1924). Consequently, three-quarters of the Bakhrushin Museum's property was appropriated by Mussovet (the Moscow city council) and relegated for other organizations' needs. That the museum survived many other attacks was due only to continued vigilance by important cultural figures.

In 1927 Bakhrushin opened the exhibition *Theatres of the October Decade*, which was a major success and the happiest event of the revolutionary years for him. With this exhibition, Bakhrushin documented the Russian stage experiments that were to amaze the world and that later became known as the Russian theatrical avant-garde (see, for example, cat. nos. 100, 109, 154).

The Bakhrushin State Central Theatrical Museum is today one of the largest educational institutions in the Soviet Union and one of the

Cat. no. 100
Alexander Khostenko-Khostov
Curtain design, *Mystery-Bouffe*,
1921

most valuable and famous theatrical collections in the world. The museum presents large-scale exhibitions both in Moscow and other cities of the Soviet Union, and regularly shows aspects of its collection abroad. Several museum affiliates in and around Moscow are adjuncts of the Bakhrushin, including those dedicated to Yermolova, the playwright Alexander Ostrovsky, Shchepkin, and the Theatrical Salon on Tverskaya Boulevard. Work is ongoing to establish a museum dedicated to Vsevolod Meyerhold.

In the good tradition of the Bakhrushin Saturdays, the museum's special subsection for educational work gears programs toward visitors of all interests. The museum continues to study theatrical history and contemporary stage processes and researches and adds to the museum's collection, mounting exhibitions, publishing, and holding conferences. The Bakhrushin Museum holdings total 1.5 million objects.

We are very pleased to introduce American art lovers to a small part of our museum's theatrical and artistic collection. *Theatre in Revolution: Russian Avant-Garde Stage Design 1913–1935* will cover a brief yet extraordinarily interesting period in our theatrical history that is related to the search for new stage imagery and artistic integrity. Introducing the viewer to one of the remarkable epochs in the worldwide evolution of the stage, the exhibition reminds one of the enormous spiritual legacy of the theatre, and of the mutual influence and enrichment of theatrical cultures worldwide.

The exhibition allows a glimpse of the Bakhrushin Museum, of its unique collection that immortalizes the ever-changing course of theatrical art. We have been very pleased to work with our American colleagues from The Fine Arts Museums of San Francisco, and thank them for their cooperation and hospitality. The Bakhrushin Museum sends its greetings to the American public and hopes that our collection will be of interest and that the exchange of exhibitions with The Fine Arts Museums will prove a testament to the friendship between our peoples.

Valerii Gubin
Director
Bakhrushin State Central Theatrical Museum
Moscow

THEATRE IN REVOLUTION
Russian Avant-Garde Stage Design
1913–1935

The Early Twentieth-Century Cultural Revival and the Russian Merchant Class

Simon Karlinsky

One of the most widespread themes in Russian drama and fiction of the nineteenth century was the backwardness, dishonesty, and rapacity of the country's merchant class. From the comedies of Nikolai Gogol (1809–1852) (cat. nos. 80, 147, 148), through the numerous and hugely successful melodramas by Alexander Ostrovsky (1823–1886) (cat. nos. 186–188) and to the now-forgotten novels by Pyotr Boborykin (1836–1921), it was traditional to paint the families of wealthy merchants and industrialists in the grimmest possible colors.[1] Their business practices were depicted as shoddy and often criminal, their employees were oppressed and exploited, and their sweet, innocent daughters were invariably forced into distasteful marriages with ugly, elderly millionaires.

Such a view of the representatives of the nascent Russian capitalism was fostered and at times demanded by the critics of the radical-utilitarian school, which dominated Russian literature from the 1860s to the end of the nineteenth century. Only Anton Chekhov (who personally knew several wealthy merchant and industrialist families), with his unique freedom from the popular stereotypes of his time, depicted members of this class as full-blooded and appealing men and women in his novellas *Three Years* and *A Woman's Kingdom* and in the character of Yermolai Lopakhin in *The Cherry Orchard*.

But even at the beginning of the twentieth century, when the fact of the wealthy merchants' support for new art museums and path-breaking art journals could no longer be ignored, we find these activities still satirized and ridiculed in such popular plays of the period as *The Price of Life* by Vladimir Nemirovich-Danchenko (one of the two founders of the Moscow Art Theatre), and Alexander Sumbatov-Yuzhin's comedy with the English title *[The] Gentleman*. Both plays portrayed in sarcastic terms various members of the Morozov family, Moscow manufacturers who, in addition to their support of liberal publications and the arts, were widely noted for their lavish philanthropy, organization of women's colleges, a free school for Moscow factory workers (the Prechistenka Evening School), and their endowment of important libraries.

With the coming of the October Revolution of 1917, the earlier financial support of educational and cultural projects by wealthy manufacturers and industrialists (by now known as capitalists, their names preceded by some compulsory adjective such as "rapacious" or "exploitative") was no longer mentioned by cultural historians. Another subject that became taboo was the often lavish subventions given by the

Cat. no. 80
Filonov School, Rebekka Leviton
Set design for act 3,
The Inspector General, 1927

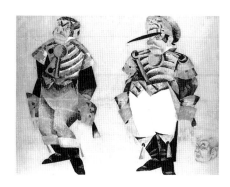

Cat. no. 147
Isaak Rabinovich
Costume designs for the Police Chief
and a Policeman, *The Inspector General*,
1920

Cat. no. 148
Isaak Rabinovich
Costume design for the Mayor,
The Inspector General, 1920

opposite:
Cat. no. 186
Vladimir Tatlin
Costume design for Drunken Klushin,
A Comic Actor of the 17th Century, 1935

merchant millionaires in prerevolutionary times to various underground revolutionary movements, including the Bolsheviks. (Savva Morozov, a major financial backer of the Moscow Art Theatre, donated millions to the revolutionary cause and committed suicide after the defeat of the 1905 Revolution.)

In more recent times, these Russian equivalents of the Carnegies, the Fricks, and the Guggenheims have been brought back from oblivion by books on art history written in the United States, such as Susan Massie's *Land of the Firebird: The Beauty of Old Russia*[2] and, especially, Beverly Whitney Kean's *All the Empty Palaces: The Merchant Patrons of Modern Art in Pre-Revolutionary Russia.*[3] Massie pays tribute to, among others, the railroad magnate Savva Mamontov, the founder of two privately financed opera houses in Moscow, which, beginning in 1888, staged dozens of previously neglected Russian operas, as well as the world premieres of Modest Mussorgsky's *Khovanshchina* and Nikolai Rimsky-Korsakov's *Sadko* and *The Golden Cockerel.* At the time when the Imperial Theatres relied on unimaginative professionals for the visual aspect of their productions, Mamontov invited the most innovative painters of his day, such as Viktor Vasnetsov, Mikhail Vrubel, and Konstantin Korovin, to design his opera sets. It was the same Savva Mamontov who at the turn of the century was one of the two principal backers of Serge Diaghilev's epochal journal *The World of Art* (Mir iskusstva).

Beverly Whitney Kean's book reminds the readers of Pavel Tretiakov (1832–1898), the art collector and the founder of the Moscow museum that today bears his name and is the greatest repository of Russian art in the world; of Konstantin Alekseyev, the heir to a textile fortune, who changed his name to Stanislavsky, founded the Moscow Art Theatre, and became the world-famous stage director and actor; and of the art collector Nikolai Riabushinsky, whose art journal *The Golden Fleece* (Zolotoe runo) proved a worthy successor to Diaghilev's *The World of Art.*[4] But the most fascinating passages of the book concentrate on the mercantile dynasties of the Morozovs and the Shchukins, whose scions at the beginning of this century were among the very first to appreciate Paul Cézanne, Henri Matisse, and Pablo Picasso, acquiring substantial collections of their art. These collections, made accessible to the general public and to the art community, helped promote the development of modernism in Russian painting a number of years earlier than, for example, the famed Armory Show in New York in 1913 made its splash in the artistic life of America.[5]

The activities of the Mamontov, Morozov, and Shchukin clans in the early twentieth century continued a tradition, going back to the 1850s, of an endless series of endowments by Moscow's merchant and industrialist families of cultural, medical, and educational projects.[6] Among the families most active in these areas were the Bakhrushins. The family originated from the town of Zaraisk in the Riasan province, where their record in the historical chronicles goes back to the seventeenth century. The earliest Bakhrushins were drovers, bringing large herds of cattle from the Volga region to the cities of central Russia. The high mortality of the animals during those treks led the Bakhrushins to take up leather manufacture.

Пьяный
Калужин

Мхати II
„Космак 17 сп"

Тр

Cat. no. 187
Vladimir Tatlin
Costume design for the Devil,
A Comic Actor of the 17th Century, 1935

Cat. no. 188
Vladimir Tatlin
Costume design for Yakov at Home,
A Comic Actor of the 17th Century, 1935

The Moscow branch of the family, headed by Alexei Feodorovich Bakhrushin (1800–1848), moved there from Zaraisk in the 1830s. Among their leatherware, kid gloves were particularly noted for their quality. In Moscow, the Bakhrushins entered into textile manufacture in addition to leather, and the family became enormously rich when appointed government suppliers during the Crimean War of 1855. As the chronicler of the cultural and philanthropic contributions of the Moscow merchants put it, "In their blood, the Bakhrushins had two passions: for charity and for amassing collections."[7] For much of the nineteenth century, the family was nicknamed "the professional philanthropists." At the end of each year, a family gathering would decide what portion of their joint income to earmark for good deeds.

Valerii Gubin's essay in this volume notes the schools, hospitals, orphanages, and retirement homes that were built by the Bakhrushin family in Moscow and maintained at the family's expense. In their native town of Zaraisk, the Bakhrushins also supported a retirement home bearing their name. Among the collections amassed by the Bakhrushins is the museum of theatrical memorabilia, also discussed by Gubin, founded by a member of the third generation of the family since the time of their move to Moscow, Alexei Alexandrovich Bakhrushin (1865–1929).

Alexei Bakhrushin first opened his private theatrical collection to the public in 1894. In 1896 he built a mansion, a portion of which, opened to the general public, housed his collection. In 1913 he donated his theatrical museum to the Academy of Sciences, an arrangement that was allowed to continue after the October Revolution. Nicholas II offered to ennoble Alexei Bakhrushin after his 1913 donation, but, as had several earlier Bakhrushins, he chose to maintain his merchant status, though he did accept the rank of a general from the monarch. Among the other Bakhrushins noted for amassing collections were Alexei's younger brother, the noted balletomane Sergei Bakhrushin, who acquired a number of canvases by Mikhail Vrubel at the time when that visionary painter was treated as a madman by much of the Russian press; and their first cousin, Alexei Petrovich Bakhrushin, whose collection of early Russian books was inherited by the Rumiantsev Museum and whose porcelain and other antiques occupied two rooms at Moscow's Historical Museum.

Alexei Bakhrushin put his museum on display just when the Russian theatre and other arts began to turn from the conventional realism of the late nineteenth century to symbolism and other modernist trends that were identified with the turn of the century. Impressionism in painting and symbolism in poetry were already in place in Russia by the mid-1890s. In 1898, two pivotal institutions appeared that gave these developments an entirely new momentum, the Moscow Art Theatre founded by Stanislavsky and Vladimir Nemirovich-Danchenko, and the influential literary and art journal *The World of Art*, created by Serge Diaghilev and his associates in the cultural movement that bore the same name as their journal. Both of these undertakings were financed, as mentioned, by private merchant funds.

Associated in its later stages with a drab socialist realism and the "method" school of acting, the Moscow Art Theatre was highly innovative and experimental during the first decade of its existence. Stanislavsky and Nemirovich-Danchenko pioneered, for the first time in Russia, the concept of a play production whose every aspect—the visual, musical, and dramatic—were under the control of one director who assumed the functions of an *auteur*, as the term is understood in later film theory. This conception of a production as a Wagnerian *Gesamtkunstwerk* was later taken over by Diaghilev in the ballet company he brought to western Europe at the end of the first decade of the twentieth century.

In addition to influences from abroad, the native sources of twentieth-century modernism in Russia included, as indicated, the journal *The World of Art*, which from its first issue challenged the supremacy of radical-utilitarian criticism with its never-ceasing demand for social relevance and photographic realism. Other sources were the eclectic early years of the Moscow Art Theatre with its famed atmospheric stagings of Chekhov's plays, symbolist dramas by Maurice Maeterlinck, and pseudosymbolist ones by Leonid Andreyev, and the artists' colony in the village of Abramtsevo, organized by Mamontov, where Russian folklore traditions were combined with art-nouveau stylizations. A new age in modernist experimentation in all artistic spheres came in the wake of the 1905 Revolution, when the moralistic and nationalistic imperial censorship was virtually abolished and the utilitarian-realistic counter-censorship in the press lost its power and influence. In literature, visual arts, theatre, and music, the modernist developments followed individual trajectories. In each sphere there were new trends and movements that challenged the styles and artistic credos of earlier groups. But in retrospect, at the distance of almost a century, it can be seen that each succeeding movement not only turned against its immediate predecessors, but also learned from them and built on their achievements. Thus, in poetry and drama, the succession of literary generations was shortened to less than a decade. The poet-playwrights of the 1890s, who brought back fantasy, mysticism, and the art of writing good and innovative verse (all banned by the utilitarians of the preceding half-century), were joined after 1905 by a new symbolist generation, oriented toward the plurality

Cat. no. 42

Alexandra Exter

Poster design for *Famira Kifared*, 1916

opposite:

Cat. no. 45

Alexandra Exter

Costume design for a Bacchante,

Famira Kifared, 1916

of worlds and a transcendental transformation of our reality.

Around 1910, symbolism in literature was attacked by new movements of the time: acmeism (more earthy and realistic successors of symbolism), futurism, and the modernist peasant-poets. In art, the aestheticism of the World of Art painters (Alexandre Benois, Konstantin Somov, and Léon Bakst) was rejected by younger painters of a neo-primitivist or abstract bent (Marc Chagall, Mikhail Larionov, Natalia Goncharova, and Vasilii Kandinsky, among so many others) early in the second decade of this century. As Valentine Marcadé's well-documented survey shows, the modernist trends and developments that continued undisturbed until ca. 1925 had all been fully formed by 1912.[8]

When Alexei Bakhrushin began to amass exhibits for his theatrical museum in the 1890s, Russian theatre could boast of celebrated actors, opera singers, and ballet dancers. But no particular drama or opera or ballet production cried out to be documented in its totality. With the appearance of Stanislavsky's more experimental stagings (such as his *Hamlet* [1911], with sets and costumes done entirely in gold, designed and co-directed by Edward Gordon Craig) and of those of his imaginative successor-directors Vsevolod Meyerhold, Alexander Tairov, and Evgenii Vakhtangov early in the second decade of the twentieth century, as well as the ballet productions of Diaghilev's company during approximately the same years, the Bakhrushin Museum had much more to document than the careers of individual actresses or singers.

The years from 1908 on were a time of unexampled freedom, diversity, and brilliance in Russian theatre and all the other arts. The levels of dynamism, inventiveness, and innovation attained were unprecedented in Russia and could stand comparison with anything then happening in the West.[9] The various rival trends not only clashed with one another, but could also on occasion collaborate. A striking example of this is Tairov's 1916 presentation of *Famira Kifared* by the poet of the senior generation of Russian symbolism, Innokentii Annensky (cat. nos. 42, 44, 45). The play amalgamates features of seventeenth-century French neoclassical tragedy with those of an ancient Greek bacchic drama and a modernist fin-de-siècle sensibility. The play makes one think of the Franco-Russian, herb-scented, art-nouveau ancient Greece of Diaghilev's productions of Claude Debussy's *Afternoon of a Faun* and Ravel's *Daphnis and Chloë*. Yet it was not one of the World of Art painters that Tairov chose as designer, but the abstractionist-constructivist Alexandra Exter, whose sets and costumes must have clashed with Annensky's text. But the resulting combination was a triumph.

The period between 1908 and ca. 1925 saw the mass emergence of talented, creative women in many branches of Russian artistic life: Zinaida Gippius, Anna Akhmatova, Elena Guro, Marina Tsvetaeva, and so many others in literature; Bronislava Nijinska in choreography; and Goncharova, Exter, Liubov Popova, Varvara Stepanova, Olga Rozanova, Nadezhda Udaltsova, and numerous others in painting and stage design.[10] The production style devised by Meyerhold and Tairov and later called *constructivist* suited the talents of such artists as Exter, Popova, and Stepanova. Like a number of their male colleagues, however, some of the most important women writers and artists (Gippius, Tsvetaeva, Goncharova, and Exter, for example) chose to

Cat. no. 44
Alexandra Exter
Frieze composition, *Famira Kifared*
(detail), 1916

emigrate to the West in the 1920s because of the lack of personal and artistic freedom under the Bolshevik regime.

Though allowed to continue into the early 1930s, the manifestations of the creative prerevolutionary modernism were eventually declared decadent and were extinguished in the Soviet Union. Among its leading exponents in the postrevolutionary period, Meyerhold was arrested and died under torture, and Tairov had his Kamerny (i.e., Chamber) Theatre taken away from him and renamed the Pushkin Theatre. (Since *perestroika* began, a plaque honoring Tairov and his actress-wife Alisa Koonen was placed in the theatre's lobby.) After the late 1930s, the splendid achievements of the pre- and postrevolutionary Russian theatre were passed over in silence or treated as an embarassing deviation in the Soviet Union. That whole avant-garde period was rediscovered by Western curators and critics in the early 1970s.[11] Like other historical phenomena banned under Stalin and Brezhnev, it has recently been officially amnestied and exonerated. Now, thanks to the museum founded by the merchant millionaire Alexei Bakhrushin, we can become cognizant of these once-buried treasures.

Notes

1. For examples of negative or invidious treatment of Russian merchants and industrialists, see the introductory chapter in the memoir by P. A. Buryshkin, *Moskva kupecheskaia*; Pavel Buryshkin, *Moscow of the Merchants* (New York: Chekhov Publishing House, 1954), 9–47.

2. Susan Massie, *Land of the Firebird: The Beauty of Old Russia* (New York: Simon & Schuster, 1980).

3. Beverly Whitney Kean, *All the Empty Palaces: The Merchant Patrons of Modern Art in Pre-Revolutionary Russia* (New York: Universe Books, 1983).

4. On *The Golden Fleece*, see William Richardson, *Zolotoe Runo and Russian Modernism* (Ann Arbor: Ardis, 1986).

5. For comparative chronology, see Whitney Kean, 300–309.

6. Buryshkin, passim.

7. Buryshkin, 127. The section on the Bakhrushin family (125-129) was written by Buryshkin with the help of their descendant, M. D. Bakhrushin.

8. Valentine Marcadé, *Le Renouveau de l'art pictorial russe 1863–1914* (Lausanne: L'Age d'homme, 1971).

9. Cf. Konstantin Rudnitsky, *Russian and Soviet Theater 1905–1932* (New York: Abrams, 1988).

10. *Russian Women Artists of the Avantgarde 1910–1930*, exh. cat. (Cologne: Galerie Gmurzynska, 1979).

11. Leonard Hutton-Hutschneker, "Introduction," and John E. Bowlt, "Artists of the World, Disunite," *Russian Avant-Garde 1908–1922*, exh. cat. (New York: Leonard Hutton Galleries, 1971), 5 and 10–14.

Design and Movement in the Theatre of the Russian Avant-Garde

Nancy Van Norman Baer

Our life is a theatre piece, in which nonobjective feeling is portrayed by objective imagery.

Kazimir Malevich, 1927[1]

At the time of the October Revolution in 1917, the average age of the thirty-eight scenic artists discussed in this book was twenty-four. Their youthful energy, idealism, optimism, and quest for relevance in life and art prompted the creation of some of this century's most radical artistic experiments. Many of these took place in the Soviet theatre where, as one American journalist observed in 1925, "such feverish activity, such boldness in the search for new forms" had never existed.[2] This statement gains added meaning when considering its source, for American theatre also experienced a period of reform in the 1920s. But in the United States the "new stagecraft," as it was called, was based on the assimilation of western European ideas; in the Soviet Union "avant-garde" theatrical experiment signified daring and radically new conceptions of stage design and stage movement.[3] While the theatre has always occupied a significant place in Russian and Soviet artistic life, only in the early twentieth century did avant-garde painters and choreographers, as well as directors, begin using the stage as a public laboratory to explore and disseminate new aesthetic ideas.

These explorations reached a high point during the Soviet Union's first half-decade, when more than 3,000 theatrical organizations flourished, serving an audience of hundreds of thousands of newly liberated workers, peasants, and intellectuals.[4] One theatre historian compared the interest to an epidemic: "Never and nowhere had such a phenomenon been witnessed in modern history."[5] Although many reasons contributed to why and how this mania for the theatre developed, the free distribution of tickets among workers and soldiers was an obvious factor. The new Soviet government realized that a theatrical performance could influence and enlighten more readily than a lecture or book, particularly when the population was largely illiterate. "Art is a powerful means of infecting those around us with ideas, feelings, and moods," wrote the Soviet Commissar of Enlightenment Anatolii Lunacharsky. "Agitation and propaganda acquire particular acuity and effectiveness when they are clothed in the attractive and mighty forms of art."[6]

Cat. no. 118
Vadim Meller
Costume design for the Blue Dancer,
Mephisto, 1920

Another element contributing to the health of the theatre was the public's desire to transcend everyday reality. The Revolution and years of civil war were a time of economic chaos and material deprivation, and people everywhere had suffered extreme hardships and shortages. The literary critic Viktor Shklovsky noted that

> In this terrifying world made of frost, stale herrings, rags, typhoid fever, arrests, bread lines and armed soldiers, one first night followed the other, and every evening theatres were jammed. Toward the middle of a show the huge unheated houses were warmed up by the breath of the audience. Lights would flicker and often go out, there was little current and no coal. . . . In operas, members of orchestras played with their fur coats on and fur caps over their ears, and steam came from brass instruments as if they were locomotive pipes or smokestacks.[7]

Despite these circumstances, the theatre was a vehicle for self-discovery, the means whereby a community became aware—might even act upon—its spiritual and artistic longings and desire for self-expression. In the absence of true enfranchisement, the theatre offered a substitute, a world in which anything was possible. Amateur dramatic groups emerged in factories, schools, hospitals, jails, and even military units, and with this explosion of activity came the agitprop sketches, revolutionary dramas, and mass spectacles that expressed hope for the new Russia.

In the professional theatre, the energy invested in production would be equally intense, particularly in the major cities of Moscow, Petrograd, and Kiev. The New Economic Policy (NEP) of 1921 would allow a partial return to the free-enterprise system; the encouragement of small-scale capitalism resulted in the creation of dozens of new studios. Appalling working conditions (1921 was a bleak, famine-stricken year and Soviet Russia verged on bankruptcy) would be offset by the relative freedom afforded to artists by commissar Lunacharsky.[8] In the atmosphere of upheaval that followed the Revolution and Civil War, nothing seemed too radical or impossible, and in virtually every artistic medium experiment prevailed.

The proliferation of theatres in early Soviet society broadened opportunities for visual artists who were well aware of the collaborative tradition between Russian painters and the stage. This tradition dated back to the late-nineteenth century when easel painters, attracted by the possibility of painting large-scale decorative canvases and having them enriched by artificial lighting, first accepted commissions to design theatrical settings. What had once been the domain of scenic craftsmen working in accordance with established formulas had become an area of legitimate artistic involvement. Between 1896 and 1899, at the art colony established by Savva Mamontov in Abramtsevo, Alexander Golovin, Kostantin Korovin, Valentin Serov, and Mikhail Vrubel were among the artists who created sets and costumes for over a dozen productions produced by Mamontov's Moscow Private Opera.[9] The collective exchange of ideas that occurred throughout the production process and commitment to creativity and craftsmanship were unique to Abramtsevo artists.

A true fusion of painting and the stage, however, still belonged to the future. It would be achieved by the World of Art (Mir iskusstva), a movement of symbolist-minded artists and writers associated with Serge Diaghilev. Based in St. Petersburg, the World of Art became, with the publication of its progressive art journal by the same name, a major influence on fin-de-siècle Russian culture.[10] Among the easel painters actively engaged in the group's activities were Léon Bakst, Alexandre Benois, Ivan Bilibin, Mstislav Dobujinsky, Golovin, Korovin, Nicholas Roerich, Serov, and Konstantin Somov.

The members of the World of Art were united in their aspiration toward artistic synthesism, the emphasis on the individual artist's creative expression, and the search for new methods of design aimed at the integration of art with everyday life. These principles would find expression a decade later in the scenic designs for Diaghilev's famed Paris seasons of Russian opera and ballet. Productions such as *Le Pavillon d'Armide* (1909, costumes and decor by Benois; music by Nicholas Tcherepnine), The Polovtsian Scenes and Dances of *Prince Igor* (1909, costumes and decor by Roerich; music by Alexander Borodin), *Schéhérazade* (1910, costumes and decor by Bakst; music by Nikolai Rimsky-Korsakov), and *L'Oiseau de feu* (Firebird) (1910, costumes by Golovin and Bakst; decor by Golovin; music by Igor Stravinsky), were seen as models of artistic harmony. Subordinating the various parts of a production to a single unified vision, they fused drama, painting, music, and movement to express the Wagnerian ideal of *Gesamtkunstwerk*, a total art work.

The activities of the World of Art artists in turn stimulated the creative initiative of the prerevolutionary avant-garde painters Natalia Goncharova and Mikhail Larionov. Commissioned by Diaghilev to design numerous Ballets Russes productions between 1914 and 1926, including *Le Coq d'or* (The Golden Cockerel) (1914, costumes and decor by Goncharova; music by Rimsky-Korsakov) and *Le Soleil de nuit* (Midnight Sun) (1915, costumes and decor by Larionov; music by Rimsky-Korsakov), they produced blueprints for sets and costumes that were semiabstract compositions. In providing a transition from the decorativeness and symbolist orientation of Diaghilev's early productions, they moved theatre design toward a modernist aesthetic. In rendered designs and onstage, painted illusion gave way to abstract representation.

Although Diaghilev's Ballets Russes was born in Russia, its success was made in the West. Inevitably, wartime isolation from his homeland and enthusiasm for the company in western Europe prompted Diaghilev to seek future collaborators among painters of the western European vanguard. In the teens and twenties, Giacomo Balla, Georges Braque, Giorgio de Chirico, Fortunato Depero, André Derain, Max Ernst, Juan Gris, Henri Matisse, Joan Miró, Pablo Picasso, and Georges Rouault received commissions to design Ballets Russes productions.[11] By the time of Diaghilev's death in 1929, the company had evolved from a vehicle for promoting Russian art and culture to a popularizer of the latest trends in European modernism.

In this same two-decade period, theatrical experiment would follow a different course in the cities of Moscow, St. Petersburg/Petrograd/ Leningrad, and Kiev. Here, Russian avant-garde painters were elaborating three-dimensional spatial ideas of decoration. Constrained by the boundaries of the canvas, they too turned to the theatre as an arena for dynamic painting.

In 1913, the year that Diaghilev presented *Le Sacre du printemps* (The Rite of Spring) with choreography by Vaslav Nijinsky, music by Stravinsky, and designs by Roerich at the Théâtre des Champs Elysées in Paris, an equally radical production entitled *Victory over the Sun* premiered at the Luna Park Theatre in St. Petersburg. Billed on Olga Rozanova's poster as one of the "First Futurist Spectacles in the World," it, like *Sacre*, broke with existing artistic, theatrical, and philosophical conventions. But whereas *Sacre* presented a vision of primal man and a society governed by instinct and nature, *Victory* envisioned a future mechanized world, no longer dependent upon anything, not even the sun.

With libretto by Alexei Kruchenykh and prologue by Velimir Khlebnikov, music by Mikhail Matiushin, and sets and costumes designed by Kazimir Malevich, *Victory over the Sun* was a pivotal work in the early avant-garde's attempt to forge a new theatrical aesthetic. The plot involved the capturing of the sun by a group of futurist strongmen and its enclosure in a square container for obscure futurist ends. As one contemporary witness put it,

> Was the author's purpose destructive or constructive? The old was thrown overboard; but what was to replace it?[12]

The text was written in the "transrational" language of *zaum*, meaning beyond the mind, beyond logic. This new language relied on neologisms, puns, and the free association of sounds and images that divested words of all predictable meaning, attempting to communicate the internal state of the speaker directly. Dissonant music combined with sound effects accompanied the actor's movement and speech. Malevich's nonobjective black-and-white sets made from cloth sheets painted with conical, spiral, and geometric forms were equally unconventional, as were his costumes—ingenious constructions of brightly colored cardboard cylinders, cones, and cubes (cat. no. 113). In addition to reshaping the human figure, the costumes dictated specific movement patterns. The Futurist Strongmen, for example, could only flex their arms upward, an action totally in keeping with their character as well as Kruchenykh's stage directions.

Malevich had originally planned for a three-dimensional stage set, but the lack of resources on the part of the producing organization (the Union of Youth) forced him to use backdrops that he painted himself.[13] In spite of this limitation, he achieved a three-dimensional, volumetric design through the distribution of freestanding geometric forms onstage and the use of mobile lighting. The poet Benedikt Livshits, who saw the production, recalled:

> Painterly stereometry was created within the confines of the scenic box for the first time, and a strict system of volumes was established, one that reduced the element of chance (which the movements of the human figures might have introduced) to a minimum. These figures were cut up by the blades of the lights and were deprived alternately of hands, legs, head, etc.,

Cat. no. 113
Kazimir Malevich
Costume design for the Attentive Worker,
Victory over the Sun, 1913

K. Малевич 1913 г.   Непріятель

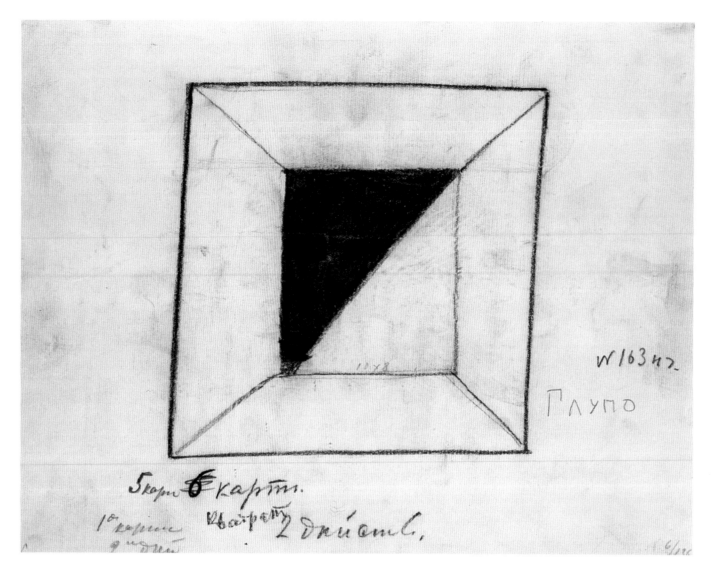

Cat. no. 115

Kazimir Malevich

Set design for act 2, scene 5,

Victory over the Sun, 1913

because, for Malevich, they were merely geometric bodies subject not only to disintegration into their component parts, but also to total dissolution in painterly space.[14]

This description supports Malevich's belief, formed in accordance with futurist principles, that "all matter disintegrates into a large number of component parts which are fully independent."[15] In Malevich's view, geometric forms were dynamically charged images that in turn could be broken apart to form a new pictorial vocabulary.

Malevich's insistence that suprematism was born in 1913, and that special significance should be given to his work on *Victory over the Sun*, confirms his move into abstraction via the theatre.[16] The overall effect of the production's geometricized design was cubofuturist, but the curtain for act 2, scene 5, consisting of a square within a square divided diagonally into unrelieved areas of black and white (cat. no. 115), was a completely abstract image. It is generally agreed that this decor suggested Malevich's painting of ca. 1915, *Black Square*, which today is regarded as the emblem of Malevich and the suprematist movement. Described as "a window in the visible universe looking into a new reality," the *Victory* backdrop is the earliest manifestation of suprematist theory.[17]

Another distinctive feature of this production was its intentional crossover of artistic disciplines. Malevich's costumes and sets were in accord with the dissonant text and music, and their visual impact was strengthened by the actor's choreographed movement. With bodies formed anew by the "armor" of their costumes, the semirobotic figures executed a limited sequence of predetermined movements that added to their grotesque appearance. By changing the way actors moved, artists' designs thus contributed to the choreographic innovations of the avant-garde theatre. The "barbarity," juvenile vitality, and mechanistic gesture that characterized the production has been linked to the fairground tradition, but also pointed the way to innovative abstraction in dance as well as painting.

The physicality that was part of *Victory* was an essential aspect of Russian avant-garde theatre. Experimental directors including Nikolai Evreinov, Fedor Komissarzhevsky, Vsevolod Meyerhold, Alexander Tairov, and Evgenii Vakhtangov recognized that movement was as essential as voice and scenic atmosphere in the creation of a three-dimensional, kinetic, interactive totality. United in their reaction against the "archeological-historical . . . realism" of Konstantin Stanislavsky's Moscow Art Theatre with its imitation of phenomenal reality, they sought to produce works of *theatrical art* that expressed rather than represented life—its situations and meaning.[18] In the experimental theatre, physical, vocal, and visual form were integrated in a display of frank theatricality; theatre became an art in and of itself, not simply a purveyor of literary works through the mouths of actors.

The same year that *Victory* was produced, Meyerhold opened a studio in St. Petersburg in 1913 to advance his theories and restore the vitality that he felt was missing in Stanislavsky's theatre of realism. Here he instituted classes in stage movement and the history and technique of commedia dell'arte in which students were taught improvisation, tumbling, and pantomime. Meyerhold had long been fascinated with the commedia tradition and had performed the role of Pierrot in his 1906 staging of Alexander Blok's *The Fairground Booth* at Vera Komissarzhevskaya's St. Petersburg theatre and in the first production of Michel Fokine's *Carnaval* (1910, music by Robert Schumann; costumes and decor by Bakst) at a charity ball organized by the St. Petersburg journal *Satyricon*. Tamara Karsavina and Nijinsky danced the ballet's leading roles and Bronislava Nijinska, partnered by Meyerhold whose "exquisite artistry" and effective stage presence she would recall, performed a polonaise.[19] In an article on theatre written that same year, Meyerhold had commented, "At the point where the spoken word fails in its power of expression the language of the dance begins."[20] Meyerhold's respect for the dance and acknowledgment of the importance of theatrical gesture also led him to investigate the techniques of ancient Greek and traditional Chinese and Japanese theatre. He particularly admired the Japanese Noh actor who was "both acrobat and dancer" and who performed all movement, even the most pedestrian, as a dance step.[21] "[The actor] must strive for complete control over his body" he wrote in 1910, a belief that laid the basis for biomechanics, the system of physical exercises he developed in the early 1920s, which will be discussed later.[22]

Alexander Tairov was another experimental director who sought a kinetic and architectonic, rather than a literary or illustrative theatrical

experience. At the Kamerny Theatre that he founded in Moscow in 1914, primary attention was paid to the actor's technique, and movement was considered a central component of the overall stage design. With the outbreak of World War I many artists had returned to Russia, including Alexandra Exter. During her frequent visits to the West between 1908 and 1914 she had become part of cubist and futurist circles, counting Picasso, Braque, Fernand Léger, and Fillipo Tommaso Marinetti among her artistic acquaintances. It was in Moscow, however, that Exter's professional career as a designer began with Tairov's invitation to create the sets and costumes for Innokentii Annensky's play *Famira Kifared* (1916). In this and future collaborations, Exter and Tairov aspired to create a dynamic fusion of drama, movement, and design that became known as "synthetic theatre."

The set that Exter built for *Famira* was radically innovative, composed of large, densely colored cubes and cones that created an environment of geometric forms (cat. no. 43). Under diffused, softly colored light, these stationary, abstract shapes created a monumental cubist landscape that surrounded a sloping staircase on the steps of which much of the dramatic action took place. According to the Soviet theatre historian Konstantin Rudnitsky, Exter's rhythmic arrangement of forms and the picturesque groupings of actors indicated by Tairov's directorial score

> obeyed the principles underlying the organization of a ballet production. . . . This essentially choreographic resolution of a dramatic [presentation] proved to be a bold and completely unexpected innovation in itself.[23]

With the premiere of *Salomé* the following year, Exter introduced dynamic elements into the architectonic scenic decor. Cloths and curtains

Cat. no. 47
Alexandra Exter
Set design for opening scene with
Jokanaan and Salomé, *Salomé*, 1917

of various colors and shapes appeared at critical moments during the play to intensify impact. A curtain painted with silver lightning streaks, for example, parted at the end of Jokanaan's first speech, revealing The Fatal Cistern and emphasizing his prophecy of doom. Later on, diagonal black banners floated down as Salomé lay dying, forming a funereal canopy. In the Exter/Tairov productions, decor functioned as an independent but equal element, interacting with the action instead of framing it and restructuring the stage as a dynamic volume (cat. no. 47).

In October–November 1917, the incongruity between the sensual and apolitical theme of *Salomé* and the Revolution that was taking place in the streets could not have been greater. Tairov lamented the "murderous atmosphere of constant uncertainty" that surrounded his theatre, but—like most of his contemporaries—he welcomed the Revolution because of the opportunity it presented to break with tradition and thereby stimulate the creation of new forms of art. When asked about the influence of the Revolution on his work, he concluded that it had greatly affected his artistic development, causing him to look for "something more quick, more truthful and more dynamic, something that matches our contemporary soul."[24] The theme of *Salomé* may have been symbolist, but the staging was radical and revolutionary.

In spite of their kinetic element, the three-dimensional constructed sets that Exter created for Tairov were not the "keyboards for the actor's playing" that he had dreamed of. This is no doubt one of the reasons why, in 1920, Tairov commissioned the constructivist artist Liubov

Cat. no. 133

Liubov Popova

Design for the garden in front of the
house, *Romeo and Juliet*, 1920

Popova to design the sets and costumes for his version of *Romeo and Juliet* (cat. no. 133). Popova's designs were rejected by Tairov, who ultimately awarded the commission to Exter. In *Romeo and Juliet* (1921), her third and last production for the Kamerny Theatre, Exter created a scenic atmosphere that was vertically dynamic with staircases, platforms, and mirrors that reflected the acting of the performers and created the illusion of multiple, intersecting spatial planes (cat. no. 60). A brilliant metaphor for the tangled intrigues of Shakespeare's tragedy, it created a three-dimensional, multileveled, cubofuturist environment but it remained a "setting" rather than an active construction. In 1922, Exter again used independent, freestanding platforms for her design of Kasian Goleizovsky's *Satanic Ballet* (not produced). For the first time, included in this project were moving elements such as hanging ladders, cables, and swings that suggested (perhaps anticipated) the constructivist sets of Liubov Popova's *The Magnanimous Cuckold* (1922), Varvara Stepanova's *The Death of Tarelkin* (1922), and Alexander Vesnin's *The Man Who Was Thursday* (1923).

The evolution from a decorative, painterly stage set to a three-dimensional stage environment, to an active stage structure, was accompanied by a change in aesthetic perceptions. The theatre was no longer an exhibition hall for pictures but a dynamic composition in which the rules of easel painting were supplanted by the search for a rhythmic, colorful, and organic construction. "We know very well that the public fears [these] so-called 'innovations'," wrote Tairov in *Notes of a Director*,

Cat. no. 60

Alexandra Exter

Set design for a square in Verona,
Romeo and Juliet, 1921

but let some time pass, and the eye of the public becomes emancipated; that which earlier seemed ugly it now accepts as a new beauty, arming itself with its former bitterness against the next new form to be born in the unending creative process.[25]

The shift from the concept of an artist-painter to that of an artist-builder is most evident in the 1921–1922 productions staged by Meyerhold. Whereas Tairov and his early collaborators (Exter as well as Boris Ferdinandov, Pavel Kuznetsov, and Serge Soudeikine) sought to create aesthetic structures that presented actors and settings in a consciously theatrical manner, Meyerhold now wished to construct an environment of participatory involvement. As Rudnitsky points out in *Meyerhold the Director*, this desire was motivated by political as well as artistic aims. Meyerhold believed that the social revolution called for a theatrical revolution, and he invented the term *Theatrical October* to express the drive for such upheaval. In 1920, as the newly appointed head of the Theatre Department of the Commissariat for Enlightenment, Meyerhold argued for the creation of aesthetic forms that would contain and express the spirit of the Revolution.

Meyerhold's first attempt in this direction was the staging of Emile Verhaeren's *Les Aubes* (The Dawns) (1920) at the RSFSR (Russian Soviet Federated Socialist Republic) Theatre No. 1 in Moscow. In preparation for this production, Meyerhold threw out what remained of the derelict theatre's moldings and decorations, bared the interior brick walls of the building, built ramps to connect the stage to the auditorium, removed the footlights, and covered the walls of the corridors with posters and slogans. In short, he did everything possible to create an atmosphere resembling the street—one suitable to a political rally and the spirit in

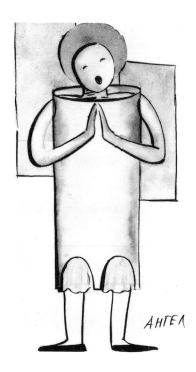

АНГЕЛ

Cat. no. 107
Anton Lavinsky
Costume design for an Angel,
Mystery-Bouffe, 1921

Cat. no. 106
Anton Lavinsky
Set design for *Mystery-Bouffe*, 1921

which he had conceived the play. Vladimir Dmitriev was invited to design *Les Aubes*, presumably with full awareness of the feelings of Meyerhold and his assistant director, Valerii Bebutov, published in *Bulletin of the Theatre*, that "'decorative' sets have no meaning; 'decoration' is for the secessionists and restaurants in Vienna and Munich; spare us 'The World of Art', 'Rococo' and the painstaking detail of museum exhibits. . . ."[26] Dmitriev only partially fulfilled the directors' wishes. Although he created a unified, nonrepresentational stage structure of raw materials—iron, wood, rope, and wire—it remained, like the earlier works of Exter, a decorative albeit brilliant cubofuturist composition of painted, stationary forms. Dmitriev's set did initiate a move toward scenic constructivism in its use of real materials to sculpt empty space, an idea that evolved from Vladimir Tatlin's earlier relief sculptures.

Meyerhold came closer to achieving his ideal stage set the following year with the production of a revised version of Vladimir Mayakovsky's *Mystery-Bouffe* (1921). Dispensing with the front curtain and the very idea of background scenery, Meyerhold asked the sculptor Anton Lavinsky and the painter Vladimir Khrakovsky to design a structure for acting that would also unite the stage and auditorium. What resulted was a system of staircases, bridges, and scaffolding surrounding a partial globe that extended into the first rows of the theatre (cat. nos. 106, 107). As one contemporary critic wrote:

> There is no stage. . . . There is a monumental platform half moved out into the auditorium. One senses that it is cramped within these walls. It requires a city square, a street. . . . It is all constructed . . . made up of wooden benches, sawhorses, boards and painted partitions. . . . It is all composed of reliefs, counter-reliefs and force lines, striking to the eye but extremely simple, fantastically interwoven. But every relief, every line . . . will obtain meaning and movement when the actor's foot steps on it and the sound of his voice strikes it. . . . [This] is no "temple" with its great lie of the "mystery" of art, this is the new proletariat art. . . .[27]

Visually, *Mystery-Bouffe* provided a link to constructivism in its organization of the stage space and introduction of principles of architectural order. Similar ideas were expressed again in Popova's and Alexander Vesnin's collaborative design for the mass festival *The Struggle and Victory of the Soviets*, also prepared by Meyerhold in spring 1921, but not produced for economic reasons. It was not until the following year that constructivist principles were fully developed in *The Magnanimous Cuckold*, the production that officially inaugurated "theatrical constructivism."

Meyerhold invited Popova to design *Cuckold* soon after she joined the teaching staff of the State Higher Theatre Workshop (GVYTM) under his direction. In this experimental laboratory for the new theatrical aesthetics, constant discussion and collective creativity was encouraged. During the time that Popova was debating Meyerhold's proposal, it was "accepted" by the brothers Georgii and Vladimir Stenberg and their friend Konstantin Medunetsky. The three student painters presented Meyerhold with a verbal image of a set built around a mill chute that allowed "processed" lovers, like sacks of grain, to descend from Stella's bedroom—a concept that the painter Georgii Yakulov later asserted "would never have occurred to a Soviet mademoiselle like Popova."[28] Since there were no preparatory sketches, the young men's ideas were more than likely relayed to Popova in her conversations with Meyerhold, along with his desire to transform the architecture of the windmill into a freestanding "workplace" for actors. This scheme provided the basis for Popova's set, and also led to the charges of plagiarism filed against her by Yakulov at the production's premiere. The subsequent investigation by the Institute of Artistic Culture (Inkhuk) brought a more disturbing accusation from those of Popova's colleagues who felt that she had betrayed constructivist ideology by applying its principles to an aesthetic use as opposed to a functional one. The following week Popova was cleared of the charges; Inkhuk established the sincerity of her productivist, utilitarian approach in the achievement of a wholly independent resolution to the design problem.[29]

The constructivist set for *Cuckold* is thoroughly discussed elsewhere in this book (see John Bowlt, Mikhail Kolesnikov, and Georgii Kovalenko), but it should be emphasized that the success of the project was largely due to the shared creative and aesthetic aspirations of Popova and Meyerhold. Both were seeking a functional and utilitarian model stripped of theatrical illusion; one that—in accordance with constructivist ideology—was reduced to its most essential form. Conceptually, such a skeletal and freestanding set could be moved from the confines of the theatre into the open air so that the results obtained in the stage laboratory (the "factory of the qualified man") could be transferred into everyday life. In her set Popova did not portray a windmill; she built a spare, rhythmically organized structure whose blades and wheels evoked a windmill, as well as the machines and mechanisms of a modern industrialized society (fig. 1). In the absence of cement, concrete, iron, glass, and skyscrapers, Popova's stage machinery represented an artist's dream of a technology that would transform the poverty-stricken country into a mechanized, electrified, and well-organized land.

The totally new environment of the constructivist stage required a

Fig. 1
The Magnanimous Cuckold, act 2, 1922

Fig. 2
Biomechanical exercises,
"Stab with the Dagger," 1922

Fig. 3
Biomechanical exercises,
"The Leap onto the Chest," 1922

new style of acting. In his theatre Meyerhold extended the constructivist aesthetic into performance through a system of actor-training that he called *biomechanics*. Based on a series of exercises derived from a variety of sources including acrobatics, dance, eurhythmics, physical culture, and sports, biomechanics aimed at achieving balance, elasticity, rhythm, and physical awareness (figs. 2, 3). When incorporated in performance, biomechanical principles magnified the scale and visual form of an actor's movement, giving each gesture added significance. In 1922 Meyerhold's students outlined the basic laws of biomechanics in regard to movement on the stage platform: 1) the body is a machine; 2) the worker is a machine operator; 3) the actor must discover his own center of gravity, his own equilibrium and stability; 4) the actor must achieve coordination of bodily movements in relation to the stage platform, stage space, and surrounding figures; 5) a gesture is a motion of the entire body; and 6) body movement is the producer of external words.[30] These laws drew on the scientific methodologies of Taylorism (a time-and-motion study) and reflexology (the study of human reflexive action)—the same methods, Meyerhold explained, that organized labor processes:

> The motions constructed on [the basis of biomechanics] are distinguished by a *dansant* quality. The labor process used by experienced workers always resembles the dance. Here, work verges on art. The sight of a person who is working correctly produces a certain satisfaction.
>
> This applies completely to the work of the actor in the theatre of the future. We are always dealing in art with the organization of material. Constructivism demands that the artist become an engineer as well. Art must be based on scientific principles; all the work done by the artist must be conscious.[31]

The physical aspect of Meyerhold's theatre was by no means unique. The Blue Blouse troupes, for example, frequently incorporated acrobatic feats in their performances. In their use of human pyramids to

Fig. 4
Blue Blouse Theatre,
"Red Star," 1925–1926

Fig. 5
Blue Blouse Theatre,
"Propeller," 1928

overleaf left:
Cat. no. 20
Sergei Eisenstein
Costume design for the First Coquette,
Good Treatment for Horses, 1922

overleaf right:
Cat. no. 21
Sergei Eisenstein
Costume design for Gipsy-Pipsy,
Good Treatment for Horses, 1922

construct symmetrical forms and revolutionary symbols such as a star
or propeller (figs. 4, 5), they relied on physical skills identical to those
required in biomechanical exercises. Founded in Moscow in 1923 by the
journalist Boris Yuzhanin, the Blue Blouse was a concept rather than
an institution. At the peak of its popularity in 1928, four hundred eighty-
four professional Blue Blouse companies existed in the Soviet Union.[32]
Developed on the lines of the spoken or "living" newspaper, they
presented simple plays with sociopolitical themes that reached directly to
the masses. Many young artists, including Nina Aizenberg and Boris
Erdman, were attracted to the Blue Blouse as designers because of its
energetic and specifically proletarian nature. Scenography was necessarily
simple and portable, the principle being to use available material in
an inventive way.

Constructivist analogues can also be found in the experimental
theatre productions of the Foregger Workshop (MASTFOR). Although
Nikolai Foregger never explicitly codified his actor-training system
known as *tye-fe-trenage*, it resembled Meyerhold's biomechanics, except
that the movement was organized musically, as in ballet. In a typical
MASTFOR performance, dialogues and monologues led from one dance
number to the next with quickness and precision. In his most famous
production, *Good Treatment for Horses* (1922), the tempo of the staging
was augmented by Sergei Yutkevich's ingeniously designed set. The
future filmmaker devised a mobile "urban" environment with moving
steps, a treadmill, suspended trampolines, flashing electric signs, rotating
decors, and "flying lights." Although everything was controlled manually
backstage, the effect was one of oiled mechanization. Sergei Eisenstein,
who also trained at MASTFOR before entering the Soviet film industry,
designed the costumes for the production, some of which were made
of nothing more than wire hoops fastened to multicolored ribbons
and strips of colored paper (cat. nos. 20, 21). Risqué even by today's
standards, they contributed to MASTFOR's "lewd" and "eccentric"
reputation.

„Хорошее отношение к лошадям"
В. МАССА.

1ая „ДАМОЧКА"

РОМВ

6/XII   ЛЕ.
                        1921.

Tenets of constructivism were more clearly defined in Foregger's *Machine Dances* of 1922–1923 in which performers simulated the parts of complex industrial machines. Principles of standardization, repetition, overlapping, and multiplication informed the mechanistic choreography that was performed to the accompaniment of factory sounds imitated by a "noise-orchestra." A performance was described by theatre historian René Fülöp-Miller, writing in 1926,

> as if priests and priestesses were celebrating in dance the new God of the Machine. Their bodies became correctly constructed appliances, they no longer moved, they "functioned." What Foregger accomplishes is a cinematics of the living organism, an analysis in dance of the human mechanism, worked out in exhaustive physiological, mechanical, and psychotechnical studies. The new dancing, in Foregger's sense, tries to express the most general movements of the human organism, rhythm no longer individual but universal. All the gestures are, therefore, as far as possible transformed into partial functions of a total movement, and strictly geometrized. The spectator is intended to recognize in the activity of each single group of muscles a motor reflex within the frame of the whole great stage machine. Dancing is intended to be nothing but a vivid demonstration of the adequate organization of the human machine."[33]

Constructivism and the use of nontraditional movement forms in the theatre seem to have been a major catalyst to ballet modernism. In the early 1920s, experimental choreographers including Kasian Goleizovsky and Fedor Lopukhov began to use acrobatic elements such as high extensions and unusual overhead lifts to enlarge the existing dance vocabulary. They too were searching for a new kind of art that was nonrepresentational and utilitarian. As Elizabeth Souritz points out in this volume, constructivist sets also helped to expand the range of choreographic possibilities. Those designed by Exter for Goleizovsky's *Satanic Ballet* (1922, not realized) and Tatiana Bruni and her husband Georgii Korshikov for Lopukhov's ballet *Bolt* (1931) allowed choreographers to realize new mise-en-scène arrangements and multilevel compositions.

Such experiments extended beyond Moscow and Leningrad to other cultural capitals of the Soviet Union. In 1919 Bronislava Nijinska had established a choreographic studio in Kiev that aimed at achieving a "new type of ballet artist" schooled in classical dance as well as the latest discoveries in movement and the visual arts. In her choreographic treatise dated 1918, at the beginning of the emerging constructivist aesthetic, she draws analogies between the body and the machine—between physical movement and mechanized motion. She speaks of the latest achievements of industry as represented by the automobile and airplane, whose "dynamic rhythm" and capacity for speed, acceleration, and "unexpected nervous breaking" she greatly admired.[34]

In Kiev, Nijinska formed a close artistic association with Exter, who in 1918 opened a nearby studio. One of the few members of the Russian avant-garde to create a "school," Exter's pupils included Boris Aronson, Alexander Bogomazov, Alexander Khostenko-Khostov, Simon Lissim, Vadim Meller, Anatolii Petritsky, Isaak Rabinovich, Pavel Tchelitchew,

Cat. no. 119
Vadim Meller
Costume design for a Male Dancer,
The City, 1921

Fig. 6
Vladimir Stenberg and Georgii Stenberg
Poster for Kamerny Theatre performances
in Paris, 6–23 March 1923
Lithograph, 69.9 × 45.7 cm
Collection Martin Muller, San Francisco

and Alexander Tyshler.[35] Presumably Exter introduced Nijinska to Meller, who created the lyrical cubofuturist designs for her first choreographic experiments, including *Fear* (1918), *Masks* (1918), *Assyrian Dances* (1919), *Mephisto* (1920) (cat. no. 118), and *The City* (1921) (cat. no. 119). Because of the acute shortage of materials in the immediate postrevolutionary period, it is doubtful that they were realized.

Kharkov was also a center of cultural activity during these turbulent years. Another member of Exter's studio, Petritsky, designed numerous productions for the city's State Opera, including *William Tell* (1927) (cat. no. 129) and *The Football Player* (1928). Petritsky's brand of constructivism displays a decorative quality that is not only distinctive but also points to the influence of national traditions. Bright colors, decorative flourishes, and a concern with formal combinations and syncopations, for example, reflect the influence of Ukrainian folk art. In the study of this period, it is important to remember that many of the modern artists and designers who are generally categorized as Russian were, in fact, Ukrainian, Georgian, Armenian, Lithuanian, Latvian, Polish, etc.

Knowledge of the extraordinary vitality of postrevolutionary art in the Soviet Union could not fail to excite the West. In 1923, the Paris performances of Tairov's Kamerny Theatre at the Théâtre des Champs-Elysées (fig. 6) presented the progressive ideas of the new Soviet state on an international stage. Although censured in the mainstream press, the productions of *Salomé* (designed by Exter), *Phèdre* (designed by Alexander Vesnin), *Princess Brambilla* (designed by Georgii Yakulov), and *Giroflé-Girofla* (designed by Yakulov) were much admired by the European avant-garde. Jean Cocteau and Léger especially expressed enthusiasm for Tairov's radical modernism; Diaghilev, according to one biographer, did not miss a single performance, watching every detail "eagerly and jealously."[36] It's not surprising to learn that in 1925, when he decided to produce a ballet depicting life in Soviet Russia, Diaghilev invited Tairov and Yakulov to be his collaborators, along with Goleizovsky and the composer Sergei Prokofiev. Although Goleizovsky, Tairov, and later Meyerhold declined his invitation to participate in the creation of *Le Pas d'acier* (1927), Yakulov and Prokofiev accepted and the ballet was eventually staged in Paris with choreography by Léonide Massine.

Elements of constructivist stage design and dance also appeared in Diaghilev's *La Chatte* of the same year. Designed by the Russian émigré artists Naum Gabo and his brother Antoine Pevsner, the ballet dealt with the central theme of metamorphosis. The set, described as a "laboratory" by Diaghilev's property master, consisted of a system of transparent forms and boxes made of celluloid, mica, and wire in which light was reflected and refracted (fig. 7). The dancers wore costumes of the same transparent material, creating a clinical, utopian atmosphere. The inventive, sculptural, and acrobatic poses of George Balanchine's choreography showed the influence of his mentor, Goleizovsky. In later years, Balanchine credited Goleizovsky and the 1921–1922 productions of the Moscow Chamber Ballet for helping to shape his thinking and ideas.[37]

Fig. 7
Naum Gabo
Model for stage set, *La Chatte*,
1926–1927, reassembled and
restored 1987
Metal, plastics, wood, and cloth,
61 × 54.5 × 79.5 cm
Courtesy Tate Gallery, London

The depiction of a future utopia as suggested by *La Chatte* was carried to a further extreme in Meyerhold's 1929 Moscow production of *The Bedbug*. By shifting the action into the future, Vladimir Mayakovsky's play permitted an optimistic view that eclipsed contemporary reality. The play was divided into two distinct parts: The first, contemporary, was designed by a group of cartoonists known as the Kukryniksy. The second, the Future, transferred the action ahead fifty years in time and was designed by Alexander Rodchenko. The two parts were separated by a stormy musical interlude composed by Dmitrii Shostakovich.

For his vision of the Future (set in the year 1979), Rodchenko created a mechanized environment of gadgets, dials, and signal lights set against a gleaming, silvery white, constructivist background. This image of a communist utopia (the new) was in sharp contrast to the Kukryniksy's crowded and chaotic street scene (the old), in which actors wore clothing purchased over the counter in Moscow shops. So, too, were the depersonalized, faceless characters of Part 2 dressed in Rodchenko's spage-age costumes (cat. nos. 156, 157). Although terrifying in their anonymity, these futuristic beings represented man freed of human limitations, emotions, and characteristics. Like Malevich's semirobotic figures in *Victory over the Sun*, they are Soviet supermen, afraid of nothing and equipped to inhabit a future utopian landscape.

Not all critics were convinced, however, and many believed that Rodchenko's antiseptic, utilitarian vision contained more than a hint of

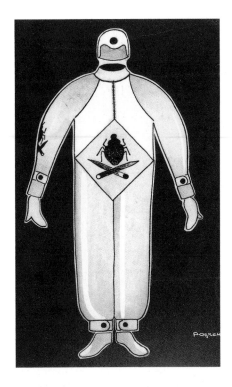

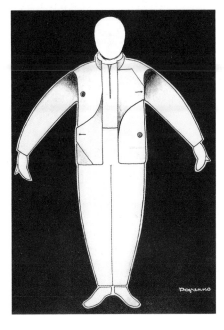

Cat. nos. 156, 157
Alexander Rodchenko
Costume designs, *The Bedbug*, 1929

satire. For some, *The Bedbug* was an inspired vision of advanced technology but for others it was a lifeless abstraction, and many suspected that it was a parody of socialism's achievements. Despite the confusion of the critics, the production was a great popular success and of all the plays staged by Meyerhold, it is the one most frequently revived.

The dreams and visions of the Russian avant-garde were to be realized only in art, and primarily in the realm of the theatre. In this creative laboratory, which existed for the most part outside a commercial enterprise system, artists sought to re-image the world by aiming their works at an audience without class distinctions. What they presented was not a depiction of life, but life itself—often disquieting, but filled with possibility. As Foregger stated in 1926, "A future historian of art will call our years the years of prophecy."[38]

In studying this period, one is inevitably left with a sense of loss in that the tremendous innovation of the era was never allowed to run its course. In 1934, it was announced at the First All-Union Congress of Soviet Writers that socialist realism, defined by the Congress as the combining of artistic representation "with the task of ideological transformation and education of the working man in the spirit of Socialism," was to be the exclusive style of Soviet writers and artists.[39] The experimentalism that had once prevailed was now banned, and art was required to submit to a program of political conformity and traditional form that would help support the Communist Party's goals of industrialization and collectivization. Individuals and institutions that failed to comply were subject to attack and administrative repression, including police surveillance, arrest, and banishment. In this climate of terror and suspicion, many artists dramatically altered their painting and writing styles, and some destroyed their work out of fear that discovery would result in imprisonment. Others suffered a more tragic fate: Mayakovsky committed suicide in 1930, and in 1939, two years after his theatre was shut down by the Soviet government, Meyerhold was arrested and subsequently died (it is not known where he is buried); his wife was murdered soon after his arrest. The achievements of the "Great Experiment" in Russian art were lost from view and, with them, the uncompromising quest for the new in art.[40] What followed was a period of rigidity, monotony, and stagnation in the arts many times greater than that which the Russian avant-garde had initially reacted against.

Notes

1. John Elderfield, "On Constructivism," *Art Forum* 9 (May 1971): 60.

2. Zakhary L. McLove, "Russian Ballet Has Risen in Revolt," *The New York Times Magazine*, 15 November 1925.

3. Representatives of the "new stagecraft" in America included Norman Bel Geddes, Robert Edmond Jones, Donald Oenslager, Jo Mielziner, Lee Simonson, and Joseph Urban. See Denis Bablet, *Revolutions in Stage Design of the XXth Century* (New York: Leon Amiel, 1977), 238-255.

4. Marc Slonim, *Russian Theater from the Empire to the Soviets* (New York: Collier Books, 1961), 261.

5. Slonim, 260.

6. From the 1920 "Theses of the Art Section of Narkompros and the Central Committee of the Union of Art Workers Concerning Basic Policy in the Field of Art," trans. in John Bowlt, ed., *Russian Art of the Avant-Garde, Theory and Criticism 1902–1934* (New York: Viking Press, 1976), 185. The literacy rate of the Russian populus in 1914 is estimated to be 40 percent. For a discussion of literacy in the Soviet Union see Jeffrey Brooks, *When Russia Learned to Read: Literacy and Popular Literature, 1861–1917* (New Jersey: Princeton University Press, 1985) and René Fueloep-Miller, *The Mind and Face of Bolshevism: An Examination of Cultural Life in Soviet Russia*, trans. from *Geist und Gesicht des Bolschewismus* (Zurich: Amalthea-Verlag, 1926) by F. S. Flint and D. F. Tait (New York: Putnam, 1965), 223–244.

7. Viktor Shklovsky, *Khod konia* (Moscow and Berlin, 1923). Quoted in Slonim, 261.

8. Known primarily for his political career, Anatolii Lunacharsky was also a critic (he reviewed Diaghilev's Paris seasons in 1912–1914) and amateur playwright whose works included *The King's Barber* (1906), *Faust and the City* (1918), *Oliver Cromwell* (1920), and *The Locksmith and the Chancellor* (1921). As a young man, he studied and traveled in western Europe, receiving a doctorate from the University of Zurich and serving as a Russian-language guide at the Musée du Louvre.

9. Lynn Garafola, *Diaghilev's Ballets Russes* (New York: Oxford University Press, 1989), 14–16.

10. For a full discussion of *Mir iskusstva* see Janet Kennedy, *The "Mir iskusstva" Group and Russian Art, 1898–1912* (New York and London: Garland, 1977) and Elena Bridgman, "Mir iskusstva: Origins of the Ballets Russes" in *The Art of Enchantment: Diaghilev's Ballets Russes, 1909–1929*, exh. cat. (San Francisco: The Fine Arts Museums of San Francisco, 1989), 26–43.

11. For a full chronology of Ballets Russes productions see *The Art of Enchantment*, 141–149.

12. Minna Tarka, "Reconstructing Victory over the Sun," *Art and Design Profile 15 Malevich 5* 5/6 (1989): 78.

13. Tarka, 79.

14. Benedikt Livshits, *The One and a Half-Eyed Archer* (Newtonville, Mass.: Oriental Research Press, 1977), English trans. by John Bowlt of 1933 Russian edition, 164.

15. Quoted in John Golding, "Supreme Suprematist," *The New York Review*, 17 January 1991, 17.

16. Susan P. Compton, "Malevich's Suprematism—The Higher Intuition," *Burlington Magazine* 117, 881 (August 1976) and Dmitrii Sarabianov, "Kazimir Malevich and His Art, 1900–1930," in *Kazimir Malevich, 1878–1935*, exh. cat. (Los Angeles: The Armand Hammer Museum of Art and Cultural Center, 1990), 166.

17. Charlotte Douglas, *Swans of Other Worlds:Kazimir Malevich and the Origins of Abstraction in Russia* (Ann Arbor, Mich.: UMI Research Press, ca. 1980), 47.

18. For a brief discussion of the Stanislavsky Method of actor training see Slonim, 173–178.

19. Bronislava Nijinska, *Early Memoirs*, trans. and ed. Irina Nijinska and Jean Rawlinson (New York: Holt, Rinehart & Winston, 1981), 287–289.

20. Quoted in *Meyerhold on Theater*, trans. and ed. Edward Braun (New York: Hill and Wang, 1969), 86. Meyerhold's interest in commedia dell'arte and the role of Pierrot can also be traced to his 1903 production of Franz von Schönthan's *The Acrobats*, a melodrama on circus life in which Meyerhold portrayed the aging clown Landowski.

21. Quoted in *Meyerhold on Theater*, 65, 149. The 1902 tour of Otodziro Kawakami's company and the 1909 St. Petersburg appearances of the actress Hanako stimulated Meyerhold's interest in Japanese theatre.

22. Quoted in *Meyerhold on Theater*, 86.

23. Konstantin Rudnitsky, *Russian and Soviet Theater 1905–1932*, (New York: Abrams, 1988), 18.

24. Nikos Kazantzakis, *Russia: A Chronicle of Three Journeys in the Aftermath of the Revolution*, trans. Michael Antonakes and Thanasis Madkaleris, (Berkeley, Calif.: Creative Arts Book Company, 1989), 177.

25. Alexander Tairov, *Notes of a Director*, trans. William Kuhlke (Coral Gables, Fla.: University of Miami Press, 1969), 117.

26. Vsevolod Meyerhold and Valerii Bebutov, "On the Staging of Verhaeren's 'The Dawn,'" *Vestnik teatra* 72–73 (Moscow, 1920), 8–10. Quoted in *Meyerhold on Theatre*, 173.

27. Konstantin Rudnitsky, *Meyerhold the Director*, trans. from Russian by George Petrov (Ann Arbor, Mich.: Ardis, 1981), 279.

28. Dmitri V. Sarabianov and Natalia L. Adaskina, *Popova*, trans. Marian

Schwartz (New York: Abrams, 1990), 251.

29. Sarabianov and Adaskina, 250-254. See also Liubov Popova, "Introduction to the Inkhuk Discussion of *The Magnanimous Cuckold*" in Sarabianov and Adaskina, 378–379.

30. Rudnitsky, *Meyerhold the Director*, 292. For Meyerhold's biomechanics see *Meyerhold on Theatre*, 197–204; Rudnitsky, 294–305; Edward Braun, *The Theatre of Meyerhold, Revolution on the Modern Stage* (New York: Drama Book Specialists, 1979), 164–168; Mel Gordon, "Meyerhold's Biomechanics," *Drama Review* 18, no. 3 (September 1974): 73–88.

31. Vsevolod Meyerhold quoted in Nikolai Gorchakov "Meyerhold's Theatre" in *Total Theatre: A Critical Anthology*, ed. E. T. Kirby (New York: Dutton, 1969), 134.

32. František Deák, "Blue Blouse," *Drama Review* 17, no. 1 (March 1973): 46.

33. Fülöp-Miller, quoted in Mel Gordon, "Foregger and the Dance of the Machines," *Drama Review* 19, no. 1 (March 1975): 72.

34. Bronislava Nijinska, "On Movement and the Theory of Movement," in *Bronislava Nijinska: A Dancer's Legacy*, exh. cat. (San Francisco: The Fine Arts Museums of San Francisco, 1986), 87.

35. John E. Bowlt, *Catalogue Raissoné of the Mr. and Mrs. Nikita D. Lobanov-Rostovsky Collection*, forthcoming.

36. Arnold L. Haskell and Walter Nouvel, *Diaghileff: His Artistic and Private Life* (New York: Simon & Schuster, 1935), 127.

37. For Goleizovsky see Elizabeth Souritz, *Soviet Choreographers in the 1920s*, trans. Lynn Visson, ed. Sally Banes (Durham, No. Car.: Duke University Press, 1990); Giora Manor, "Before Balanchine: Kasyan Goleizovsky's Russian Revolution," *Dance Magazine* (January–February, 1989); Lydia Joffe, "Kasian Goleizovsky: Some Notes on a Great Choreographer," *The Dancing Times* (June 1966); Yuri Slonimsky, "Balanchine, The Early Years," trans. John Andrews, *Ballet Review* 5, no. 3 (1975–1976): 37–38.

38. Nikolai Foregger, "Experiments in the Art of the Dance," trans. David Miller, *Drama Review* 19, no. 1 (March 1975): 77.

39. Slonim, *Russian Theater*, 332.

40. This is a reference to Camilla Gray's impressive study of the Russian avant-garde. See Camilla Gray, *The Russian Experiment in Art: 1863–1922* (New York: Abrams, 1971).

The Construction of Caprice: The Russian Avant-Garde Onstage

John E. Bowlt

One of the most important events in the history of the modern Russian theatre was the exhibition *Stage Design in the USSR during the Decade 1917–1927*, held at the Academy of Arts in Leningrad in 1927.[1] This enormous survey of set and costume designs, organized by the critic Erik Gollerbakh, the painter Alexander Golovin, and the collector Levkii Zheverzheev, served as a vivid panorama of sketches, maquettes, and posters by prominent artists such as Natan Altman, Vladimir Dmitriev, Boris Erdman, Alexandra Exter, Valentina Khodasevich, Anatolii Petritsky, Liubov Popova, and Alexander Rodchenko—and also as a timely critical evaluation of the many styles that had been generated by the various principles of stage design elaborated just after the October Revolution of 1917.

Among the contributions to the catalogue of this impressive exhibition, Gollerbakh's article on "Theatre as Spectacle" deserves particular attention. In discussing what then seemed to be the most radical achievements in stage design, the author delineated certain ideas and concepts that today help us to understand more clearly the context of our own exhibition, *Theatre in Revolution: Russian Avant-Garde Stage Design 1913–1935*. Gollerbakh's essay makes fascinating reading, because it carries both general and particular statements, often provocative, on the aims and applications of the visual arts to the modern stage. We learn, for example, that "until the footlights have been 'overcome,' the theatre—as spectacle—has every right to exist,"[2] and that, with regard to plastic expressivity, "the ideal costume, is, of course, the absence of any costume at all."[3] Of direct relevance to our own exhibition is Gollerbakh's observation that the new, revolutionary theatre differed from its nineteenth-century precursor by its sharp orientation away from decoration toward construction, from the stage as an extension of the framed painting toward an architectural, volumetrical complex. Gollerbakh and other enlightened critics of his time indicated that this orientation was accompanied by a parallel concentration on other elements—on the incorporation of mechanical movement (an obvious example being Popova's scenic contraption for Vsevolod Meyerhold's production of *The Magnanimous Cuckold* of 1922), on "facturality" or the natural textures of surfaces (as in Vladimir Tatlin's wooden boards for *Zangezi* of 1923), and on improvisation, spontaneity, and process (we think of Boris Erdman's designs for Kasian Goleizovsky's *Eccentric Dances* of 1923) (cat. no. 36). These are primary characteristics

Cat. no. 53
Alexandra Exter
Costume design for Herodias, *Salomé*,
1917

Cat. no. 36
Boris Erdman
Costume sketch, *Foxtrot Championship*,
1923

of the Russian avant-garde onstage during the 1910s and 1920s and the
notion of *Bühnenarchitektur*, in particular, can be associated with many
of the images included in our exhibition. As Alexander Yanov, a leading
theorist of stage design wrote in 1926, "However simplified, however
primitive the decoration, its skeleton, its basic structures (constructions)
must have an architectural logic."[4]

Of course, scenic prerequisites such as architectonic construction,
kinetic mechanism, and emotional caprice were not new in the history of
the theatre and its design. The common Italian *presepe*—the renarration
of the Nativity—often depends on architectural likeness and moving parts
for its effect; the mummers and buffoons of Old Russia, so beloved by
modern Russian artists (from Alexandre Benois to Tatlin), were surely no
less spontaneous in their performances than the outlandish personages
invented by Sergei Eisenstein and Sergei Yutkevich for the Vladimir Mass/
Vladimir Mayakovsky *Good Treatment for Horses* (1922) (cat. no. 210);
and Max Reinhardt in Munich, i.e., outside Russia, with his "stage in
relief and light effects, controlled by a single pictorial style, revealed new
means for resolving the architectonic problems of the theatre."[5] Even so,
in very general terms, it is reasonable to propose that the "retheatralization
of the Russian theatre"[6] just before and after the Revolution came
about precisely as a result of this unprecedented attention to architecture
(volume), speed (instantaneity), and spontaneity (arbitrariness).

This becomes especially clear when we compare the main
achievements of constructivist design of the early 1920s such as Popova's
Cuckold and Varvara Stepanova's sets and costumes for *The Death of
Tarelkin* (1922) with the first phase of Serge Diaghilev's Ballets Russes
(1909–1914). Ballets Russes painters such as Léon Bakst, Benois, and
their colleagues tended to overwhelm the audience with splendid
coloration or meticulous historicity—sometimes to such a degree that
the other components of the production (dancing, singing, mime, and
music) were lost from view. As the critic Alexander Kugel once said of
Diaghilev's artists, "with them the cult of beautification replaced the cult
of beauty."[7] True, the Ballets Russes never performed in Russia, but
something of their luxurious decadence was manifest on the stages of
Moscow and St. Petersburg, too. In fact, the more we study the history
of the prerevolutionary theatre, the more we realize that its leading
representatives, above all Exter and Alexander Tairov, owed just as much
to Michel Fokine and Bakst as they did to Adolphe Appia and Edward
Gordon Craig, and they supported rather than undermined what Yurii
Annenkov called the "dictatorship of the painter."[8] Is it so very far from
Bakst's ample sultanas in *Schérérazade* (1910) to Exter's wonderful
bacchantes and satyrs for *Famira Kifared* (1916)? Is it perhaps not mere
historical coincidence that the voluptuous story of Salomé occupied
a prominent place in the repertories of Diaghilev, Nikolai Evreinov,
and Vera Komissarzhevskaya as well as of Goleizovsky, Konstantin
Mardzhanov, Tairov, and even Meyerhold? *Salomé*—this invitation to a
beheading mesmerized the artists of Russia's theatrical renaissance, from
Isaak Rabinovich to Serge Soudeikine, and when Exter created her lavish
costumes for Salomé, Herodias (cat. no. 53), and Herod for Tairov's 1917
production, she was drawing on a recent and very rich tradition of
Salomé interpretations. True, her costumes were dynamic and her sets

opposite:
Cat. no. 210
Sergei Yutkevich
Costume design for the dancer Ludmilla
Semenova, *Good Treatment for Horses*,
1922

эскизъ для Л Н СЕМЕНОВОЙ

"ХОРОШЕЕ ОТНОШЕНИЕ К ЛОШАДЯМ"

Fig. 1
Scene from *Aelita*,
Yakov Protazanov's film, 1924.

Fig. 2
L'Annonce faite à Marie, act 1, 1920

architectonic, and, in spite of the billowing Bakstian veils, she was already anticipating the more structured and economical forms of *Aelita* (the science-fiction movie that she designed in 1924) (fig. 1). Even so, Exter, like Tairov, may have been more fin de siècle than we care to admit; essentially, her combination of "silvery black and silvery blue costumes sparkling against the background of drapery"[9] was as extravagant as Nikolai Kalmakov's scandalous designs for the Komissarzhevskaya/Evreinov interpretation (not realized) of October 1908. As a matter of fact, this much discussed "non-production" is of crucial importance to the development of the modernist stage in Russia, because it was precisely against this kind of decorative luxury that the constructivists revolted. Moreover, Exter herself accomplished this move from ornamental surface to spatial construction, as can be seen from a comparison of her *Salomé* of 1917 with her scenographic projects of the 1920s that were collected and reproduced as *Alexandra Exter: Décors de Théâtre*.[10] Some idea of the kind of heady excess that troubled the constructivists can be gained from the following description of the Kalmakov *Salomé*:

> The bloody tragedy, saturated with monstrous vice and sensuality, unfolds against a background of a dark blue, ominous sky with occasional stars of fanciful form and a huge sickle of the moon concealing the misty form of a naked woman. . . .The hangman Naaman with bright red hands and feet is as black as the night, the Syrian Narrab is as tender as a child, the handsome page of Herodias bows with his naked body blindingly white like marble; and they all seem to be convex, motionless, frozen idols. . . .[11]

While Exter's own interpretation of *Salomé* in 1917 owed something to Kalmakov's spectacle, she also managed to transcend the confines of the pictorial surface and to organize forms in their interaction with space. When the critic Yakov Tugendkhold observed of *Famira Kifared* that Exter and Tairov had "made an organic connection between the moving actors and the objects at rest,"[12] he indicated that the artist was about to reformulate the stage as a dynamic volume. Indeed, it was precisely in *Famira* and *Salomé* that the old conventions were replaced by a kinetic resolution in which the actors and the scenery played equal roles. Exter's concentration on the "rhythmically organized space"[13] pointed forward to her constructivist creations, when she would build rather than decorate the stage. As early as 1917, in her initial project for *Romeo and Juliet*, Exter filled up the "box of the stage from top to bottom with bridges and platforms."[14]

Even so, Tairov's Kamerny Theatre in Moscow, where these works of Exter were staged, was a place of compromise, and perhaps for this reason better survived the horrors of the Stalin era than did other theatres. By and large, its repertory was classical (*Phèdre, Romeo and Juliet*) and its decorations decorative—such as Boris Ferdinandov and Pavel Kuznetsov for *Sakuntala* (1914), and Soudeikine for *Le Mariage de Figaro* (1915) and *King Harlequin* (1917). To a considerable extent, too, the Kamerny Theatre "legalized" the symbolist heritage with its productions of Innokentii Annensky's version of *Famira* (1916), Paul Claudel's *L'Annonce faite à Marie* (1920) (fig. 2), Arthur Schnitzler's

Fig. 3
The Man Who Was Thursday, 1923

Fig. 4
The Magnanimous Cuckold, 1922

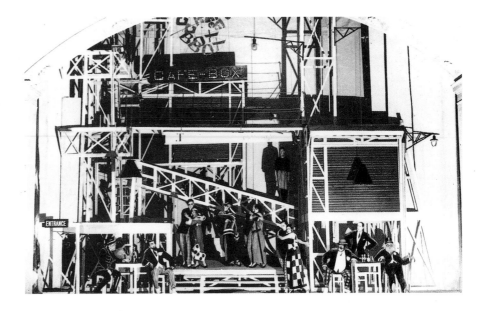

Der Schleier der Pierrette (The Veil of Pierrette) (1916), and Oscar Wilde's *Salomé* (1917). If it had not been for Exter's brilliant designs, the Kamerny Theatre would hardly be recognized as a radical and revolutionary theatre, for even the constructivist wizardries of Alexander Vesnin and Georgii Yakulov, e.g., for *The Man Who Was Thursday* (1923) (fig. 3) and *Giroflé-Girofla* (October 1922) were derivative variations on Popova's *Cuckold* (April 1922) (fig. 4), as some observers were quick to point out:

> A couple of words about the artist G. Yakulov. For some reason, most critics are delighted by his work. But, actually, the style of the backdrop construction has been borrowed from Popova (*Cuckold*); the trick doors and other accessories have also been taken from there.
> But what Popova resolved in a rigorous manner, Yakulov has twisted and convoluted.[15]

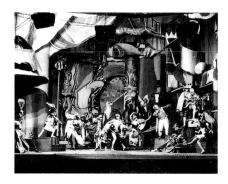

Fig. 5
Princess Brambilla, 1920

But Yakulov published a "counter-attack," arguing that the theatre was twenty years behind painting and, "while being objective in my judgment of the Kamerny Theatre, I must say that the presence of technical possibilities really limits the acuity of certain aspects of the spectacle."[16]

In deference to Yakulov, we should emphasize that his art cannot be contained within one stylistic category or by one theatrical allegiance. He gave his artistic allegiance neither to cubism, futurism, or constructivism, and yet he derived much of his strength from all these movements. It was in two productions in particular—*Princess Brambilla* (1920, in which Yakulov himself performed) and *Giroflé-Girofla*, both of which were given at the Kamerny Theatre (cat. no. 206, fig. 5)—that Yakulov demonstrated his innate sense of the theatre. As a matter of fact, Yakulov's set and costume designs for these two spectacles seemed destined more for the circus or "happenings" than for the conventional stage. Yakulov used chance, coincidence, and intuition, which resulted either in remarkable success (as in *Giroflé-Girofla*) or in abrupt failure (as in *Signor Formica* of 1922). This element of guesswork imbued Yakulov's art with spontaneity and immediacy that appealed to a broad public. As he once said, "Art exists for the ignoramus. The greatness of art lies in its right to be illiterate."[17] Consequently, Yakulov tended to regard the theatre precisely as a circus experience and, in turn, tried to emphasize its simplest and most basic ingredient—"the principle of perpetual motion."[18] In order to express this movement in *Giroflé-Girofla*, Yakulov resorted to an involved system of machines that "moved forward some parts, removed others, rolled out platforms, let down ladders, opened up traps, constructed passageways."[19] This crazy, chaotic spectacle, which Yakulov repeated in modified form in his conception of *Le Pas d'acier* (produced by Diaghilev in Paris in 1927), could not fail to evoke mirth, and it was the most popular entertainment in Moscow in 1922.

In spite of Exter's and Yakulov's brilliant contributions, the Kamerny Theatre remained, in the eyes of many contemporaries, passé. It was not necessarily technological misapplication or plagiarism, but rather the weight of tradition that hindered its advance toward the status of a truly revolutionary theatre. As the critic Sergei Ignatov wrote in 1923, the repertory of the Kamerny Theatre moved from "harlequinade to tragedy, and from tragedy back to harlequinade."[20] In this sense, the Kamerny Theatre with its classical repertory, its prima donna (Alisa Koonen), and its very title (the Chamber Theatre), maintained the conventional notion of the theatre as an intimate spectacle played to an elite public. Consequently, for more extreme transformations in Russian stage design and theatrical performance we should look elsewhere—to the theatre of mass action, to the alternative genres of cabaret, music hall, vaudeville, and circus, to Meyerhold's experiments, and also, perhaps unexpectedly, to the theory and practice of the artist and writer Yurii Annenkov.

The importance of the Meyerhold productions such as *Cuckold*, *The Death of Tarelkin*, and *The Bedbug* (1929) designed by Popova, Stepanova, and Rodchenko respectively, is, of course, undeniable and much has been written about them. There can be no question that these experiments broke sharply with the theatrical traditions still upheld by Meyerhold's rival, Tairov. Justifiably, *Theatre in Revolution* contains

Cat. 206
Georgii Yakulov
Set design, *Princess Brambilla*, 1920

many pertinent designs. Even a glance tells us that the installations constructed by Popova for *Cuckold* and *The Earth in Turmoil* (1923) and Stepanova's universal furniture for *Tarelkin* related directly to the elements of volume, dynamics, and spontaneity emphasized above. However, in order to appreciate these radical designs more fully, we should turn our attention to a production often neglected in discussions of the modern theatre. This was the Meyerhold/Annenkov production of Leo Tolstoy's play *The First Distiller* that Annenkov designed for the Hermitage Theatre in Petrograd in September 1919.

For the second act of this comedy (the scene in hell) Annenkov introduced a system of trapezes with trapeze artists, which elicited immediate associations with the circus. In turn, this audacious intervention paralleled or anticipated the general "circusization"[21] of the early Soviet theatre manifest in Nikolai Petrov's productions at the Theatre of Popular Comedy in Petrograd, in Ferdinandov's adaptation of circus techniques to his Experimental-Heroic Theatre in Moscow, and to specific events such as the interpretation of *Mystery-Bouffe* of 1921 by the artist Altman and director Efim Ravdel that was actually played out in the Salomonsky Circus in Moscow. In any case, Annenkov's ingenious conception prompted one critic to regard the spectacle as a "modernized *lubok* with its elements of the music hall and the circus."[22] It seems probable that the whole enterprise inspired the foundation of the eccentrist group of actors and artists in 1921 led by Grigorii Kozintsev, Georgii Kryzhitsky, and Leonid Trauberg. Incidentally, Meyerhold remembered *The First Distiller* when he came to work on *Cuckold* three years later, because there, too, he introduced "unprecedented, purely 'circus,' acrobatic numbers."[23]

Viktor Shklovsky described Annenkov's interpretation of *The First Distiller* as "a vivid thing, naked in its composition." He added, "Annenkov has done the following to Tolstoy's text":

> He has taken it as a scenario, and has elaborated it, incorporating harmonica players, popular songs, a clown, acrobats, etc. These insertions were motivated in the following way: the popular songs were included as songs being sung by the peasants drunk with the "devil's brew"; the harmonica players and choir were included on the stage during the drunk scene, while the acrobats were presented as devils, i.e., the circus has been introduced into the play as a depiction of hell. Finally, the clown in his ginger wig and baggy "customized" pants has been inserted without any motive at all. The gingerman just happened to turn up and wanders around hell. . . .
>
> This mix of farce and *moralité* interrupting and even complementing each other—this is the real merit of this merry and talented production.[24]

In his review Shklovsky also compared this production of *The First Distiller* with the 1911 production of *The Emperor Maximilian and His Disobedient Son, Adolf*, for which Tatlin had designed sets and costumes. Although these lacked the volumetrical dimension that he emphasized in *The Flying Dutchman* (1915–1918, not realized) and *Zangezi* (1923), Tatlin applied his interpretation of the neoprimitivist concerns of Natalia Goncharova and Mikhail Larionov to *The Emperor*, regarding the entire event as a folk or *lubochnaia* drama and emphasizing the elements of chance and casuality just as Annenkov did in *The First Distiller*.

The same was true of the famous opera *Victory over the Sun*, produced at the Luna Park Theatre, St. Petersburg, in December 1913 with libretto by Alexei Kruchenykh and Velimir Khlebnikov, music by Mikhail Matiushin, and designs by Kazimir Malevich. There is no need to repeat the basic information on *Victory over the Sun* since it has been the subject of much research and critics have often commented on its parallels with the circus and the *balagan* (fairground booth). Malevich's characters relate more to some riotous street performance than to an opera; indeed, their entire artistic environment seemed to be one of vulgarity and farce, as the following description makes clear:

> The opera was preceded by V. Khlebnikov's "prologue" under the title "Blackcreative Newslets." A. Kruchenykh "read" the prologue against the background of a curtain made out of just a regular bedsheet with "portraits" of Kruchenykh himself, Malevich, and Matiushin daubed on it. You can judge what kind of "prologue" this was from the fact that it was dominated by such inhuman expressions as:
> "Bytavy, ukravy, mytavy . . . ."
> Actually, the audience did understand something, i.e., that the sounds of some kind of "trumpeting" would soon be flying toward them.
> Since the futurists don't want to be like "everyone else," the curtain—after the prologue—was not pulled apart, but ripped in half.
> After which there proceeded the "opera," if I may call it that.

Cat. no. 96
Valentina Khodasevich
Design for stage construction,
Archangel Michael, 1922

In the end it became boring, and it was the audience itself that came to the rescue of the weary futurists. Almost every cue was followed by some witty word or other, and soon the theatre was hosting not one, but two performances: one onstage, and the other in the auditorium. Whistling and booing replaced the "music" which, by the way, harmonized very well with the crazy decors and the delirium that resounded from the stage. . . .[25]

"Inhuman expressions" and "delirium" were, however, primary ingredients of Russian cubofuturism, and they provided the new theatre with a juvenile vitality that it had lacked for too long. Malevich's funfair figures and transrational sets for *Victory over the Sun* were an abrupt challenge to the conventional dramatic theatre; their dissonance and "barbarity" left an imprint on many subsequent productions—from the Meyerhold arrangement of Mayakovsky's *Mystery-Bouffe* in 1921 (with designs by Viktor Kiselev and Anton Lavinsky) to Valentina Khodasevich's work on *Archangel Michael* in 1922 (cat. nos. 96, 98, 99).

Although Annenkov is now remembered more for his incisive graphic portraits of political and cultural leaders and his book illustrations, he was also one of the leading theoreticians of the stage and its design just before and after the Revolution. His acute observations on the theatre are worth recalling, especially the key statements in his primary tract entitled "The Theatre of Pure Method," which he first gave as a lecture at the Petrograd House of Arts in April 1921.

overleaf left:
Cat. no. 99
Valentina Khodasevich
Costume design for a Man,
Archangel Michael, 1922

overleaf right:
Cat. no. 98
Valentina Khodasevich
Costume design for Lucille,
Archangel Michael, 1922

69   The Construction of Caprice

Affirming that the theatre of the past had been accommodated within numerous aesthetic categories, Annenkov contended that their point of derivation had always been the same false one, i.e., that

> the theatre is not an independent, self-sufficient, pure form of art, but merely a treaty drawn up by a bunch of different arts, a treaty according to which they promise to reproduce, supplement, explain, and reveal—by visual and acoustic media—the fortuitous, miraculous elements of the theatre. . . .
>
> Hitherto, the theatre has been merely a medium, a means of presentation, but not an end in itself . . . there has been no theatre of pure method. . . .
>
> Basically, theatre is dynamic. . . .
>
> Hitherto, decors have served as backgrounds for the scenic presentation, an environment for the dramatis personae of the play. . . .
>
> There is no place in the theatre for dead pictures, for all is in movement. But until the decor stirs from its place and starts to run around the stage, we will not see a single, organically fused theatrical presentation.
>
> Bakst, Anisfeld, Soudeikine—least of all are they stage designers.
>
> Artistically organized, i.e., rhythmically organized, movement is theatrical form.[26]

One of Annenkov's most interesting points of scenic analysis was that the distance between the proscenium and the auditorium, between "there" and "here," was being overcome, i.e., that the traditional hierarchy of the theatre (perpetuated by the position of the diva vis-à-vis the public or the dividing line between "high" tragedy and "low" music hall) was destined to disappear with the "democratization of the theatre":

> Is it not true that Meyerhold interrupted [Emile] Verhaeren with the speech and proclamations of revolution?
>
> Is it not true that, concurrently with Meyerhold, Max Reinhardt introduced the spectator into the action by distributing a crowd of Parisians along the levels of the auditorium in his *Danton*?
>
> Is it not true that we attempted to seize the great majesty of the crowd in the mass presentations on the squares of Petersburg?[27]

Annenkov's reference to the "mass presentations" is not casual, because he and his colleague Evreinov produced and designed *The Storming of the Winter Palace* in Petrograd in November 1920—one of the most impressive mass actions involving 6,000 actors, 500 musicians, and 100,000 spectators who viewed the action from Uritsky (now Winter Palace) Square. *The Storming of the Winter Palace* was one of several mass actions planned for the major cities just after the Revolution, but few were realized. Although the genre of the mass action was international and of long standing (cf. the elaborate, organized mass festivals at the time of the French Revolution), its apologists in Soviet Russia felt that it could and should be adjusted directly to their own ideological needs. Alexei Gan, one of the enthusiastic supporters of the movement, explained that the mass action is not an invention or a fantasy, but is an absolute and organic necessity deriving from the very essence of Communism. . . . The mass action under Communism is not the action of a civic society, but of a human one—wherein material production will fuse with intellectual production. This intellectual/material culture is mobilizing all its strength and means so as to subordinate unto itself not only nature, but also the whole, universal cosmos.[28]

However, *The Storming of the Winter Palace* was an ambitious but ill-conceived enterprise since, in relying on the "masses" as an integral part, it required enormous manpower that could not be satisfactorily controlled. Annenkov recorded the details of the White, or Right, Tribune in the production:

125 ballet dancers
100 circus people
1,750 supernumeraries and students
200 women, preferably students
260 secondary actors and
150 assistants. . . .[29]

Ultimately, the spectacle merely regenerated and confirmed historical facts and called for no interpretation or act of imagination on the part of the audience. As one of the producers wrote:

The spectacle begins. . . . We have flags, telephones, electric bells in our hands. Actors come out on to the steps of the Stock Exchange. . . . It was obvious that they were not touched or excited by the idea of the scenario or by the project itself."[30]

However, to a considerable extent, *The Storming of the Winter Palace* served as a practical illustration of Annenkov's theatre of pure method. In spite of (or because of) its partial derivation from the medieval mystery or morality play and public carnival, it broke the rules of conventional theatre, especially in its transformation or, rather, incorporation, of the audience into the cast. No doubt, what also attracted Annenkov, Gan, and other constructivists to the mass action was its potential mobility. May Day celebrations and other more metaphorical dramatizations such as *The Struggle and Victory of the Soviets* (cat. no. 136), designed by Popova and Vesnin for the Congress of the Third International in 1921 (rehearsed by Meyerhold, but not realized), did not need a fixed location, text, or even particular distribution of roles. With a projected cast of 200 cavalry, 2,300 infantry, 16 artillery batteries, tanks, motorcycles, and 5 airplanes carrying projectors, *Struggle and Victory* was impractical to produce, but it did give Popova valuable experience for her less ambitious scheme for *The Earth in Turmoil* two years later.

Sometimes the result of the mass actions was chaos, but the universality and uncontrollability that characterized such street theatre were unimaginable within the respectable walls of the Kamerny Theatre or the Moscow Art Theatre. The lack of discipline and even public

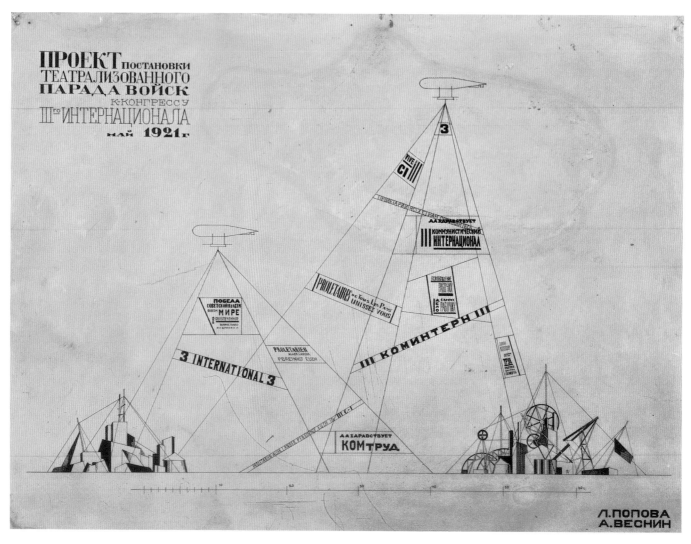

Cat. no. 136
Liubov Popova and Alexander Vesnin
Set design, *The Struggle and Victory
of the Soviets*, 1921

indifference that often accompanied the mass actions are elements that relate directly to the concept of the *peredvizhnoi* or movable theatre of the 1920s, both literally (this was the actual name of a particular theatre founded in Petrograd in 1922) and symbolically (a play could be instantly performed at any time and any place). Once again, we are reminded of the traveling troupes and wandering minstrels and mummers of Old Russia, but in the 1920s the movable theatre also represented a novel approach that led to the transitory and experimental nature of much constructivist theatre. To some extent, such concepts also help to explain the numerous nonproductions of the avant-garde, for one of its paradoxes is the lasting fame or notoriety generated by projects for certain spectacles that never reached the stage. Several images from these constructivist nonconstructions are included in *Theatre in Revolution*, such as *Romeo and Juliet* designed by Popova in 1920, *The Love for Three Oranges* designed by Alexander Khostenko-Khostov in 1926, and *I Want a Child* designed by El Lissitzky in 1928 (cat. no. 112). As Sergei Tretiakov wrote in 1922, it was the "sketch, the rehearsal, and the moving around of decorations"[31] that had become more important than the finished product, especially as the conventional plotline gave way to special effects, quick changes, and improvisation. As music hall and vaudeville such as the Blue Blouse revues (fashioned so energetically by Nina Aizenberg) gained ascendance, so critics concluded that "serious"

Cat. no. 112
El Lissitzky
Maquette of stage and auditorium,
I Want a Child (reconstructed by
N. Kustov), n.d.

theatre no longer existed. How appropriate, then, that the leading theatre journals of the early 1920s carried advertisements for depilators, shaving creams, hair restorers, and other cosmetics next to their articles about constructivist performance.[32]

In this respect, Meyerhold's experimental presentations in the early and mid-1920s take on an even greater significance, for they relied as much on accident and unpredictability (for example, Stepanova's furniture for *The Death of Tarelkin* did not always function in the way it was supposed to) as on the directives of the producer and artist. Ultimately, perhaps it was this very combination of the ludicrous and the streamlined that distinguished the constructivist movement. Constructivism affected not only the decorative aspect of the theatre, transforming the stage into a truly three-dimensional experience, but also the dramatic text, the music (or other) accompaniment, and the actors themselves. Meyerhold's system of biomechanics, with its debt to the eurhythmic principles of Emile Jaques-Dalcroze, the work-study programs of Frederick Winslow Taylor, and the devices of the Japanese theatre, was a principal element in the constructivist concept of the performer: "Maximum effect through minimum means" and "function determines form" were the basic assumptions on which Meyerhold constructed his system and that he taught to students such as Ilia Shlepianov and Elizaveta Yakunina at his State Higher Directors' Workshop (GVYRM) from 1922 onward.

In 1920 Meyerhold was given the premises of the former Zon Theatre in Moscow. Stripping the stage bare and revealing the original bricks of the walls, Meyerhold turned this once elegant theatre into a loft or alternative space. Meyerhold opened his new enterprise—the RSFSR (Russian Soviet Federated Socialist Republic) Theatre No. 1—in November 1920 with a production of Verhaeren's *Les Aubes* (The Dawns) with designs by Vladimir Dmitriev. The play was politically relevant in that its subject was a capitalist war that turned into a revolution of the international proletariat. But the audience found certain methods, such as the presence of a Greek chorus in the orchestra pit, the interruption of the narrative by episodes of a purely agitational nature, and the abstract cylinders, spheres, cones, and disks scattered onstage to be perplexing and illogical. Clearly, both Meyerhold and Dmitriev wished to renounce the use of illustrative decor, but the conglomeration of shapes produced merely another kind of superficial decoration. Fortunately, Dmitriev did better in his subsequent designs, e.g., for *The Love for Three Oranges* of 1926, but what Meyerhold needed immediately was a designer who above all would be able to use material in three dimensions in close conjunction with the integral component of movement onstage. Meyerhold found this support in the art of Rodchenko, Stepanova, and, above all, Popova.

Popova was first involved in stage design in 1920 when she was commissioned to design costumes for the children's play *The Tale of the Country Priest and His Dunderhead Servant*. In 1920 she designed costumes and sets for Anatolii Lunacharsky's play, *The Locksmith and the Chancellor* (cat. no. 135), and also prepared sets and costumes for the unrealized production of *Romeo and Juliet* at the Kamerny Theatre. The same year she worked with Vesnin and Meyerhold on *The Struggle and Victory of the Soviets* mentioned above. But the turning point in Popova's career and in the evolution of constructivist theatre came in September 1921. In that month the famous exhibition *5 × 5 = 25* opened in Moscow, at which five artists—Exter, Popova, Rodchenko, Stepanova, and Vesnin—contributed five abstract works each. One of the visitors was Meyerhold, who, on seeing the works of Popova and her colleagues, concluded that they could be used as the basis of stage designs. The result was that Meyerhold invited Popova to compile a program for a course in material, three-dimensional stage design at his State Higher Theatre Workshop (GVYTM), and it was here that Popova developed the basic ideas for her extraordinary construction for *The Magnanimous Cuckold*, staged by Meyerhold on 25 April 1922.

Meyerhold took Fernand Crommelynck's rather indecent farce about a miller who suspects his adulterous wife but who is constantly duped, and used it merely as an experiment in pure acting and pure form, "taking the circus, not literature as his departure-point."[33] Although Popova is generally credited with the visual design of this spectacle, it should be remembered that she started with suggestions by other artists already working in the Workshops, including Sergei Eisenstein, and with a model developed by Vladimir Liutse. Still, the definitive conception belonged to Popova. The artist Louis Lozowick recalled his impression of the production:

> The stage was bare—no curtain, no proscenium arch, wings, backdrop, floodlights. On the background of the bare wall of the building with its open brickwork, one saw a simple, skeleton-like construction, a scaffolding designed by Popova consisting of one large black wheel and two small ones, red and white. Several platforms at various levels, revolving doors, stairs, ladders, chutes; square, triangular, and rectangular shapes.[34]

Inevitably, Popova's construction elicited censure as well as praise. Ippolit Sokolov, for example, felt it necessary to write after seeing the performance that

it is difficult to imagine anything more vulgar, coarse, and more tasteless than the revolving red-and-black wheels of Popova's construction for *The Cuckold* [that were used to expand] the emotions of jealousy or sensuality.[35]

Whatever the responses to *Cuckold*, neither Popova nor Meyerhold regarded it as a standard prototype, although it certainly influenced many other theatrical resolutions of the 1920s, including Stepanova's designs for *Tarelkin* and Vesnin's *The Man Who Was Thursday*. In fact, as indicated above, Vesnin even disputed the significance of the Popova/Meyerhold collaboration, arguing that it was *The Man Who Was Thursday* that had really established the move toward construction onstage.[36] Popova's next and last theatrical endeavor, her design for Meyerhold's production of *The Earth in Turmoil* of 1923, relied on a totally representational setting and employed a real automobile, a real tractor, real telephones, etc. Rodchenko also incorporated real objects into the theatre for his rendering of Meyerhold's production of Mayakovsky's *The Bedbug* in 1929.

No doubt, Popova's work on *Cuckold* also provided a valuable

Fig. 6
Varvara Stepanova
Designs for sports clothes, 1923

stimulus to Stepanova in her constructivist inventions for *Tarelkin* even though she did not admit this. Certainly, Stepanova seems to have been repeating Popova's basic effort

> to transfer the issue from the aesthetic to the productivist dimension [and to present] the organization of the material elements of the spectacle as an apparatus, a kind of installation or contrivance for the given action.[37]

In any case, Stepanova's use of a series of wooden constructions of abstract form produced an unprecedented, variable scenario. As the actors moved about the stage, their formal, physical definitions changed constantly because the laths and slats of the constructions served as a kind of op-art mechanism. As she asserted in a conversation with Gan immediately after the premiere of *Tarelkin*,

> In *The Death of Tarelkin* I managed finally to show spatial objects in their utilitarian context and where I wanted to supply real objects—a table, a chair, armchairs, screens, etc. As a totality, they integrated the material environment wherein the live human material was meant to act.[38]

From the costumes for *Tarelkin*, it is clear that Stepanova was concerned with simplicity of form and maximum of efficiency. As in her *sportodezhda* (sports clothes) of 1923 (fig. 6), Stepanova regarded emotion, illusion, and ornament as alien to the utilitarian aspect of constructivism, and maintained that each profession—factory worker, doctor, actor, or sportsman—required its own costume, which should be constructed according to the norms of expediency and convenience dictated by that profession. The most exciting instance of Stepanova's experiments in this area were, indeed, her designs for sports clothes (not unlike the stage costumes for the characters Tarelkin (cat. no. 173) or Raspliuev (cat. no. 175) in *Tarelkin*, incorporating lightness of form (for mobility), economy of material (to restrain the body's temperature), and clear colors (for identification). They were not mass produced, but *Tarelkin* provided her with the opportunity to test her uniforms within a three-dimensional, living environment.

But not all were happy with *Tarelkin*. Sergei Bobrov, painter and poet and one-time friend of Goncharova and Larionov, complained in his review, "A Kind of Ideological Struggle: The History of Tarelkin's Murder," that

> Stepanova is guilty of attempting to murder the virtuous Tarelkin . . . but the general result of all this is trashy, downright pretentious furniture that has nothing to do with the play and that, therefore, merely gets in the way.[39]

Vladimir Bezard, too, in his article, "Meyerhold and the Russian Theatre," also refused to recognize the novelty of Stepanova's designs:

> Meyerhold has really been unlucky with his artists. *The Death of Tarelkin*, too, suffers as a result of its installation. The furniture is weak. The numerous bits of paper and documents are badly done. The costumes are a

ТАРЕЛКИН

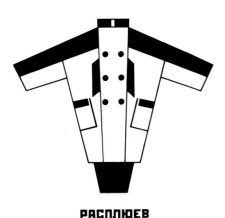

РАСПЛЮЕВ

Cat. no. 173
Varvara Stepanova
Costume design for Tarelkin,
The Death of Tarelkin, 1922

Cat. no. 175
Varvara Stepanova
Costume design for Raspliuev, Chief
of Police, *The Death of Tarelkin*, 1922

failure, even though, for some reason or other, they are called *prozodezhda* —in spite of the obvious aestheticism of all these strips of material, pieces sewn on, and little pockets.[40]

Perhaps the real reason for the widespread hostility toward the scenic resolutions in Meyerhold's theatre lay in their mechanical gadgets often hampering rather than enhancing the actors and their acting. True, for constructivists such as Nikolai Foregger, Gan, and Sokolov, the human body itself was a potential machine that had still to be streamlined, regulated, and made efficient. The fact that the actor in *Cuckold* and *Tarelkin*, therefore, moved as a mechanical component or as a piece of furniture, was—or should have been—fully expressive of their artistic ethos. It was all part of what Gan called the "passage from composition (an aesthetic symptom) to construction (a productional principle)."[41] But to those who valued "life" above "technology," such as Tairov and Yanov, author of a major theoretical manual on stage design in 1926, the result of the constructivists' material constructions onstage did not mean "that the actor was liberated from the power of objects, but that he got stuck to various steps and ladders."[42] Tairov was especially adamant in his stand against this "dehumanization":

> The mechanization of art is a malicious reaction both in art and in life— pathetic spanners in the works of the locomotive of human progress.[43]

Even Boris Arvatov, one of the leading apologists of constructivism and the machine aesthetic, complained that the contemporary theatre had become "technologized" for the sake not of society but of technology alone, although he did recognize that constructivist design had vanquished the nonfigurative art of "our enemies" Malevich and Tatlin.[44] In any case, Meyerhold's artists had little experience of scenic installation and structural engineering, so that the wheels in *Cuckold* often stuck and the revolving stage that Rodchenko projected for *One-Sixth of the World* in 1931 never revolved. Viktor Shestakov, one of Meyerhold's designers, was aware of this failing:

> A technical process or the process whereby spatial and material form is resolved is incomprehensible in a preparatory drawing. Yet this form is one of the basic qualities in the creative resolution of the spectacle.[45]

An evident cause for dissatisfaction also lay in the blatant irony inherent in the endeavor to present sophisticated technology within the comfortable isolation of the theatre when the Soviet economy was in shambles—and when, as one critic has written recently,

> the artist was so absorbed in the creation of systems that for a long time he gave no thought to those he was creating for—the people of the future. Who were they, these people facing the prospect of migrating to the future under the protection of blooming mills, Towers to the Third International, or skyscrapers on stilts? This question, raised in the staging of Mayakovsky's comedies, where the conflicts are based entirely on the move from today to the future and back again, found an answer in Vsevolod

Cat. no. 123
Ignatii Nivinsky
Costume design for Brighella,
Princess Turandot, 1921

Cat. no. 124
Ignatii Nivinsky
Costume design for Prince Calaf,
Princess Turandot, 1921

Meyerhold's and Rodchenko's staging of *The Bedbug*. The people of the future appeared on stage—in uniforms.[46]

It was this divorce of art from life in the 1920s that prompted Arvatov to dismiss, at least implicitly, the entire phenomenon of contemporary theatre and to urge its artists to become designers of "life," not of "art":

> Abandon the stages, the ramps, and the spectacles. Go into life, train and retrain. Learn not aesthetic methods, but the methods of life itself, of social construction. Be engineers, be the assembly workers of everyday life. The working class wants real, scientifically organized forms, not illusions. It needs the construction of life, not its imitation.[47]

But although constructivism was a primary creative expression of Soviet Russia of the 1920s, it was, of course, not the only style supported in the visual arts. Although *Theatre in Revolution* emphasizes these extreme experiments, it should be remembered that many other scenic systems were elaborated in the theatres of Moscow and Petrograd/Leningrad— from Boris Kustodiev's "mercantile primitivism" for Alexei Dikii's production of *The Flea* in 1926 to the expressionist fantasies by the Filonov School for *The Inspector General* in 1927. Nevertheless, more often than not, it was a "soft" and lyrical interpretation of constructivism that held sway in which the severe, monochromatic surfaces of Rodchenko and Stepanova were adulterated with bright colors, allegorical ornaments, and the "piquancy of a refined, tavern-like eroticism."[48] Alexander Fevralsky sensed the danger as early as 1923 when he noted that "decorative constructivism" was becoming increasingly prominent at the Kamerny Theatre, the studios of the Moscow Art Theatre, and the Habimah Theatre. "What we have is a danger of aesthetic constructivism (a self-contradiction), a vulgarization, the substitution of construction by decoration."[49] Certainly, the tinted geometries of Ignatii Nivinsky for Evgenii Vakhtangov's production of *Princess Turandot* in 1922 (cat. nos. 122–124), Konstantin Vialov's for Valerii Bebutov's production of *Stenka Razin* in 1924 (cat. no. 205), or Goleizovsky's sensual harlequinades are more intimate, more accessible, and more "human" than the mechanical anonymities of Rodchenko and Stepanova.

When we take account of this plurality of styles in the early Soviet theatre and realize that the rigorous economy of constructivism was the exception rather than the rule, we can understand why—conversely—one of the leitmotifs of the avant-garde critics and artists was a call to cleanse the theatre of excess. At first this "convalescence campaign"[50] was directed at petit-bourgeois triviality, inasmuch as constructivism was regarded as the purifying agent that "cleansed [the theatre] for the actor's play."[51] The theatre needed a "radical disinfection," declared Annenkov.[52] Similarly, other supporters of the theatre of pure method demanded the "deaestheticization" of the theatre, for "it is much more important for us to end this eau-de-cologne, candy aestheticism in all this Goleizovsky stuff."[53] Actually, the most radical application of this hygiene control was the Taylorized gymnastics of "industrial gesticulation" that Sokolov proposed in 1922–1923, arguing that this

Cat. no. 122
Ignatii Nivinsky
Set design for *Princess Turandot*, 1921

Cat. no. 205
Konstantin Vialov
Costume design for Stenka Razin,
Stenka Razin, 1924

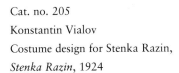

should be the Soviet style in the same way that the baroque, the rococo, the Empire, etc., had provided the artistic expressions of the imperial and capitalist regimes.[54] Ironically, it was but a short step from Sokolov's extension of biomechanical efficiency to the mass-gymnastic displays and military parades of the Stalin era.

The tragedy of the Russian avant-garde onstage is that it hardly touched the audience for whom, ostensibly, it was intended. The new consumer of cultural invention was often ingenuous and illiterate and had little understanding of the complexities of cubofuturism and constructivism. Furthermore, the very denominator to which the proletarian public might have related directly—the human body—was often deformed, eclipsed, and lost from view. As the critic Alexander Briantsev wrote in the catalogue to *Stage Design in the USSR during the Decade 1917–1927,*

> Above all, the untried spectator will seek an *explanation* of the place and time in the decor, because what he needs is the *logical* interconnection of all three concepts: place, time, and action.[55]

Socialist realism restored place, time, and action to the theatre. It replaced the "inhuman expressions" and "delirium" of the avant-garde with a logical and florid decoration that appealed to many more members of the new Soviet society than had the avant-garde. As we examine *Theatre in Revolution*, we should not forget this vital aspect of theatre, i.e., the degree of audience participation and the relevance or irrelevance of these remarkable sets and costumes to the human dimension. One result of our inquiry may well be that we begin to question our blind enthusiasm for the avant-garde and mollify our traditional censure of socialist realism, the cruel, but eminently theatrical movement that replaced and destroyed it.

Notes

1. See Erik Gollerbakh, Alexander Golovin, and Levkii Zheverzheev, eds., *Teatralno-dekoratsionnoe iskusstvo v SSSR 1917–1927* (Stage Design in the USSR during the Decade 1917–1927) (Leningrad: Komitet vystavki teatralno-dekoratsionnogo iskusstva, 1927).
2. Erik Gollerbakh, "Teatr kak zrelishche" (Theatre as Spectacle), in Gollerbakh et al., 39.
3. Gollerbakh et al., 42.
4. Alexander Yanov, *Teatralnaia dekoratsiia* (Theatre Design) (Leningrad: Blago, 1926), 40.
5. Gollerbakh et al., 20.
6. Gollerbakh et al., 34.
7. Alexander Kugel, "Balet" (Ballet), *Zhizn iskusstva* [Petrograd], 1923, no. 18:2.
8. Yurii Annenkov, "Teatr chistogo metoda" (The Theatre of Pure Method), 1921, Manuscript, F.2613, op. 1, ed. khr. 14, 1.8, TsGALI (Central State Archive of Literature and Art, Moscow).
9. Konstantin Rudnitsky, *Russian and Soviet Theater 1905–1932* (New York: Abrams, 1988), 18.
10. (Paris: Editions des Quatre Chemins, 1930).
11. M. Veikone, "Na generalnoi repetitsii 'Salomei' v teatre V.F. Komissarzhevskoi" (At the Dress Rehearsal for *Salomé* at the Komissarzhevskaya Theatre), in *Alkonost* (St. Petersburg: Peredvizhnoi teatre P.P. Gaideburova i N.F. Skarskoi, 1911), 140.
12. Yakov Tugendkhold, "Pismo iz Moskvy" (Letter From Moscow), *Apollon* [Petrograd], 1917, no. 1:72.
13. Konstantin Derzhavin, *Kniga o Kamernom teatre* (The Book of the KamernyTheatre) (Leningrad: Khudozhestvennaia literatura, 1934), 70.
14. Nina Giliarovskaia, *Teatralno-dekoratsionnoe iskusstva za 5 let* (Five Years of Theatrical Design Art), exh. cat. (Kazan, 1924), 29.
15. Abbat-Fanfreliush, "Kamernyi" (The Kamerny), in *Zrelishcha* [Moscow], 1922, no. 7:9.
16. Georgii Yakulov, "Moia kontr-ataka" (My Counterattack), *Ermitazh* [Moscow], 1922, no. 7:11.
17. Quoted in Giliarovskaia, 46.
18. Giliarovskaia, 45.
19. Abram Efros, *Kamernyi teatr i ego khudozhniki 1914–1934* (The Kamerny Theatre and Its Artists 1914–1934) (Moscow: VTO, 1934), xxxvi.
20. Sergei Ignatov, "Moskovskii Kamernyi teatr" (Moscow Kamerny Theatre), *Teatr* [Berlin], 1923, no. 1:5.
21. D. Zolotnitsky, "Oktiabr i opyty agit-komedii" (October and the Experiment of Agit-Comedy), in Yurii Golovashenko, ed., *Teatr i dramaturgiia* (Theatre and Dramatic Art) (Leningrad: Leningradskii gosudarstvennyi institut teatra, muzyki i kinematografii, 1974), 48.
22. N.N-v., "Pervyi vinokur" (The First Distiller), *Zhizn iskusstva*, 1919, no. 259–60:2.
23. "Khronika" (Chronicle), *Ermitazh*, 1922, no. 1:8. (A discussion of the Theatre of Popular Comedy and the eccentrist artists is in Mel Gordon's essay in this volume.)
24. Viktor Shklovsky, "Dopolnennyi Tolstoi" (The Supplemental Tolstoi), *Zhizn iskusstva*, 1919, no. 259–60, 2.
25. "Petersburg," *Muzy* [Kiev], 1913, no. 1:20.
26. Annenkov, 1.8–9.
27. Annenkov, 1.6.
28. Alexei Gan, "Borba za massovoe deistvo" (The Struggle for a Mass Action), in Ivan Aksionov et al., *O teatre* (About Theatre), Tver: Tverskoe izdatelstvo, 1922), 73.
29. Yurii Annenkov, "Revoliutsiia i teatr" (Revolution and Theatre), in *Parizhskii vestnik* [Paris, published by the Embassy of the USSR], 1925, no. 66:3.
30. Quoted in Evgenii Znosko-Borovsky, *Russkii teatr nachala XX veka* (Early Twentieth-Century Russian Theatre) (Prague: Plamia, 1925), 428–29.
31. Sergei Tretiakov, "Velikodushnyi rogonosets" (The Magnanimous Cuckold), *Zrelishcha*, 1922, no. 8:12.
32. See, for example, *Teatr i zrelishcha* (Theatre and Spectacle) (supplement to *Zhizn iskusstva*, 1927, no. 18:3. (A discussion of the Blue Blouse revues is in Nancy Baer's essay in this volume.)
33. "Khronika" (Chronicle), in *Ermitazh*, 1922, no. 1:8.
34. Louis Lozowick, "Survivor from a Dead Age," 30, undated, Manuscript, collection of Adele Lozowick, New York.
35. Ippolit Sokolov, "Teatralnyi konstruktivizm" (Theatrical Constructivism), *Teatr i muzyka* [Moscow], 1922. no. 12:288.
36. Alexander Vesnin, "Pismo v redaktsiiu" (Letter to the Editor), *Zrelishcha*, 1922, no. 4:15.
37. From a lecture that Popova gave at the Institute of Artistic Culture, Moscow, on 27 April 1922. Translated from the French in Natalia Adaskina and Dmitri Sarabianov, *Liubov Popova* (Paris: Sers, 1989), 378.
38. [Alexei Gan], "Beseda s V.F. Stepanovoi" (Conversation with V. F. Stepanova), *Zrelishcha*, 1922, no. 16:11.
39. Sergei Bobrov, "V poriadke ideologicheskoi borby: Istoriia ubiistva Tarelkina" (A Kind of Ideological Struggle: The History of Tarelkin's Murder), *Zrelishcha*, 1922, no. 18:10.
40. Vladimir Bezard, "Meierkhold i russkii teatr" (Meyerhold and the Russian Theatre), *Zrelishcha*, 1922, no. 15:9.
41. [Alexei Gan], "Konstruktivisty" (The Constructivists), *Ermitazh*, 1922, no. 13:3.
42. V. Azov, "Portnoi Ivanov iz Londona i Parizha" (The Tailor Ivanov from London and Paris), *Zhizn iskusstva*, 1923, no. 6:12.

43. Alexander Tairov, "Iz zapisnoi knizhki" (From the Notebook), *Gostinitsa dlia puteshestvuiushchikh v prekrasnom* [Moscow], 1922, no. 8:9.

44. Boris Arvatov, "Dve gruppirovki" (Two Groups), *Zrelishcha*, 1922, no. 8:9.

45. Viktor Shestakov, "Mysli o rabote khudozhnika teatra" (Thoughts on the Work of a Theatre Artist), ca. 1930–1940, Manuscript, F.2343, ed. khr. 304, op. 1, 1.81, TsGALI (see note 8).

46. Boris Brodsky, "The Psychology of Urban Design in the 1920s and 1930s," *The Journal of Decorative and Propaganda Arts*, 1987, no. 5:81.

47. Boris Arvatov, "Ot rezhissiory teatra k montazhu byta" (From Theatre Directing to the Montage of Existence), *Ermitazh*, 1922, no. 11:3.

48. Khrisanf Khersonsky, "Pisma iz Moskvy" (Letters from Moscow), *Zhizn iskusstva*, 1923, no. 6:4.

49. Alexander Fevralsky, "Detskaia bolezn pravizny i konstruktivizma" (A Childhood Disease of Righteousness and Constructivism), *Zrelishcha*, 1923, no. 34:6.

50. "Ko dniu pechati" (By the Day of Printing), *Zhizn iskusstva*, 1927, no. 18:1.

51. Alexei Gvozdev, "Ledianaia Deva" (The Ice Maiden), *Zhizn iskusstva*, 1927, no. 18:5.

52. Annenkov, "Teatr chistogo metoda," 1.109 (verso).

53. Vladimir Mass, "DEestetizatsiia iskusstva" (Deaestheticizing Art), *Zrelishcha*, 1922, no. 5:7.

54. Ippolit Sokolov, "Stil RSFSR" (The Style of the Russian Soviet Federated Socialist Republic), *Teatr i muzyka*, 1922, no. 1:3. (The effect of Taylorism on theories of movement is discussed in Nicoletta Misler's essay in this volume.)

55. Alexander Briantsev, "Stsenicheskaia veshch i stsenicheskii chelovek" (The Object Onstage and the Person Onstage), in Gollerbakh et al., 180.

The Russian Avant-Garde and the Theatre of the Artist

Mikhail Kolesnikov

From the moment of the emergence of avant-garde trends in the Russian visual arts in the 1900s–1910s, and in pace with their formation, the role of the artist in the theatre acquired an extraordinary dynamic, which led toward a revolution in stage design. The intensity of that artistic process, with its continuous influx of new ideas and aesthetic concepts, resulted in the coexistence of a multitude of styles. Every aspect of theatrical production, from scenic design and costumes to the movement of the actor was reevaluated and reconceived.

Of course, this kind of re-envisioning became possible only after the emergence of nonobjective art at the beginning of the 1910s. Only the artist-innovator could reject the age-old system of defining stage space with flat, painted decorations and could instead build onstage a three-dimensional, volumetric construction. Further experiments in the 1920s turned the stage set into a functional machine, a contraption for the actor's play. Because such construction referred to the place of action by only a few details, decoration had a symbolic, even abstract, character.

Vladimir Tatlin was one of several Russian avant-garde artists who came to the theatre at the very beginning of their professional careers and worked as scenic designers virtually to the end, while at the same time remaining first and foremost easel painters.[1] Each of Tatlin's productions of the 1910s to the 1920s was an event and deserves a separate discussion. However, I shall only mention three of his projects in which Tatlin outlined future discoveries in the sphere of stage design.

In 1913–1914 Tatlin created his design for Mikhail Glinka's opera, *A Life for the Czar* (or *Ivan Susanin*), in full format, which included preparatory studies of all stage sets and costumes, including mass scenes. This unproduced work was notable for its use of three-dimensional decoration, the first in Russian theatrical design by a scenic artist.

Tatlin continued his exploration in the next, also never-realized, design for Richard Wagner's opera, *The Flying Dutchman*, which he worked on over the following three years (the designs have been dated 1915 to 1918) (cat. nos. 177, 178). His few sketches of the masts represent engineering outlines executed with the help of drafting instruments. The stage design for the single set is reminiscent of an enormous sailing ship. Tatlin was the first to break up the surface of the stage, building several planes tilted at different angles and intersecting each other at different levels, which opened up new and promising possibilities for the actors' dynamic and plastic movement. On his

Cat. no. 194
Alexander Vesnin
Program cover design, *Phèdre*, 1922

Cat. no. 177
Vladimir Tatlin
Design for a Ship, *The Flying Dutchman*,
1915–1918

Cat. no. 178
Vladimir Talin
Design for a Mast, *The Flying Dutchman*,
1915–1918

intersecting decks the artist built enormous masts with sails that were
more than just decorative. Actor-sailors were expected to climb them
as part of the action, which allowed the use not only of the horizontal
plane and depth, but also of the vertical space. Most importantly, in
The Flying Dutchman Tatlin for the first time introduced the concept of a
construction onstage. Just a year later, in 1919, the first drafts of Tatlin's
"tower" appeared, which culminated in the famous open spiral structure,
the Monument to the Third International.

Tatlin's next work in the theatre was devoted to the memory of
Velimir Khlebnikov. In 1923, an amateur company of the Experimental
Theatre of the Museum of Artistic Culture in Petrograd produced
Zangezi, for which Tatlin served as the author of the play based on
Khlebnikov's poem of the same name, director, actor, and, of course,
scenic artist. To Khlebnikov's construction of words, where sound was
the principal building element, Tatlin attempted to find a counterpart in a
tangible construction, built with a variety of materials of different surfaces
and different shapes. According to the artist's conception, certain combinations of colors and forms corresponded to certain sounds; light and costumes
also played an important role in the production (cat. nos. 183, 184).
Unfortunately, the play was a failure, primarily because of the difficulty
of unifying disparate elements into a coherent theatrical performance.

In the 1920s, the evolution of Russian art was characterized by
the frequent change and cross-pollination of styles and tendencies. The
artist-innovator was extremely important to the new theatre, just as a
pilot is indispensable in turbulent and unfamiliar waters. Tatlin, however,
represented the reverse—an artist in need of the theatre. Why was theatre
so attractive to avant-garde visual artists, especially during those years
when experimentation in their studios was at its most intense? The
answer lies in the nature of theatre itself. Canvas, paint, paper, clay,
wood, metal—nothing in an artist's studio could replace what the stage

Cat. no. 183
Vladimir Tatlin
Costume design for Grief, *Zangezi*, 1923

Cat. no. 184
Vladimir Tatlin
Costume design for Laughter, *Zangezi*,
1923

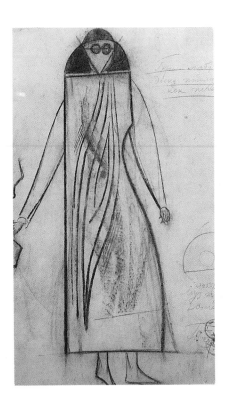 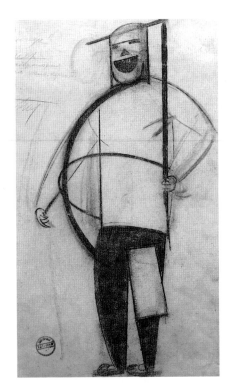

offered, three-dimensional space combined with movement.

The Moscow Kamerny Theatre, founded in 1914, became a
laboratory for new ways to design for the stage. Its founder and sole
leader, the director Alexander Tairov, strove to overcome the naturalistic
tendencies that then prevailed onstage by creating a new, synthetic type
of theatre. In this theatre the artist played the most important role.
Tairov kept abreast of developments in contemporary painting, and for
each of his first productions he invited, as if to try them out, new artists
of diverse and at times diametrically opposed aesthetic convictions.
Throughout the 1910s and 1920s, the Kamerny Theatre employed
such outstanding representatives of different generations and artistic
orientations as Pavel Kuznetsov, Serge Soudeikine, Aristarkh Lentulov,
Alexandra Exter, Georgii Yakulov, Alexander Vesnin, and the brothers
Vladimir and Georgii Stenberg. Productions created by them in
collaboration with Tairov played an important part in the development
of avant-garde stage design, and the Kamerny Theatre can rightfully be
called the theatre of the artist.

In 1916 Tairov invited Exter, who had never before worked in the
theatre, to design sets for Innokentii Annensky's bacchic drama *Famira
Kifared*. Her debut could hardly be described as timid. It was more akin
to a volcanic explosion. Exter literally took over the entire theatre. The
foyer, vestibule, and stairs were covered with her nonobjective painting;
the stage portal and curtain were also executed according to her sketches
(cat. no. 41); and onstage, among Exter's constructions, the actors, whose
costumes she also designed and whose bodies she painted, performed.
It would be wrong to assume that Exter and Tairov invented three-
dimensional volumetric stage sets, for numerous attempts in that
direction had already been undertaken by such renowned directors
as Max Reinhardt, Adolphe Appia, and Edward Gordon Craig (here
it is appropriate to mention Craig's famous production of *Hamlet* in

Cat. no. 41
Alexandra Exter
Curtain and portal design for the
Kamerny Theatre, 1916

1911 at the Moscow Art Theatre). Yet it was with *Famira Kifared* that
the principle of volumetric stage design as it related to directing and
performing was first realized on the Russian stage at its most consistent
and complete level.

Among Russian avant-garde painters, Exter was an artist without
an original creative conception. Her individual style was a synthesis of
the diverse artistic directions with which she felt an affinity. Most stage
sets designed by the artist-innovators reflected the influence of two or
more artistic concepts. Many such productions suffered from eclecticism,
but once in a while the synthesis of styles in a play turned out to be so
coherent and convincing that it signaled the emergence of an entirely
new stylistic order, whose origins could not be conclusively determined.
Perhaps the most widespread style in the 1910s and 1920s was the one
that characterized the Russian avant-garde—cubofuturism.

As an artist-innovator, Exter continuously experimented in many
areas of painting and decorative arts, so theatre gave her new horizons
in form, color, and movement. Each of her theatrical works was an
important step in the development of theatrical decorative art. Exter's
and Tairov's next collaborative production—Oscar Wilde's *Salomé*,
produced in 1917 at the Kamerny Theatre—was one of those works.
An attempt was made to create a dynamic set, which foretold future
attempts at kinetic stage design. The action took place within the
framework of a single set, but Exter used moving elements—curtains

Cat. no. 48
Alexandra Exter
Set design for death scene and finale,
Salomé, 1917

and various flat, colored forms at the back of the stage (cat. no. 48)—
to achieve unexpected effects.

Exter's third, and last, stage design at the Kamerny Theatre, for
Shakespeare's tragedy *Romeo and Juliet* in 1921, was yet another
experiment. For this production Exter built a vertical set that filled the
entire stage space. Seven multilevel platforms allowed Tairov to achieve a
monumental effect in the mass scenes that were so abundant in the play.

Apart from his work with Exter, Tairov established similar
relationships with other artists in his search for new ways to design stage
sets. During the early 1920s a series of productions were undertaken at
the Kamerny Theatre that were true events in its life. In these works the
producer and the artists, by enhancing each other's effort, fully succeeded
in realizing Tairov's concept of the synthetic theatre, which was based on
emotionally charged, dynamic stage action. The success of the productions
testified that the artists had a clear understanding of their tasks and could
effectively reinterpret the results of their studio experiments on canvas
and paper for the stage space. Among such successful collaborations
should be mentioned the sets for the capriccio after E.T.A. Hoffmann's
Princess Brambilla and Charles Lecocq's operetta *Giroflé-Girofla*,
designed with passion and imagination by Yakulov, and the severe,
monumental style of Vesnin's sets for Paul Claudel's *L'Annonce faite à
Marie* of 1920 (see, for example, cat. no. 191) and Jean Racine's tragedy,
Phèdre (cat. no. 194), of 1922.

The 1923 production of G.K. Chesterton's *The Man Who Was
Thursday*, with sets by Vesnin, introduced a qualitatively new phase
in the experiments conducted at the Kamerny Theatre. In complete
accordance with constructivist canons, the artist erected onstage a
"skeleton" of a contemporary Western industrial metropolis, with
elevators rising and falling, moving sidewalks, and "live" advertisements.
It was this production that generated debate within theatrical circles
and the press among the adherents of the two leaders of the theatre,
Meyerhold and Tairov. One concern was which production more
faithfully and convincingly created a model of a contemporary Western

Figs. 1, 2
Biomechanical exercises, n.d.

opposite:
Cat. no. 191
Alexander Vesnin
Costume design for Violaine,
L'Annonce faite à Marie, 1920

metropolis, satirizing its mechanical quality—Tairov's and Vesnin's *The Man Who Was Thursday* or Alexei Faiko's *Lake Lyul,* produced by Meyerhold and designed by Viktor Shestakov. Another argument had to do with who first built a construction onstage—Vesnin in *Thursday* or Popova in the famous production by Meyerhold of *The Magnanimous Cuckold* of 1922.

The artists themselves attributed no great importance to these arguments. Popova and Vesnin shared common creative interests; they collaborated on the set design for the mass theatrical performance *The Struggle and Victory of the Soviets* in honor of the Congress of the Third International. That theatricalized, gigantic military parade, which was to have been assembled by Meyerhold in 1921 on the Khodinskoe Field, Moscow, was supposed to be witnessed by an audience of 30,000, although this production was not realized. It was for *Struggle and Victory* that the very first constructions were built by Popova and Vesnin, becoming, it seems, the basis for further experiments in that direction.

Without answering the question of who invented theatrical constructivism, it seems true that Meyerhold's and Popova's production of *Cuckold* was perhaps the only effort to consistently realize constructivist principles onstage in all aspects of theatrical action, including the invention of a principally new system of actor training, which he called *biomechanics.*

The idea of the creation of a new human being, perfected through the principles of mechanization and thus ideally suited to the machine age, was in part responsible for the emergence of biomechanics. The central principles of biomechanics were codified in 1921 and 1922 by Meyerhold in his studio with the assistance of his young students. Based on observation of the human body, biomechanics attempted to guide individuals in the careful study of their bodies, in order to control the body fully and perfect it. The exact, analytic reproduction of every motion, the coordination of body movements and the spoken word, and attention to geometric, linear motions were biomechanical principles. In this way, biomechanics was directly connected to the constructivist aesthetic and the machines that it deified. As the critic Ivan Aksionov noted, *Cuckold,* which introduced biomechanics to the stage, "was supposed to unveil the hidden aesthetic of the labor process."[2]

Onstage, the well-regulated human mechanism was meant to enlighten and serve as a model for imitation. Meyerhold managed to get his actors to work so closely and so intensely with each other that instead of individual actors onstage, the audience saw two-bodied, three-bodied, and multiple-bodied characters (figs. 1, 2). It was felt that this new acting technique, which involved groups of actors, would eventually facilitate harmonic interactions of large groups offstage; thus these plays were to have been the first step in the creation of a future mass theatre.

Popova's design for *Cuckold* played a crucial role in that production. Indeed, many constructivists saw Popova's work as an important step in creating a new human being. Sergei Tretiakov wrote of Popova's construction that

> this is the scaffolding of a house in the process of construction. These are the ladders and passageways, which our muscles must overcome.[3]

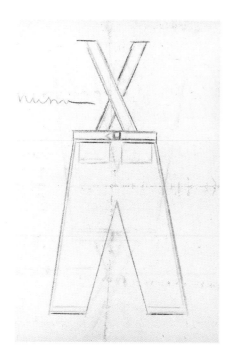

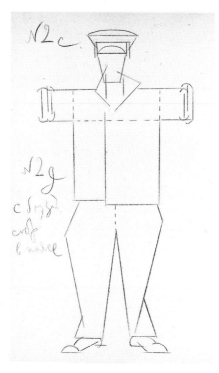

Cat. nos. 141, 142
Liubov Popova
Work uniform designs,
The Magnanimous Cuckold, 1922

Actors could forget the existence of a painted backdrop, but they could not help taking all the elements of the construction into account as its spaces and rhythms defined all of their movement possibilities. The use of such a construction in *Cuckold* demanded not just actors trained in Meyerhold's biomechanics, but also a new kind of theatrical costume. All the actors were dressed in identical work uniforms (*prozodezhda*) (cat. nos. 141, 142).

The rational core of the construction, its connection with the action onstage, its proportion and rhythms, grew directly from the central conception of the production. In Popova's design, the theorists of constructivism saw the scaffolding of the stage set as supporting the edifice of the new, future world then under construction. Yet that did not prevent Popova's colleagues, the artist-functionalists, from subjecting her to a "comrades' trial" for betraying constructivist ideals, which initially denied theatre's right to exist.

It was during the 1920s and 1930s that constructivism monopolized Russian theatrical stages, or at least its avant-garde ones. It seems paradoxical that constructivists in their first statements declared the obsolescence of theatre,[4] or at least its old forms, but that a few years later many of them were actively working there. That contradiction can be explained by the harsh economic realities that prevailed at the time and that prevented constructivists from completing the enormous number of new projects and experiments being born in their studios. The theatre thus became the testing ground for their new ideas.

Meyerhold, who had become the undisputed leader of the theatrical avant-garde, set out to overhaul and rejuvenate the theatre by creating entirely new forms of theatrical spectacles. With *Cuckold* the concept of the theatre of the artist took a quantum leap, proving that the new type of constructivist stage set and Meyerhold's new system of acting had the artistic right to exist. In fact, some of the most extreme aspects of the production were the most warmly received by audiences.

Following *Cuckold*, the 1922 production of Alexander Sukhovo-Kobylin's play *The Death of Tarelkin*, with stage design by Varvara Stepanova, was Meyerhold's next constructivist experiment. If the set for *Cuckold* was a single unit and still hinted at the real-world setting of the play, the set for *Tarelkin* broke up the unit into a group of separate, abstract, constructivist sections, which completely eliminated the slightest hint as to where the action took place (fig. 3). Aksionov wrote that

> the fact that the details have been separated from each other and given the form of mundane objects—a table, a chair, a stool—completely demolished the last hints at stage decoration and abolished the very memories of the theatre.[5]

This anti-furniture had no flat surfaces, only latticed openings; it served as circus props for various stage tricks (fig. 4). One table rolled around loudly on its legs, another turned into a bed or a coffin, chair backs collapsed at strategic moments, stools turned—one even shooting blanks at the same time. The play recalled the aesthetics of the puppet show and the outdoor folk theatre. Meyerhold felt that this kind of show would give audiences a healthy outlook on life, in keeping with the

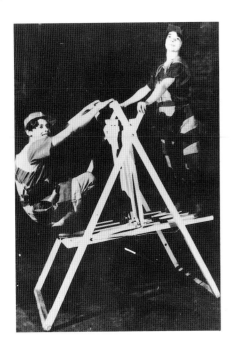

Fig. 4
The Death of Tarelkin, 1922

Fig. 3
The Death of Tarelkin, act 3, 1922

demands of the day. The Punch-and-Judy atmosphere onstage was supposed to infect the spectators. The prompter, dressed in the same uniform as the actors, was placed in the first row of the orchestra. Varicolored balls floated through the theatre, gigantic fake apples were thrown from the balcony during the entr'actes, which the audience tried to catch. Posters saying "Death to Tarelkins, long live Meyerholds" were tossed into the hall.

Stepanova's answer to Popova's work uniform was the so-called actor's "uni-form" (cat. nos. 172, 174, 176). Although Stepanova's costumes were identical in design, each was differentiated by rhythmic linear patterns. Recognizing that her costumes represented a turning-away from the principles of collective uniformity, Stepanova patterned them so that the lines and dots varied rhythmically as the actors positioned themselves in groups. Each group movement formed a rhythmic structure, a living constructivist structure.

It was during her work on this production that Stepanova developed a series of sport clothes, which were used not just for special gymnastic exercises and sports parades, but also mass-produced for everyday use. In this period, constructivist artists such as Alexander Rodchenko and Tatlin were already actively working on designs for new kinds of everyday clothing, but constructivists who worked in the theatre made a major contribution as well. For example, Exter's designs for street dress typified constructivists' attempts to solve social problems in purely artistic ways. In her designs Exter tried to create a new type of clothing that "should cheer up and shape up our unfocused and badly put-together Russians."[6] Exter's street clothes used primary colors often derived from Russian folk costumes, which she thought would lessen bureaucratic grayness and coldness.[7] As the product of the long-term, collective creativity of the people, the folk costume, Exter felt, could serve as an ideological and practical model for contemporary urban clothing.[8]

During the same period Meyerhold continued to develop one of the main ideological principles of constructivism—the creation of a new human being. In his musical *D.E. (Give Us Europe)* of 1923, Meyerhold

93   Theatre of the Artist

ДОКТОР

ВАРРАВИН

ПОЛУТАТАРИНОВ

contrasted the old bourgeois world with the newly emerging revolutionary order. A live jazz band, in its first appearance on the Soviet stage, symbolized the degenerate West. According to one critic, jazz dances in their debauchery characterized collapsing bourgeois society; the biomechanical exercises and the acrobatic polka in the play showed the health and desire for labor of the Red youth. In this contrast of the old and the new, the advantages of the new socialist existence were made so clear that the theatre was turned into a powerful means of agitation.

In this period other forms of constructivist theatre also made advances. Particularly notable were such innovative choreographers as Nikolai Foregger and Kasian Goleizovsky, whose pioneering experiments attempted to renew the Soviet ballet. At the foundation of their experiments lay a number of constructivist principles, which they developed further, particularly in the direction of biomechanics and the movement of the human body. They searched for new and unexpected combinations of musical and body rhythm, which were usually explored in choreographic miniatures as individual dances or small group numbers.

During the 1920s, representatives of the Russian artistic avant-garde continued to enrich theatrical/decorative art with new plastic forms. It was during this time that in the very core of the theatre of the artist, and its various manifestations, a new profession was born—the artist of the theatre in the contemporary understanding of the word.

Cat. no. 172
Varvara Stepanova
Costume design for a Doctor,
The Death of Tarelkin, 1922

Cat. no. 174
Varvara Stepanova
Costume design for Varravin,
The Death of Tarelkin, 1922

Cat. no. 176
Varvara Stepanova
Costume design for Polutatarinov,
The Death of Tarelkin, 1922

Notes

1. Under the conditions imposed by the forcible entrenchment of socialist realism in Soviet art that began around 1930, Tatlin could no longer teach because art colleges were being closed and formalist creativity was no longer considered a safe aesthetic stance, even in the privacy of an artist's studio. Thus the theatre became perhaps the only form of activity available to the artist.

2. Ivan Aksionov, "Prostranstvennyi konstruktivizm na stsene" (Spatial Constructivism Onstage), in *Teatralnyi Oktiabr* (Leningrad-Moscow, 1926), 33.

3. Sergei Tretiakov, "Velikodushnyi rogonosets" (The Magnanimous Cuckold), *Zrelishcha*, 1922, no. 8:12.

4. Aksionov, 33.

5. Aksionov, 33.

6. Alexandra Exter, "V poiskakh novoi odezhdy" (In Search of New Clothing), exh. cat., *Vserossiiskaia vystavka iskusstva* (All-Russian Exhibition of Industrial Arts), 1923, no. 2:17.

7. Exter, 17.

8. Alexandra Exter, "Russkaia moda" (Russian Fashion), *Krasnoe pole*, 1923, no. 30.

Внимательный рабочий.

15

167

East Meets West: Russian Stage Design and the European Avant-Garde

Steven A. Nash

Gertrude Stein's famous comment that Pablo Picasso's sets and costumes for the ballet *Parade* of 1917 put cubism onstage and helped win its "war" of acceptance is only partly correct.[1] While *Parade* provides a benchmark for cubism's popular accessibility, Stein's attribution of historical precedence is misplaced. Cubism, at least in its cubofuturist guise, had already reached the stage in Russia in the brilliant designs by Kazimir Malevich for *Victory over the Sun* in 1913 (cat. no. 114).

Indeed, as the present exhibition *Theatre in Revolution: Russian Avant-Garde Stage Design 1913–1935* and its catalogue abundantly illustrate, Malevich and such associates in the Russian avant-garde as Natalia Goncharova, Vladimir Tatlin, and Alexandra Exter from about 1912 to 1917 initiated a revolution in stage design that pushed theatrical experience into new visual and spatial realms, helping to open the way for the triumph of constructivism in all the visual arts in the late 1910s and 1920s. Behind this phenomenon was a powerful dynamic of stylistic change, based on the absorption of new foreign influences into native lines of development. Not allowing their geographic distance from artistic centers in the West to isolate them culturally, Russian artists followed with surprising timeliness trends emerging in France, Italy, Germany, and elsewhere. Freedom and frequency of travel back and forth to the West, the circulation of Western publications and photographs of new art, exhibitions organized in Russia exposing major European avant-garde artists, and the entry of works by many of these artists into Russian collections all promoted the revolutionary impact of modernist ideas.

A complex mixture of different Western models vied for attention. Fauvism, cubism, futurism, and German expressionism were primary, all stimulating a cacophonous experimentation and runaway eclecticism that Diaghilev parodied in his description of the formative avant-garde:

> Twenty schools spring up in a month. Futurism, cubism, antiquity, pre-history. . . . Mototism dethrones automatism, to be surpassed by trepidism and vibrism, which cease to exist because planism, serenism, exacerbism, omnism and *néisme* arise.[2]

With such influences, however, came fundamental lessons in the structural qualities of art, the liberating power of pure color, the basic autonomy of the art work from perceptual experience, and, for some

Cat. no. 114
Kazimir Malevich
Costume design for the Enemy,
Victory over the Sun, 1913

Fig. 1
Henri Matisse
Statuette and Vase on an Oriental Carpet,
1908
Oil on canvas, 89 × 105 cm
The Pushkin Museum of Fine Arts,
Moscow

Fig. 2
Natalia Goncharova
Stone Woman (Still Life) (also known as
Nature morte à l'ananas), 1908
Oil on canvas, 130 × 146 cm
Private collection, Paris

artists, insights into what was felt to be a higher realm of existence, all of which, when melded into native traditions and concerns, helped stimulate the creation of still newer visual languages. This dialectic of absorption and transformation was evident in all the arts but certainly not least of all in stage design, where ideas from different media interacted in what was seen as a total environmental art form. To understand better how the reaction to foreign influences affected prerevolutionary Russian stage design is to see more clearly both its artistic roots and its creative achievement.[3]

Long admired as exemplary modernizations of traditional Russian themes and motifs, the stage designs of Goncharova speak clearly of this tie with the European avant-garde. The influence is one of many but nonetheless fundamental.

As for many other artists of her generation, the pull toward the West was strong in Goncharova's early years. Her work of ca. 1906–1910 is marked by experimentation with such sources as Pierre Bonnard's postimpressionist still lifes, German expressionism, cubism (she later claimed to have been the first cubist painter in Russia),[4] and fauvism; her later development with Mikhail Larionov of a nearly abstract rayonist style relied heavily on Italian futurism. No one approach predominated for long, although a natural attraction to native arts was a steady theme that eventually took control in her neoprimitivism of 1910–1912, and it underlay her brilliant debut as a stage designer with the folkloric costumes and sets for Diaghilev's 1914 production of *Le Coq d'or* (The Golden Cockerel).[5] Also important for these designs, however, were the lessons in color and decorative pattern she derived from the great works by Matisse she was able to see in the Moscow collections of Ivan Morozov and Sergei Shchukin (figs. 1, 2).[6]

Although Goncharova asserted in 1913 that she had completely turned her back on Western influences in favor of Eastern traditions,[7] it was these two complementary interests—the sophisticated colorism of Matisse and Russian folk culture as found in *lubki*, signboards, folk costumes, and painted and carved decorative arts—that combined to give the pulsating rhythms and decoration of *Le Coq d'or* such force.[8] The free manipulation of form and sequence in the designs echoes aspects of futurism, but it was their hedonistic abundance of pattern that most counted.

In designs for other, mostly unrealized, theatrical projects that Goncharova produced before settling in Paris in 1917, the stylistic balancing act she maintained tipped in one direction then another, from exercises in folk imagery and Byzantine-like stylization to variations on rayonism.[9] The general dominance of the decorative side of her sensibility, however, put her out of step with the formalist experiments going on around her. From as early as 1911–1912, the strongly geometric and mechanistic direction of progressive Russian art had made itself felt, largely under the influence at first of cubism and futurism. While the term cubofuturism is generally invoked to describe the particular amalgams of these styles that arose in Russia, the emerging points of view were too complex to be easily classified. One of the artists who most significantly redefined and extended cubist principles, and transferred these principles from the canvas to the stage, was Vladimir Tatlin.

Fig. 3
Vladimir Tatlin
Set design for *A Life for the Czar*, 1912

The story of Tatlin's early development of ca. 1910–1915 is now well known. Often cited are its grounding in traditional Russian folk art and icon painting, the crucial impact of cubism (particularly Tatlin's visits to Picasso in Paris in 1914), followed by pioneering work with ruggedly abstract reliefs in metal, wood, and glass.[10] Less thoroughly discussed is the role that stage design played in this evolution, as evidenced by his work on *The Emperor Maximilian and His Disobedient Son, Adolf*, of 1911 and *A Life for the Czar* (or *Ivan Susanin*) of 1913 (never produced).[11]

Most authors stress the folkloric content of Tatlin's designs for these plays and hence their relationship with Goncharova's slightly later work, particularly in the use of florid patterns for costumes and backdrops and a neoprimitive style that reduces form to flattened, sharply linear designs. By 1913, however, the abstract tendency inherent in Tatlin's approach had become more dominant, moving him in a direction different from Goncharova. In one of the best-known studies for *A Life for the Czar*, for example, theatrical space is articulated with a collage-like buildup of large, angular planes forming the background, wings, and stage furnishings and even intersecting across the floor (fig. 3). Although the production was never staged, it is clear that Tatlin envisioned not just a flat backdrop against which the drama would unfold, but rather, a total environment organized according to geometric principles, with actors in elegantly simplified costumes (designed with hard-edged arcs, sharp angles, and flat surfaces that would have challenged any seamstress!) serving as extensions of the set. Illusionist description is largely sacrificed to new formal demands, and colorful period detail gives way to the sterner pleasures of purified form in dynamic interaction. Produced at a time when Tatlin was just beginning to move into sculpture, such designs seem to have given him a vehicle for thinking three-dimensionally. The spatial implications of cubism are explored on a large projected scale, and an introduction is seen to the compositional ideas that would guide his relief sculpture for several years thereafter.

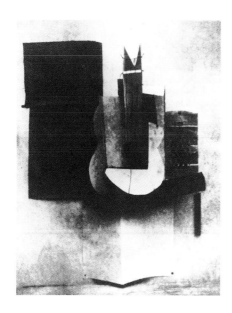

Fig. 4
Pablo Picasso
Still Life with Guitar and Bottle, 1912
Mixed media construction. Destroyed.
Illustrated in *Soirées de Paris*, no. 18,
15 November 1913

While the exact chronology of these designs is hard to establish, a firm *terminus ante quem* is provided by Tatlin having included a sizeable group of them in the World of Art exhibitions at St. Petersburg and Moscow in November and December 1913.[12] They may have substantially predated his earliest relief sculptures, which very likely commenced late in 1913.[13] At any rate, their stylistic generation was based on a knowledge of cubism already advanced by this time, well before Tatlin's eventful trip to Paris in early 1914.[14] Major cubist paintings by Picasso had entered the Shchukin collection around 1911–1912 and were available for viewing to interested students and artists, and among the other avenues of information on cubism were, for example, various publications on contemporary art emanating from Paris, works by Fernand Léger, Picasso, Albert Gleizes, and Henri Le Fauconnier exhibited at the 1912 *Jack of Diamonds* show, and the reports and artistic responses of the many Russian artists visiting Paris. Tatlin's paintings and drawings from 1911–1912 had begun to submit to a geometric stylization that, in its complexity and sophistication, goes well beyond neoprimitivism toward cubist models.

Although it is impossible to determine when Tatlin first learned of constructed sculptures by Picasso such as his famous *Guitar* of 1912 or *Still Life with Guitar and Bottle* from one year later (fig. 4), a comparison of these works with designs for *A Life for the Czar* shows similar formal devices at work, whether expressed in reliefs or theatrical settings. The simplification of form to geometric planes, the finlike structures that project from the wall or backdrop to activate surrounding space, the stacking of levels, and the rhythmic play of sharp edge versus flat and curving planes are all related, emphasizing the similarity of approach and the importance of these designs to Tatlin's transition from flat surface to real space.

Tatlin was well primed for the lessons of the art he would find on view in Paris both publicly and privately. In retrospect, we know it was the sculptures he saw that had the most lasting impact. In his legendary encounter with Picasso, he would have been able to study around the studio various three-dimensional constructions, some of them quite large and environmental.[15] He almost certainly met the Russian émigré Alexander Archipenko, whose *Medrano I* of 1912 and *Head* of 1913 added new dimensions to the theme of constructed sculpture, and possibly also Vladimir Baranoff-Rossiné, another countryman living in Paris who was making painted cubist works from diverse materials. Tatlin's further development of these ideas was immediate and powerful. In the sculptures he produced after his return, he pushed geometric construction in new and uncompromising directions, with assemblages of metal and wood exploring both abstract composition and the notion of *faktura*, or the expressive life of materials per se. His work for the stage was a key step in this development, and opened paths to the later achievements of such artist-designers as Alexandra Exter.

Italian futurism's influence was simultaneous with the influx of cubism into Russia and often inextricable from it. Both styles challenged inherited renaissance conventions and both affected stage design as much as painting and sculpture. Backdrops by Iosif Shkolnik from 1913, for example, indicate how the principles of futurism could be regurgitated

more or less whole, while Malevich's famous work for the stage from the same year, as discussed below, demonstrates a more creatively synthetic approach.

Despite later attempts to disassociate themselves from futurist connections, the initial response of many Russian artists and theorists to the work of Umberto Boccioni, Giacomo Balla, Gino Severini, Filippo Tomasso Marinetti, and other Italians was intense. Just how rapidly such influences disseminated in Russia is evidenced in numerous ways. Larionov's *luchizm* or rayonism gestured emphatically toward futurist theories of lines of force dividing form into energized segments. The Russian Izdebsky Salon of 1909–1910 included four works by Balla. Major exhibitions of futurist art in Paris in 1912 and 1913 received notice in the Russian press and undoubtedly drew many Russian visitors, and Boccioni's important sculpture exhibition at Galerie de la Boëtie in June 1913 was reviewed, for example, in both *Den* and *Apollon*.[16] The production of Italian futurist manifestos attained a high point in 1912 and many reached Russia both in the original and in translation, such as the reprinting in Russian of Boccioni's *Technical Manifesto of Futurist Painting* of 1911 in the June 1912 bulletin of the Union of Youth group. In the raucously creative and defiant demonstrations by certain self-proclaimed futurist organizations of artists and writers, such as the Burliuk brothers' Hylaea group and Larionov's and Goncharova's Tavern of the 13, conscious imitation was made of similar efforts to *épater le bourgeoisie* by the Italian futurists. In painting, theoretical interest merged with practical application in works that show a direct reliance on Italian models, as with the Balla-like representation of movement through the simultaneous depiction of forms in Malevich's *Knife-Grinder* of 1912 and Goncharova's *The Cyclist* of 1912–1913. Numerous other examples exist by Russian artists who appropriated motifs or stylistic devices directly from Italian contemporaries.

In regard to theatre, one of the most potent influences came from Italian futurist performances of various kinds (fig. 5) via the similar and even more extreme "happenings" they helped stimulate in Russian cafés

Fig. 6

Iosif Shkolnik

Set design for *Vladimir Mayakovsky*, 1913

and cabarets.[17] Not uncommon in these productions were unusual lighting effects, walls or flats painted with wild designs, audience involvement in the action, costumes and even body painting in modern patterns, and rapidly changed costumes and sets. Such experiments and assertions of artistic license must have encouraged those artists and writers who sought almost literally to break down the doors of theatrical tradition. As Vladimir Mayakovsky put it in 1913,

> The great break-up which we have begun in all spheres of beauty, in the name of the art of the future—the art of the Futurists—will not stop and indeed cannot stop at the door of the theater.[18]

The first major blast in this attack came at the Luna Park Theatre in St. Petersburg from 2–5 December 1913, with back-to-back presentations of Mayakovsky's tragedy *Vladimir Mayakovsky* and Mikhail Matiushin's opera *Victory over the Sun* with libretto by Alexei Kruchenykh.

For Mayakovsky's play, Pavel Filonov produced a backdrop for the prologue and epilogue, costumes, and large cardboard figures connoting some of Mayakovsky's fantasy images; these fascinating solutions unfortunately are known only through description.[19] The previously referred-to designs by Shkolnik for backdrops to acts 1 and 2 depict cities in tangled states of upheaval (fig. 6).[20] A comparison with Boccioni's *The Street Enters the House* of 1911 (fig. 7) shows how directly Shkolnik's imagery was dependent upon the Italian futurist vision of modern cities in a dynamic flux of simultaneous collapse and expansion. Shkolnik's rather tepid reprises, however, miss the Italian's true apocalyptic fervor.

Fig. 7
Umberto Boccioni
The Street Enters the House, 1911–1912
Oil on canvas, 100 × 100 cm
Kunstmuseum Hannover mit Sammlung
Sprengel, Hannover

For a more inspired vision and a more creative response to futurism, one must consider Malevich's designs for *Victory over the Sun*.

Although Malevich did not visit Germany until much later in life and never traveled to France or Italy, a knowledge of western European painting constantly surfaced in his presuprematist work of 1910–1915, which draws in equal measures upon cubist and futurist precedents. His range of reference was widespread, as he moved inquiringly from one artistic idea to another while pursuing his own clear path of development. The important role played by Léger's machinelike, tubular shapes in his formalized primitivism of ca. 1912–1913, for example, is frequently noted.[21] Less well recognized is the compositional influence that Léger's earlier cubism had upon the scaffoldings of line and plane in Malevich's cubofuturist or so-called alogist paintings of 1913–1914.[22] The semantic explorations of verbal meaning versus symbolic form typical of these paintings grew out of Russian *zaum* (transrational poetry) but also relates to the disjunctive imagery of cubism and futurism. And numerous motifs and devices can be traced to the same general sources, including the use in certain works of futurist force lines and composite movement.[23] Most importantly, Western modernism provided models for a release from natural appearance which, when joined with the metaphysical aspect of Malevich's work that had been strong since his symbolist beginnings, propelled him toward suprematism and the search for new meanings in art through abstraction.

Victory over the Sun was an important step in that progression. Elements of Malevich's decor are commonly seen as presaging the black-and-white minimalism of his early suprematist paintings.[24] In any event, the designs brought his cubofuturist style to a resounding,

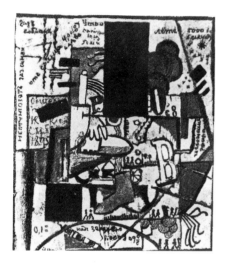

Fig. 8
Albert Gleizes
The City and the River, 1913
Ink, 19.5 × 16 cm
Solomon R. Guggenheim Museum,
New York

Fig. 9
Kazimir Malevich
Curtain design, *Victory over
the Sun*, 1913
Original drawing lost.
Reproduced in *Kazimir Malevich
1878–1935*, exh. cat. (Los Angeles:
The Armand Hammer Museum of Art
and Cultural Center, 1990), 9, fig. 9

fully three-dimensional climax that represents a milestone in Russian avant-garde theatre.

A statement by Malevich concerning his later designs for Mayakovsky's revolutionary allegory *Mystery-Bouffe* (from which none of the drawings or sets survive) is highly revealing of his conception of theatrical space:

> I saw the box-stage as the frame of a picture and the actors as contrasting elements (in Cubism every object is a contrasting element in relation to another object). Planning the action on three or four levels, I tried to deploy the actors in space predominantly in vertical compositions in the manner of the latest style of painting; the actors' movements were meant to accord rhythmically with the elements of the setting. I depicted a number of planes on a single canvas; I treated space not as illusionary but as cubist. I saw my task not as the creation of associations with a reality existing beyond the limits of the stage, but as the creation of a new reality.[25]

In other words, Malevich considered the stage a forum for the three-dimensional, real-space realization of the principles of cubist painting. As in his own alogist paintings of 1913–1914, some of which bear a strong resemblance to decor designs for *Victory over the Sun*, Malevich looked not to the analytical cubism of Picasso and Georges Braque for his lead, but to the less immaterial, more solidly structured compositions of Léger, synthetic cubism, and the lesser cubist painters such as Gleizes and Jean Metzinger. A print by Gleizes from this period shows the same basic formal syntax and black-and-white language as Malevich's backdrop designs (figs. 8, 9).

Unlike Tatlin, Malevich was not both sculptor and painter, but during this period he used collage on some of his canvases—a distinctly cubist device—both for a shift into literal reality and the play of real depth. The impulse to extend this use of space even further may possibly have been encouraged by Boccioni, whose work Malevich knew and borrowed from and whose *Technical Manifesto of Futurist Sculpture* of 1912 had so strong an impact throughout the art world.[26] Boccioni argued for new art forms based on the incorporation of space into sculpture and sculpture into the environment:

> There can be no renewal unless it is through Environmental Sculpture, since only by this means can plastic art develop and come to model the atmosphere which surrounds our objects.

In his call for "the marvelous mathematical and geometrical" elements of modern life, the use of diverse materials, the fragmentation of real objects and their fusion with abstract planes and volumes, and the extension of these dynamic constructions into depth, one finds almost a prescription for Malevich's aggressively modern stage inventions.

His costumes may also have had futurist connections. A different source, the so-called simultaneous dresses of Sonia Delaunay, has been posited but seems less likely.[27] Delaunay made her first dresses in summer 1913 using brilliantly colored appliqués of segmented geometric shapes based on Robert Delaunay's concept of simultaneous contrasts.

Some of her fabric designs were exhibited at the Erster Deutscher Herbstsalon in Berlin in October 1913, and an evening dedicated to both Robert and Sonia Delaunay had been arranged at the Stray Dog cabaret in St. Petersburg in July 1913, so Malevich was certainly generally aware of their work. Through Italian futurist performances and other futurist organs, however, concepts of daringly new, sometimes outlandish clothing for the modern man and woman had become so widespread that even the popular press by early 1913 could attempt, with tongue in cheek, the creation of "futurist" fashions (fig. 10). Such vernacular ideas must have come to Malevich's attention and may well have helped inspire the spirited geometry of his costumes.

As part of his effort to unify and utilize the full space of the stage, Malevich built freestanding geometric volumes that echoed in design the costumes and backdrops. The movement of the actors was emphasized by kinetic spotlights that sliced across already segmented and dynamic forms. Extensions *back* into space were created by some of the backdrops composed as a box within a box, with diagonal lines connecting the corners and establishing an inner perspective that is pushed against by Malevich's jarring mixtures of painted words, symbols, and shapes. An energy distinctive to cubofuturism inheres in these blocky, purposefully disjunctive and alogical compositions, and the large black quadrilaterals floating in space are prescient of his later suprematism, but the figurative images again recall Western precedents. In keeping with the opera's theme of the need to transcend present existence, Malevich's iconography of future life invokes speed, technology, and the machine through fragments of airplanes, bombs, wheels, cosmic bodies, T-squares, clocks, and other mechanical paraphernalia, a vocabulary that obviously owes much to Italian futurism and certain cubists as well. *In toto*, Malevich's designs realized on a grand scale the mode of painted and constructed cubist sculpture that extended from Archipenko and Baranoff-Rossiné in France to later work by Exter, Ivan Kliun, and Ivan Puni in Russia, while adding the movement of actors and lights, assertive abstract form, and an assault of modernist imagery that proclaimed loudly the birth of a new era. Malevich's robotized figures, lumbering slowly around the stage, contributed to this twentieth-century vision and to the futurist characterization of depersonalized, mechanized humanity that would reach an apogee in later constructivist theatre.

Malevich had absorbed, reshuffled, and fully transformed his different sources. What emerged, despite Kruchenykh's difficult libretto, was a unique theatrical experience, part of the excitement of which is captured in Benedikt Livshits's eyewitness report:

> [With his play of light and space] what K. S. Malevich did in *Victory over the Sun* could not but astound the spectators—who ceased to feel like an audience the moment the black gulf of the "contemplacle" yawned before them. Out of the primordial night the tentacles of projectors seized on parts now of this object, now of that, and, saturating it with colour, gave it life. . . . Principles accepted by painting since Impressionism were transferred for the first time into a sphere of three dimensions. . . . Abstract form was the only reality, a form which completely absorbed the entire Luciferan futility of the world. . . .[28]

Fig. 10

"Futurist Fashions for 1913,"

The Bystander, London, January 1913

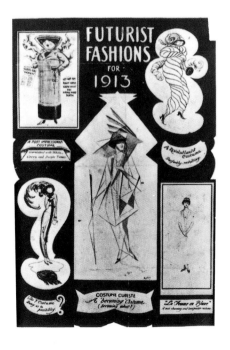

Although performed only twice, *Victory over the Sun* had a lasting impact, as evidenced by its revival just seven years later by the Unovis group (Union of the New Art or Affirmers of the New Art) in Vitebsk. In a very practical sense, it demonstrated to the new avant-garde what was possible through a merger of ambitious artistic and theatrical ideas.

Further steps in the same direction were taken by Exter in such productions as *Famira Kifared* (1916) and *Salomé* (1917) (cat. nos. 49, 50, 52).[29] Building upon the achievements of Tatlin and Malevich, while also keeping an eye on developments in the West, Exter designed the most purely geometric and sculptural ensembles of sets and costumes seen anywhere to date. Indeed, her work can properly be understood only as effecting a rapprochement between theatre design and the contemporaneous abstract paintings of Liubov Popova, Malevich, and Exter herself, so insistently did they synthesize geometric form with the full space of the stage, using the actors as compositional elements.

The most cosmopolitan member of the Russian avant-garde, Exter had begun to make frequent trips to western Europe in 1908, providing a valuable source of regular information on new developments there. Her own work passed through a skillful if predictable series of investigations of different Western styles, from fauvism to cubism and futurism, before it matured about 1915–1916 into her own brand of abstraction, highly charged with color and movement. Her first theatrical designs, commissioned at about the same time by Alexander Tairov, fit importantly into this emerging, new artistic personality, while also showing lingering traces of her affiliations with the West.

The pictorial rhythms that activate Exter's abstract paintings from 1916–1917, featuring rotating and swirling projections of angular or pointed forms, derive at least in part from similar vocabularies in Balla's futurist paintings and sculpture of ca. 1914–1915. Exter applied the same general principles to her three-dimensional costume and set designs for the theatre, although the final, actual sets are generally more severely geometric.[30] A comparison, for example, of Balla's *Bandiera sull'altare della patria* of 1915 with the watercolor design for *Salomé* shows the relationship that existed (figs. 11, 12). Her stage maquette for the same production might profitably be compared, its densely woven lobes dissecting a box space, to the relief by Balla from 1915 entitled *Velocità*.[31]

Exter's devotion to the dynamic interaction of all compositional elements, whether on a flat surface or the stage, linked her to the futurist concept of figure-cum-environment involving the depiction of composite movement and the passage of time. As with Malevich, her designs for extravagantly stylized costumes may well owe a debt to the futurist vision of new clothes for the new twentieth-century body, as illustrated, for example, in Balla's *Il Vestito antineutrale: Manifesto futurista* of 11 September 1914.[32] And although the resemblance seems to be coincidental rather than a matter of direct influence one way or the other, Exter's work of this period shares much in common with designs by Balla and Fortunato Depero from late 1916 for Igor Stravinsky's *Feu d'artifice* (Fireworks; 1917) (presented only once) and *Le Chant du rossignol* (Song of the Nightingale) (not produced), which were likely sources for stage designs soon to follow by Larionov.[33]

opposite:

Cat. no. 49

Alexandra Exter

Costume design for Three Slaves, *Salomé*, 1917

overleaf left:

Cat. no. 50

Alexandra Exter

Costume design for Salomé, *Salomé*, 1917

overleaf right:

Cat. no. 52

Alexandra Exter

Costume design for Two Jews, *Salomé*, 1917

Fig. 11

Giacomo Balla

Bandiera sull'altare della patria

(*Flags at the Country's Altar*), 1915

Oil on canvas, 100 × 100 cm

Collection Donna Benedetta Marinetti,

Rome

Exter's success with *Famira Kifared* and *Salomé* led to further collaboration with Tairov in the postrevolutionary period on a production of *Romeo and Juliet* (1921). Such presentations had a powerful influence on other artists working in the theatre, including Alexander Vesnin and Vladimir Dmitriev. Although the abstractly geometric approach she helped pioneer with Tatlin and Malevich was, among progressive designers and producers, soon competing for allegiance with a more technological, machine-oriented aesthetic, she can be said to have firmly established one branch of the constructivist theatre. These two main divergent strains actually merged in Exter's extraordinarily inventive costumes for Yakov Protazanov's 1924 film *Aelita*, although even here we may see a distant memory in her transparent, faceted, and strutted constructions of Balla's "plastic complexes" of 1914–1915.[34]

As these many examples demonstrate, Dostoevsky's famous cultural aphorism that "We Russians have two homelands: Russia and Europe" was as valid in the early twentieth century as in the nineteenth. With Exter, as with the other leading artist-stage designers in the early Russian avant-garde, however, European influence was a matter more of stimulation than imitation. It opened up new avenues of inquiry that, when implanted into an indigenous cultural context, helped fuel the chemistry of change that resulted in a distinctly new Russian art of worldwide significance. Knowledge of European modernism came at a time when these artists were deeply committed to an analysis of pictorial structure and material values. It liberated them from the outworn

Fig. 12
Alexandra Exter
Set design, *Salomé*, 1917

conventions of realism, impressionism, and symbolism and gave them the basic tools to build new visual structures. It could be said that constructivism would have been impossible without cubism and futurism, but the distance that Russian artists progressed beyond such sources can be measured by the strong reversal of influence from East to West that occurred during the 1920s and for many years thereafter. To see the lasting legacy of the Russian avant-garde stage, one need only consider, for example, the theatrical experiments at Germany's Bauhaus in the 1920s or Léger's enthusiastic praise to Tairov of his production of *Phèdre* in France in 1923: "I assure you that there is nothing in Paris to compare with this. . . . My dream is to tackle the problem of plasticity on the stage as you have done."[35] Western influence had come full circle.

Notes

1. Gertrude Stein, *Picasso* (Boston: Beacon Press, 1959), 29. Jeffrey Weiss has pointed out an earlier, and possibly the first, incursion of cubism onto the popular stage, with the appearance of a *cubiste* among the otherwise everyday characters in Robert Dieudonné's revue *Et Voila!* first performed at the Théâtre des Capucines on 12 October 1911. See Jeffrey S. Weiss, "Picasso, Collage, and the Music Hall," *Modern Art and Public Culture: Readings in High and Low* (New York: Museum of Modern Art and Abrams, 1991) 83, fig. 77.

2. Quoted from Georges Michel, *Pall Mall* (Paris: 1913) by Mary Chamot, "The Early Work of Goncharova and Larionov," *Burlington Magazine* 97, no. 627 (June 1955): 173.

3. The subject of European influences on the Russian avant-garde is a vast one, involving deep cultural interactions that warrant a lengthy, specialized study. The present essay can address only a few of the most salient points as related to the early history of avant-garde theatre design. Some useful studies that are more general in scope include: Charlotte Douglas, "The New Russian Art and Italian Futurism," *Art Journal* 34, no. 3 (Spring 1975): 229–39 and "Cubisme français/cubo-futurisme russe," *Cahiers du Musée d'art moderne* 2 (Paris, 1979): 184–93; Susan P. Compton, "Italian Futurism and Russia," *Art Journal* 41, no. 4 (Winter 1981): 343–48; *Futurism and the International Avant-Garde*, exh. cat. (Philadelphia: Philadelphia Museum of Art, October 1980–January 1981), passim.

4. See Mary Chamot, *Goncharova: Stage Designs and Paintings* (London: Oresko Books Limited, 1979), 30.

5. The neoprimitivist movement in Russia can be seen in part as a direct renunciation of Western influence and an assertion of traditional, national values versus the technological and materialist character of modern Europe. This mood of nationalism led certain theorists to proclaim Russia not only the birthplace of neoprimitivism but also of cubism and futurism. See John Bowlt, *Russian Stage Design: Scenic Innovation, 1900–1930*, exh. cat. (Jackson: Mississippi Museum of Art, 1982), 28, 189. For information and bibliography on *Le Coq d'or*, see among many other sources, Chamot, passim, and Bowlt, 148–49.

6. Matisse's *Statuette and Vase on an Oriental Carpet* entered the Shchukin collection in 1908, the year it was painted. It was absorbed in 1918 into the new Museum of Modern Western Art in Moscow and transferred in 1948 to the Pushkin Museum.

7. "I turn away from the West. . . . For me the East means the creation of new forms, an extending and deepening of the problems of color. . . ." From the preface to the catalogue of Goncharova's one-woman exhibition in Moscow in 1913, trans. in John Bowlt, ed., *Russian Art of the Avant-Garde: Theory and Criticism 1902–1934* (New York: Viking Press, 1976), 55–58.

8. Guillaume Apollinaire recognized this merger in Goncharova's art between modern French painting and orientalism in his introduction to the catalogue of her exhibition at the Paul Guillaume gallery in Paris in 1914. See Chamot, 15.

9. See Chamot, pls. 45–50, VII.

10. See, for example, John Milner, *Vladimir Tatlin and the Russian Avant-Garde* (New Haven and London: Yale University Press, 1983), chaps. 1–3.

11. On these projects, see especially Bowlt, *Russian Stage Design*, 294–95, and Larissa Alexeevna Zhadova, ed., *Tatlin* (New York: Rizzoli, 1984), cat. 509–10, pls. 38–41, 137–55. Although a connection is made in the Tatlin literature between his stage designs and sculpture, the primacy of date of the former, and hence their key formative role, is not stressed.

12. They frequently are given the erroneous dates of 1913–1914.

13. Listings in early exhibition catalogues containing works by Tatlin indicate that the first reliefs date from 1913. Among the surviving reliefs and those known from photographic documentation, only *The Bottle* (Zhadova, pl. 111, cat. 507) is consistently dated to 1913. The close similarity of the bottle motif in this work —cut from a sheet of metal and crisscrossed with thin lines—to the corresponding motif in Picasso's *Still Life with Guitar and Bottle* of 1913 strongly suggests that the former was based directly upon the latter. Picasso's sculpture was published in *Les Soirées de Paris* 2, no. 3 (15 November 1913), a source that would eventually have been known to Tatlin and that provides a tentative *terminus post quem* for *The Bottle*.

14. Although the year of this trip is frequently given as 1913, it has been proven conclusively that it took place in 1914. See the letter published and dated to early 1914 in Zhadova, 181–82. Anatolii Strigalev has located Tatlin's passport, which documents the 1914 date (information kindly provided by John Bowlt).

15. See Pierre Daix, *Picasso: The Cubist Years 1907–1916* (London: Thames and Hudson, 1979), cat. nos. 578, 629a.

16. The April 1912 issue of the Union of Youth bulletin, for example, published the introduction from the catalogue of the large futurist exhibition in Paris. Earlier, Marinetti's first manifesto of 1909 had appeared almost immediately in a St. Petersburg newspaper, and the July–August 1910 issue of *Apollon* translated nearly in entirety the *Technical Manifesto of Futurist Painting*.

17. The single best source on futurist soirees and performances of other kinds is Michael Kirby and Victoria Nes Kirby, *Futurist Performance* (New York: PAJ Publications, 1986). Boccioni's caricature (fig. 5) depicts onstage, from the left, Boccioni, Pratella, Marinetti, Carra, and Russolo. On Russian cabarets of this period and their conjunctions with the art world, see John Bowlt, "Natalia Goncharova and Futurist Theater," *Art Journal* 49, no. 1 (Spring 1990): esp. 47–48, and "When Life was a Cabaret," *Art News* 83, no. 10 (December 1984): 122–27; and Benedikt Livshits's entertaining descriptions of the Stray Dog cabaret in St. Petersburg in his recollections, *The One and a Half-Eyed Archer* (Newtonville, Mass.: Oriental Research Press, 1977), English trans. by John Bowlt of 1933 Russian edition, esp. 214–23.

18. Quoted in Konstantin Rudnitsky, *Russian and Soviet Theater 1905–1932* (New York: Abrams, 1988), 11, from V. V. Mayakovsky, *Teatro i kino* (Theatre and Film), vol. 1 (Moscow, 1954), 379–81.

19. Rudnitsky, 13, and Livshits, 160–62, 179 n. 23.

20. A second, similar design by Shkolnik is illustrated in *Russia 1900–1930: L'Arte della scena* (Milan: Electa, 1990), 123, pl. 70. Shkolnik was assisted with his sets for Mayakovsky by Olga Rozanova, whose highly energetic poster design advertising the Luna Park program of 2–5 December shows the principles of futurism extended into the realm of abstraction (Rudnitsky, 27).

21. For example, Léger's *Essai pour trois portraits* of 1911, which was shown in Moscow in the *Jack of Diamonds* exhibition of 1912, is discussed by Edward Fry as a major influence on Malevich in *Fernand Léger*, exh. cat. (Buffalo: Albright-Knox Art Gallery, 1982) 12, and Compton, "Italian Futurism and Russia," 345.

22. Comparisons of compositional structure can be made, for example, between Léger's *Les Fumées sur les toits* (1911) and *Le Passage à niveau* (1912) and Malevich's *The Guardsman* and *Woman at the Tram Stop*, both from 1913.

23. Other sources are pointed out, for example, by John Bowlt in *Journey into Non-Objectivity: The Graphic Work of Kazimir Malevich and Other Members of the Russian Avant-Garde*, exh. cat. (Dallas: Dallas Museum of Fine Arts, 1980), 11; Douglas in "Cubisme français/ cubo-futurism russe," 192, and in *Swans of Other Worlds: Kazimir Malevich and the Origins of Abstraction in Russia* (Ann Arbor: UMI Research Press, ca. 1980), 50–51. Another possible borrowing is the ruler-like string of piano keys in Malevich's *Portrait of M. V. Matiushin*, with its echo of the long easel bar or guide that dissects Boccioni's *Fusion of a Head and Window*.

24. See Douglas, *Swans of Other Worlds*, 59, and "Birth of a 'Royal Infant': Malevich and 'Victory Over the Sun,'" *Art in America* 62, no. 2 (March–April 1974): esp. 49–50, who discusses both the primary role of the square in Malevich's designs and the question of whether the famous drawing of a square divided into black and white triangles is meant to be abstract or a cropped image of the sun's surface.

25. Quoted by A. Fevralsky in A. Anastasev and E. Peregudova, eds., *Spektakli i gody* (Plays and Years) (Moscow, 1969) 13, and in Edward Braun, "Constructivism in the Theater," *Art in Revolution*, exh. cat. (London: Hayward Gallery, 1971), 60.

26. See Umbrio Apollonio, ed. *Futurist Manifestos* (New York: Viking Press, 1973), 51–65.

27. Marianne Martin, *Futurist Art and Theory 1909–1915* (Oxford: Clarendon Press, 1968), 188 n. 1, and *Sonia Delaunay: A Retrospective*, exh. cat. (Buffalo: Albright-Knox Art Gallery, 1980), 35, 37–38, 113 n. 61, particularly Blaise Cendrars's contention that Delaunay's designs influenced the Russian futurists.

28. Livshits, 163–64.

29. Rudnitsky, 18–19, 30–33.

30. The solid, angular quality of the sets caused one contemporary critic to note that they were all "cubes and cones," representing the "triumphal parade of cubism." Quoted in Rudnitsky, 18, from A. M. Efros, *Kamernyi teatr i ego khudozhniki* (The Kamerny Theatre and the Artist) (Moscow, 1934), xxiv. The rhythmical and coloristic elements in Exter's drawings, however, link her more closely with the futurists.

31. The maquette is illustrated in Andrei Nakov, *Alexandra Exter*, exh. cat. (Paris: Galerie Jean Chauvelin, May–June 1972), 23, and Balla's relief is shown in Martin, *Futurist Art and Theory*, fig. 218.

32. Martin, pl. 14.

33. For the work by Balla and Depero for Stravinsky and Diaghilev, see Marianne Martin, "The Ballet *Parade*: A Dialogue Between Cubism and Futurism," *Art Quarterly* 1, no. 2 (Spring 1978): 92, 101, and *L'Arte della scena*, 53–55. Depero was incensed by what he felt were plagiarisms by Larionov from his work. See John Bowlt, "From Studio to Stage: The Painters of the Ballets Russes," *The Art of Enchantment: Diaghilev's Ballets Russes 1909–1929*, exh. cat. (San Francisco: The Fine Arts Museums of San Francisco, 1989), 56.

34. Published in Balla and Depero's *Riconstruzione futurista dell'universo* of 11 March 1915; see Martin, "The Ballet *Parade*," 94.

35. From A. Tairov, *O Teatr* (Moscow, 1970), 543; quoted by Braun, 66; Léger's letter dated 9 March 1923.

Russian Eccentric Theatre: The Rhythm of America on the Early Soviet Stage

Mel Gordon

W*e revere Charlie Chaplin's ass more than the hands of Eleonora Duse!*

Factory of the Eccentric
Actor manifesto, 1921[1]

The extraordinary Soviet love affair with American culture began in the experimental theatre studios of Moscow and Petrograd in the early twenties. Among the prerevolutionary Russian intelligentsia, the New World was a mere cipher for utopian happiness or mad capitalist exploitation—sensationalized topics more suitable for the publishers of cheap German and Scandinavian novels. Theatrically, the graphic images of Ellis Island and the New York skyline, of Galveston and the northern Mississippi farmlands, could only be seen on the makeshift stages of the Finnish, Polish, Ukrainian, and Yiddish-speaking minorities scattered throughout the fringe regions of the czarist empire.

In Russia proper, the land of Columbus held little aesthetic appeal to the purveyors of either early twentieth-century realism or its nascent challenger, symbolism. Typically, the Moscow Art Theatre's extensive repertory (with the single exception of Henning Berger's *The Deluge*, 1915, staged by the independent First Studio)[2] completely ignored the colossus across the Atlantic. And even after the revolutionary year 1917, Muscovite cinema-goers doted on the mild comedies of the western European silent film stars Max Linder and André Deed. Charlie Chaplin, the preeminent icon of American popular entertainment at that time, was known only by hearsay, except in the world of the constructivist theatre.

Although the top-hatted figure of Woodrow Wilson occasionally appeared on the pageant stages of Soviet spectacles during the heady "war communism" period (1918–1920), capitalism was almost always represented by treacherous French and British leaders or by ubiquitous, pot-bellied western European financiers. The earliest identifiable American stage characters appeared in Petrograd during the 1919–1920 season of the Theatre of Popular Comedy. Led by Sergei Radlov, the Popular Comedy sought to "Americanize" old European classics and melodramas from the seventeenth and nineteenth centuries by updating the original dramatic material and pressing it through a mesh of modern entertainment forms. Radlov combined the established scenic techniques of turn-of-the-century British music hall and clowning, American circus, minstrel shows, vaudeville, and comic film acting into a single, slapstick performance style. He called it *eccentrism*. Under other rubrics, like *urbanism*, *chaplinism*, or *pinkertonism*, Radlov's novel genre would shape Soviet theatre and cinema for more than a decade.[3]

Russian audiences were certainly familiar with grotesque stylizing in theatrical art since the days of Nikolai Gogol (1809–1852). But Radlov declared that there was a special "Anglo-American genius" for the production of a mass culture that unmasked the absurdity and the hectic pace of modern life. Without any regard for history, logic, or nineteenth-century perspective, American eccentrism found its expression on the popular stage as well as in flashing advertising displays, improbable adventure novels, detective serials, illustrated joke books, garish promotions of penny dreadfuls, working-class amusement parks, and dime museums that displayed weird artifacts of the marvelous. According to Radlov, eccentrism alone understood the dynamic rhythms of Western city life with its startling visual juxtapositions, piercing machine and street sounds, endless transformations, and commercialized exposés of human folly.[4]

Typical products of the Popular Comedy's "Americanization of theatre" were its 1920 presentations of *The Dead Man's Bride* and *The Foster Child*. In *The Dead Man's Bride*, a Russian sailor fell in love with the daughter of J.P. Morgan, the American banker. A contemporary Pantalone, Morgan frantically ran around the stage, spewing poetry about his celebrated trading abilities to exchange "Negroes" for diamonds and vice versa. And while Morgan confided to the audience that "Time is money," his ancient mother (played by the circus clown Alexander Alexandrov, in a ridiculous dress) lustily pursued the hapless sailor by executing astounding acrobatic feats. Petrograd's young spectators responded enthusiastically to this electrified commedia.[5]

For *The Foster Child*, Radlov borrowed a number of essential scenic ideas and characters from Nate Pinkerton's adventure series, which chronicled the escapades of America's first self-proclaimed private detective. Here in the main street of an unnamed Western city, the adopted son of a rich capitalist, Serge (played by the circus acrobat Serge Alexander) was handed some crucial documents by a wounded revolutionary. Chased by legions of police and government agents across the mysterious urban landscape, the boy scaled cul-de-sacs and rooftops, temporarily ducking into a restaurant and the tiny space between two skyscrapers. Twice cornered, Serge negotiated a hundred-and-fifty foot tightrope over the audience and leaped forty feet to the stage floor. In the finale, Serge was rescued from his relentless, whistle-blowing pursuers when a rope ladder was unfurled from an unseen Russian airplane above the proscenium arch. Clenching the precious papers in his mouth, Serge climbed the rope to be flown to the ultimate safety of the Soviet Union.

Inspired by Radlov's experiments and Filippo Tommaso Marinetti's Italian futurist program, a young artistic group in Petrograd once again pronounced the triumph of modern American culture. More provocative and radical in spirit than the Popular Comedy, they called themselves FEKS, an acronym for the Factory of the Eccentric Actor. Led by the sixteen-year-old artist Grigorii Kozintsev, FEKS proved itself an effective public-relations vehicle for pinkertonism.[6] In its first free-for-all evening on 5 December 1921, Kozintsev declaimed:

YESTERDAY: Museums, temples, libraries.
TODAY: Factories, plants, bustling ports.
YESTERDAY: European culture.
TODAY: American Technology. . . .
Today's rhythm is the Rhythm of the Machine, concentrated in America.[7]

Leonid Trauberg announced that "Today's street scene is the circus, cinema, music hall, Pinkerton. We're [FEKS] as modest as American advertising."[8] Sergei Yutkevich followed with the provocation, "We rate a Pinkerton book cover higher than the inventions of Picasso!!!"[9] And the old man of the group, thirty-year-old Georgii Kryzhitsky maintained that "Pinkerton is more convincing than Aristotle."[10]

In September 1922, FEKS mounted its first major production based on Gogol's *The Marriage*. Plastered across Petrograd were eccentric FEKS posters for *The Marriage: A Gag in Three Acts* with the slightly ungrammatical American phrase, "Times is Money!!!" (A second poster simply proclaimed, "Amerika Forward!")[11] Since the actors, now trained with the "mathematical precision of the American comic and detective films,"[12] were still rehearsing more than an hour past curtain time, Soviet militiamen had to be called to restore order outside the theatre. Onstage, a performer playing Gogol sat on a chamber pot, which sent imaginary shocks of electricity into his posterior. Suddenly the film short "Charlie Chaplin and Little Betsy" was projected onto the backdrop. Gogol's main characters were transformed by the FEKS writers into Charlie Chaplin and "Musichall Kinematografovich Pinkerton." The love interest in *Marriage* was supplied by a Miss Agatha who spoke with simultaneous English and Ukrainian accents. As FEKS's wild parody gained momentum, two thoroughly irritating clown-prompters named Albert and Einstein taunted both the actors and spectators into a balloon-tossing frenzy.

FEKS's 1923 spring production, *Foreign Trade on the Eiffel Tower, or "Hamlet" Reworked*, borrowed more directly from Radlov's bag of urbanist tricks. An American inventor, Mr. Hugely, has come to Paris with a formula for "blue coal"—a fuel that can be extracted from thin air. Realizing that this discovery will ruin their capitalist trust, the World Fuel Corporation sets out to destroy both the inventor and his formula. A seven-year-old Russian girl (played by the clown Serge) and the Frenchman Pepo manage to rescue Hugely and his invention after battling the Corporation agents on the floors of the Eiffel Tower and in the sewers of Paris.

At the First Workers Theatre of the Proletkult in Moscow, eccentrism took a more political turn. In March 1921 an adaptation of Jack London's short story, "The Mexican," opened to much acclaim. Designed by a twenty-two-year-old Sergei Eisenstein, *The Mexican* (cat. no. 13) not only followed the basic plot of London's satiric melodrama about a down-and-out Mexican revolutionary who resorts to prize-fighting, but also suggested the tabloid madness of American society. In the Prologue and second act, twenty leggy Tiller Girls (American precision dancers), blackface minstrels, Stetson-hatted cowboys, blankfaced

Cat. no. 13

Sergei Eisenstein

Set design, *The Mexican*, 1921

Indians, miners, corrupt judges, and storkish-looking reporters on the prowl (all Eisenstein additions) cheered on the braggart Champion, who, despite his physical prowess and strength, is knocked out by the Mexican amateur.[13]

During summer 1922 in Petrograd, Eisenstein joined Yutkevich to pen the ultimate eccentric satire, *Columbine's Garter*, a parody of Arthur Schnitzler's pantomime, *Der Schleier der Pierrette* (The Veil of Pierrette) (retitled in 1910 by Vsevolod Meyerhold *Columbine's Scarf*). Here all the features of pinkertonism came to life. Pierrot, an old Bostonian capitalist, morphine addict, and writer, grooms himself as he salaciously awaits Columbine, a treacherous erotic dancer, who will soon strangle him with a steel garter. Meanwhile at the Metropolitan Hotel, Columbine's parents, Ma and Pa, two old Russian émigrés (dressed as an automat restaurant and a flush toilet), prepare for the wedding of their daughter and Arlecchino, the owner of the garter factory. Various decadent American types dance to syncopated music of the hotel jazz band. Suddenly realizing that her deadly garter has been left behind, Columbine returns to Pierrot's apartment, where she is electrocuted by Ned Rocker, "Detective, USA, New York," the real Arlecchino.

Eisenstein/Yutkevich's unrealized project was written for Nikolai Foregger's MASTFOR (an acronym of the Foregger Workshop) (cat. no. 86), a celebrated Moscow cabaret. The sole descendant of an aristocratic

Cat. no. 18
Sergei Eisenstein
Costume design for Etoile,
Good Treatment for Horses, 1922

Cat. no. 19
Sergei Eisenstein
Costume design for a Woman
in the scene "Hands Up,"
Good Treatment for Horses, 1922

Cat. no. 86
Nikolai Foregger
Uniform and logo design for
the Foregger Workshop (MASTFOR),
1922–1923

Russo-German family, Foregger was considered one of the most innovative and controversial of all the Soviet directors and choreographers of the early twenties. His effete appearance and eccentric ways earned him the rubric *The American*. In December 1921, his bitingly satiric burlesque, *The Parody Show*, cleverly designed by Yutkevich and Eisenstein,[14] demonstrated that perfectly executed eccentric and stylized acting could occupy a new niche between theatre and dance. Attacking the theatrical pretensions of the Moscow Art Theatre and Alexander Tairov's Kamerny Theatre as well as the naiveties of the current agitprop, MASTFOR quickly became the focal point of a theatre-obsessed Moscow.[15]

In January 1922 Foregger presented his most famous production, *Good Treatment for Horses* (cat. nos. 18, 19). Written by Vladimir Mass, *Good Treatment* touched on the greed of Russia's artistic bourgeoisie and the new entrepreneurial class created by Lenin's New Economic Policy (NEP) of 1921–1928 as an American impresario tours Moscow in search of local talent. Brought to a decadent Russian cabaret—rather like the real MASTFOR—the cosmopolitan American is amazed by the novelty dances and "hot" music of the New Russia. Combining *tye-fe-trenage* (MASTFOR's special movement grid of three hundred cartoon-like gestures and actions) with poses from a Berlin manual on American jazz music, Foregger created an entirely new kind of eccentric dance theatre. Mobile sets and scantily attired characters, including a hooknosed Isadora Duncan dancer, and "American" routines like "Mucky from Kentucky" and the "Dance of the Ku Klux Klan," dazzled Muscovite audiences in search of the latest Western entertainments.[16]

As MASTFOR's popularity grew, so did Foregger's inventiveness: Foxtrots, tangos, apache dances, and shimmies merged with aerial somersaults, pyramid-climbing displays, acrobatic leaps, and Tiller-Girlish mechanical steps and turns. A series of "acting-machines" were

Fig. 1
Blue Blouse Theatre
Us and Henry Ford, n.d.

opposite:
Cat. no. 168
Vladimir Stenberg and Georgii Stenberg
Costume design for a Man,
Day and Night, 1926

even placed in MASTFOR's foyer in order to teach the audience "how to act" in the patented *tye-fe-trenage* style. Between 1922 and 1924, Foregger offered over forty quick-paced constructivist programs of daring, satirical political sketches, erotic dances, and agit-mimes called *chaplinades*. Embodying the annihilation of the dramatic rules of the past, ascribed to the pace of American life, Foregger and his MASTFOR quickly symbolized the felicitous marriage of American popular culture and twenties' Soviet art.[17]

MASTFOR's most influential scenic innovation, the machine dance, took Foregger's most bitter enemies by surprise when it was first presented in February 1923. "Celebrating the new god of the Machine"[18] and the rhythm of industrial America, MASTFOR dancers created—with shocking precision—the movement and internal workings of the modern factory. Human enactments of lynch-pin rotations on locomotive wheels, pistons within expanding cylinders, turning flywheels, transmission bands, handpumps, and spinning lathes impressed both the NEP spectators and their working-class counterparts. Eccentric aspects of MASTFOR's productions imbued the Soviet agitprop theatre with Americanisms long after the theatre's demise in 1924. Dozens of amateur theatres and dance troupes demonstrated their own blank-faced "American" versions of living machinery, underscored by "music" from human noise orchestras.[19] And borrowing directly from MASTFOR's arsenal, the fabled Blue Blouse movement—numbering some 100,000 members across the Soviet Union—created such machine-dance paeans to American industry as "Us and Henry Ford" (fig. 1).

In 1924 one of Foregger's disciples, Vitalii Zhemchuzhny, directed the anti-illiteracy comedy *An Evening of the Books*, made famous by Varvara Stepanova's striking set design, a ten-foot book from which each performer magically appeared.[20] At the beginning of *Evening*, capitalist authors and storybook characters, led by Nate Pinkerton, Tarzan (the "Bourgeois Dream"), God, and the romance-writer Anastasia Verbitskaya, scheme to destroy the Soviet state presses. They are thwarted and then crushed by John Reed, James Fenimore Cooper's Pathfinder, and Upton Sinclair. Once captured by the defenders of "Good Literature," God offers to be "a walk-on for Meyerhold" as a means of doing penance for his previous antirevolutionary activities.

If Soviet critics and theatre historians have generally been unkind to Alexander Tairov's Kamerny Theatre, Muscovite spectators in the twenties and thirties were not.[21] A ticket to the Kamerny Theatre was among the most difficult to find and often provided an experience similar to performances of the Swedish Ballet in Paris or a Broadway extravaganza (for example, cat. nos. 168, 169). Tairov's personal manner and cosmopolitan tastes were more closely aligned with the directors of New York's Theatre Guild than with the standard bearers of Russian theatre culture Stanislavsky and Meyerhold. Although nearly all of the Kamerny Theatre productions stunned their audiences with the most up-to-date and artistic mise-en-scenes and stylized performances, Tairov himself developed few lasting or influential ideas about scenic design or acting technique. Tairov promulgated no true training "systems" and rarely carried on about the theatre's unique social mission. In this sense, Tairov resembled a typical American director of the twenties.

Cat. no. 26
Sergei Eisenstein
Set design, *Heartbreak House*, 1922

opposite:
Cat. no. 197
Alexander Vesnin
Costume design for Phèdre, *Phèdre*, 1922

What made the Kamerny Theatre unusual for Soviet audiences was its extensive and sophisticated dramatic repertory. Asian and European playwrights from the fourth-century Indian poet Kalidasa to the French neoclassicist Jean Racine (cat. no. 197), and from George Bernard Shaw (cat. no. 26) to Bertolt Brecht (cat. no. 171), were all represented in various eclectic and modernist productions. Yet throughout the NEP period, Tairov's interest in American life and art grew. Almost four years after Radlov pioneered the "Americanization" of Soviet theatre, Tairov turned his attention to eccentrism.

In December 1923 Tairov mounted a stage version of G. K. Chesterton's novel, *The Man Who Was Thursday*. Alexander Vesnin's urbanist environment, which depicted the Western city's dynamic attractions and claustrophobic entrapments for revolutionary and foe alike, was considered one of the greatest achievements in constructivist stage design. Filling the entire proscenium space vertically and horizontally, like an Eiffel-Tower metropolis, was a multileveled construction that supported three working elevator shafts, an escalator, one swing crane, and three rotating billboards. Robotic sandwich-board men advertised their wares while mackintoshed proletariats trundled off to their derrick-framed workhouses. Meanwhile, during twenty-three cinematic-like episodes, bomb-carrying anarchists and detectives chased one another in confused and mistakened pursuit. Watching all of this in

Дорогой Алисе Георгиевне
в память наших исканий
образа Флоры.
Л. Весн
19 ²⁰⁄ᵢᵢ 22 г.

Cat. no. 198
Alexander Vesnin
Costume design for Wednesday,
The Man Who Was Thursday, 1923

Cat. no. 200
Alexander Vesnin
Costume design for a Woman,
The Man Who Was Thursday, 1923

mysterious delight were menacing capitalists (cat. no. 198) with their eccentrically garbed girlfriends (cat. no. 200).

After directing Shaw's *St. Joan* (1924), Tairov returned to eccentrism in November 1925 with the political revue called *Kukirol*. Attempting to profit from the lure of decadent entertainments found in American nightclubs and western European cabarets while officially condemning their lavish life-styles, *Kukirol* attracted large houses as it received blistering reviews from the critics. Later that year, Tairov staged an adaptation of the Hollywood film *Rosita*—a probable first European borrowing from American cinema. And between 1926 and 1929, Tairov directed three Eugene O'Neill plays—*The Hairy Ape* (1926) (cat. no. 170), *Desire under the Elms* (1926), and *All God's Chillun Got Wings* (1929), entitled *The Negro*—in appropriately lurid and expressionist modes. By the end of the twenties, in the last era before the mandate of socialist realism, Tairov was considered the champion of O'Neill and serious American drama in Europe.

Historically, Meyerhold, the director most associated with constructivism and eccentrism, came to American themes somewhat late in the superheated theatrical atmosphere of the twenties. Almost a generation older than the devotees of Charlie Chaplin and pinkertonism, Meyerhold integrated certain Americanisms within a broad spectrum of earlier popular European forms like commedia dell'arte and Russian fairground performances.[22] Vulgar caricatures of NEP speculators or German bourgeoisie in Alexei Faiko's comedies, *Lake Lyul* (November 1923), which takes place "somewhere in the far West, or extreme East" of Russia, and *Bubus, the Teacher* (January 1925), set in postwar Germany, acted as substitute American eccentrics, rather than true American types.

Not so much its comedic forms, but America's technical expertise appealed to Meyerhold's notion of the New World as a citadel of boundless modernity and wondrous scientific efficiency. The stream-lined movements that Frederick Winslow Taylor designed for American industrial workers in the teens, for instance, inspired Meyerhold to develop his own psycho-physical system of actor training known as *biomechanics*.[23] Actively preparing over a period of months, rather than in a traditional four- or five-year regimen, acting students in Meyerhold's studio (the State Higher Theatre Workshop or GVYTM) could learn to emote with kinesthetic precision while following the scenic dictates of their "director-engineer." The ideology of Taylor, through primitive time-and-motion studies, was applied to scripts and audience response as well as to acting work at Meyerhold's studios.[24]

Virtually all of the Americanisms of the early Soviet theatre could be found in Meyerhold's agitprop production of *D.E. (Give Us Europe)* (June 1924).[25] Adapted by Mikhail Podgaetsky and a cadre of his civil engineering students from Ilia Ehrenburg's 1922 science-fiction novel, *D.E.* revealed capitalism's unrestrained attempt to annihilate Europe and Soviet Russia's defense of it in the future years between 1927 and 1940. A Dutch adventurer is in league with three American billionaires who pepper Europe with plagues, deadly love potions, and endless internecine wars so that American commerce may flourish without the impediments of bolshevism or progressive European labor. In the final episode,

Cat. no. 171
Vladimir Stenberg and Georgii Stenberg
Set design, *The Beggar's Opera*, 1930

however, the Red Army, in a superhuman effort, manages to complete a secret Leningrad–New York City tunnel to defeat the forces of international reaction.

The seventeen episodes of *D.E.* unfolded in a rhythmically shocking array of competing stylistic and cinematic modes. Titles, illustrations, and images were continually projected onto three screens as moving platforms and panels reassembled to create new mise-en-scènes across the North American and European battleground. Meyerhold's performers, enacting multiple roles of Ku Klux Klansmen, German cabaret dancers, Red Army militiamen, Afro-American revolutionaries, corrupt Polish officials, French fascists, and scientists of all stripes, dazzled Soviet spectators with their vibrant and instantaneous transformational skills. In the First Episode alone, Erast Garin played seven different eccentric inventors, each in his own slapstick style and vocal pattern. (An eye-like opening in a panel revealed Garin's changes of disguise before bemused Soviet audiences.) Chaplinesque routines of cannibalism conducted by British lords in rocking chairs alternated with vigorous displays of biomechanical etudes by Red sailors, followed by the lugubrious machinations of the world's capitalist and fascist leaders, followed still by wild apache dance numbers to the music of Moscow's first live jazz band.

Switching between fast and slow motion, communist propaganda and American filmic comedy, French farce and Kabuki, Soviet athleticism

Cat. no. 170
Vladimir Stenberg and Georgii Stenberg
Set design, *The Hairy Ape*, 1926

and decadent stand-up/fall-down dances, and melodrama and science fiction, *D.E.* brought eccentrism to a full circle. Meyerhold's ability to tap into "Anglo-American genius" was unparalleled. Like a perfect Ziegfeld revue, *D.E.* could not be surpassed. Therefore, over the next six years, it remained on the Soviet stage in constantly mutating versions. And it was during those years that eccentrism, the American-Russian invention, lost its novelty on Moscow's stages and entered newly formed into the world of Soviet cinema.

Notes

1. Grigorii Kozintsev, "AB!" in *Ekstsentrizm* (Petrograd: Ekstsentropolis, 1922), 3.

2. Set in the Rocky Mountains, *The Deluge* exposed the sad corruption of New World life. To this Danish cautionary drama, Evgenii Vakhtangov, the First Studio director, added the redeeming power of Tolstoyan philosophy.

3. For a description of Sergei Radlov's early Soviet career, see Mel Gordon, "Radlov's Theatre of Popular Comedy," *The Drama Review* 19, no.4 (December 1975):113–116.

4. See Sergei Radlov, ("Elektrifikatsiia teatra" (The Electrification of Theatre), in *Desiat let v teatre* (Twenty Years in the Theatre) (Leningrad: Priboi, 1929), 95–101.

5. A.C. Alexandrov, in E. Kuznetzov, ed., *Sovetskii tsirk 1918–1938* (The Soviet Circus, 1918–1938) (Moscow-Leningrad: Iskusstvo, 1938), 95.

6. See FEK's pamphlet, *Eccentrism*, František Deák, intro., in *The Drama Review* 19, no. 4 (December 1975):88–94. Lynn Ball, trans. from Russian, 95–109. The fullest treatment of FEKS in any language can be found in Giusi Rapisarda, *Cinema e Avanguardia in Unione Sovietica, La Feks: Kozincev e Trauberg* (Rome: Officini Edzioni, 1975).

7. Kozintsev, 2.

8. Leonid Trauberg, "The Filmmaker as Denouncer," quoted from Ball, 104.

9. Sergei Yutkevich, "Eccentrism, Painting, Publicity," quoted from Ball, 107.

10. Georgii Kryzhitsky, *The Philosophical Showbooth* (Petrograd: Ekstsentropolis, 1922), 3. Translated for the author by Alma Law.

11. Vladimir Nedobrovo, *FEKS: G. Kozintsev i L. Trauberg* (Moscow-Leningrad: Iskusstvo, 1928), 89.

12. Sergei Gerassimov, in Luda Schnitzer and Jean Schnitzer, eds., *Cinema in Revolution*, trans. and with additional material by David Robinson (New York: Hill & Wang, 1973), 114.

13. A great deal of confusion exists among film scholars over Eisenstein's contribution to *The Mexican* and its sequence within Eisenstein's theatrical career. This is because of Eisenstein's deliberately muddled account given in *Film Sense* (New York: Harcourt Brace, 1942), 219 passim. In fact, two separate productions of *The Mexican* were staged at the Proletkult Theatre: The first, designed by Eisenstein in January 1921, was a realistic, agitprop presentation; the second, revised, eccentric production was directed by Eisenstein in March 1923.

14. Once again, in his various autobiographical accounts, Eisenstein jumbled the dates of his participation in Foregger's *The Parody Show* and *Good Treatment for Horses*. Confusion over the MASTFOR chronology has been further compounded by revised versions of *Good Treatment* that were produced fall 1923, entitled *Better Treatment for Horses* and *Even Better Treatment for Horses*.

15. See Mel Gordon, "Foregger and the Dance of the Machines," *The Drama Review* 19, no. 1 (March 1975):68–73.

16. See Li [A. Cherepnin], "Foregger," *Zrelishcha*, 1924, no. 82:11.

17. Nikolai Foregger, "Pesa, siuzhet, triuk" (Play, Plot, Trick), *Zrelishcha*, 1922, no. 7:11.

18. René Fülöp-Miller, *The Mind and Face of Bolshevism* (New York: Knopf, 1928), 260. Trans. from German by F. S. Flint and D. F. Trait.

19. Fülöp-Miller, 261.

20. Photographs of Varvara Stepanova's set appear in David Elliott, *New Worlds: Russian Art and Society 1900–1937* (New York: Rizzoli, 1986), 100-101, and Alexander Lavrentiev, *Varvara Stepanova: The Complete Work*, ed. John E. Bowlt (The MIT Press: Cambridge, 1988), 112–115.

21. See Nick Worrall, *Modernism to Realism on the Soviet Stage* (Cambridge: Cambridge University Press, 1989), 15–75.

22. Among the dozen English-language accounts of Meyerhold's work in actor training, Edward Braun's *The Theatre of Meyerhold* (New York: Drama Book Specialists, 1979) is the most useful and reliable.

23. See Mel Gordon, "Meyerhold's Biomechanics," *The Drama Review* 18, no. 3 (September 1974):73–88.

24. See Richard Stourac and Kathleen McCreery, *Theatre as a Weapon: Workers' Theatre in the Soviet Union, Germany, and Britain, 1917–1934* (London: Routledge & Kegan Paul, 1986), 20.

25. Descriptions of *D. E.* can be found in Llewellyn H. Hegbeth, "Meyerhold's 'D.E.,'" *The Drama Review* 19, no. 2 (June 1975):23–36; and Mel Gordon, "Agit-Fantasy," forthcoming in *Theater* (Spring 1991).

Constructivism and Dance

Elizabeth Souritz

During the first years following the October Revolution of 1917, the art of dance in Russia fell under a variety of influences. At that time, numerous studios opened that were involved in dance, stage movement, plastic movement, rhythmics, and gymnastics. Each studio in its own way developed and interpreted the ideas of Isadora Duncan and Emile Jaques-Dalcroze, experimented with expressionist choreography akin to the German *ausdruckstanz*, and gave birth to new choreographic forms such as the machine-dance. Undoubtedly, the new dance was influenced by the artist-experimenters who created stage sets and designed costumes for the dancer-actors, and constructivism was therefore an essential source for its development.

But did constructivist dance and constructivist ballet actually exist? Probably not. At the very core of the concept of constructivism was the deaestheticizing of stage design; i.e., the real object had to take the place of the image. Therefore the idea of constructivism contradicted the essence of theatre—and dance. What we will address here are the distinct manifestations of constructivism in theatre and dance, the repercussions from constructivist ideas, and their influence.

Constructivism could exert its influence first of all through stage design, then also through stage movement, and through music of the mechanistic kind, which reproduced the rhythm of industrial machines in action. Moreover, in stage design constructivism was rarely encountered in a pure form but rather in combination with other styles—cubism, cubofuturism, suprematism, etc.—and it instinctively tended toward representation, toward theatrical illusion.

Attempts to make constructivist stage design available for dance and ballet were first made in 1922. Several constructivist sets were created for Kasian Goleizovsky's Moscow Chamber Ballet. The Bakhrushin State Central Theatrical Museum has in its collection a preliminary study by an anonymous artist, dated 1922, for the ballet *Sarcasms*, with music by Sergei Prokofiev, as well as a sketch of the same date by Alexandra Exter for *Satanic Ballet* (cat. no. 68), with music by Alexander Scriabin. The former represents a construction made of wooden boards; a scaffold; a suspended, flat triangular shape; and ropes stretched across the stage. Exter's design depicts multiple ladders and platforms placed above a fragment of a large wheel, around which were rope ladders, cables, and swings with figures climbing on them. We do not know if these sketches were ever used in production, or what dances accompanied such stage

Cat. no. 68
Alexandra Exter
Sketch of stage construction,
Satanic Ballet, 1922

designs. Much more is known about Goleizovsky's other works, especially *Salomé*, with music by Richard Strauss and stage sets by Nikolai Musatov, and *Faun*, with music by Claude Debussy and stage sets by Boris Erdman, which premiered respectively in July and August 1922. In both cases, stage design of a novel type had been created—a construction where the place of action as well as costumes and stage props were functional but devoid of obvious representation.

For *Salomé* Musatov built a scaffold against a background of triangular forms. When Salomé appeared on it, the forms parted and a huge moon appeared against the black velvet backdrop, so that Salomé seemed to be surrounded with radiance. The culmination of her dance was her jump into the arms of several young men standing by the scaffold below, to whom she proceeded to give away her veils until she was almost nude. In spite of the constructivist stage set, the representational principle was sufficiently strong. The movable triangles resembled pyramids and mountains, and the scaffold, though neutral, was no longer perceived as a working platform but as an atmospheric environment. Infused with tense sensuality, the set conjured the Orient, a mysterious night permeated perhaps with a promise of love, perhaps with a threat of death.

Goleizovsky's choreography was the component least responsive to the concept of constructivism. This is largely because his choreographic premise was based on emotion, rather than on the idea of "building" supra-emotional forms, which would have been closer to constructivism. Although Goleizovsky purified the dance of anything accidental, just as had been done in "pure" classical dance, his choreography remained permeated with sensuality, a fact that caused him to be perennially reproached for his eroticism. Even the acrobatic movements that he liberally introduced into his dances appeared not as something dispassionate or mechanistic, but as yet another expression of the carnal. It would seem that the austere wooden constructions, devoid of even a hint of representation, would be at odds with such an approach. Yet the result was completely the opposite and a well-integrated union of dance and action was born. It was not a "constructivist ballet" by any measure, but rather a ballet in which constructivism played a role in helping the choreographer to realize his purpose. It was hardly a coincidence that in 1922, in an article entitled "The Old and the New," he wrote that a choreographer who aspired to create something new needed stage design in which

> he must regard every unexpected turn, twist, elevation, step, etc. as a subject for thought, as a possibility for enhancing the movement.[1]

Erdman provided Goleizovsky with that opportunity again in *Faun*. The stage held a wooden structure made of several platforms and framed by two ladders. The structure was painted white, which emphasized its neutrality and utility. The set was only platforms and steps, a crisscrossing of white planes and lines that represented nothing. Such constructivist sets required purely utilitarian costumes—*prozodezhda* (a work uniform) —neutral and conducive to the industrial activity of actors.

But, of course neutral clothing is not always neutral. Ballet dancers

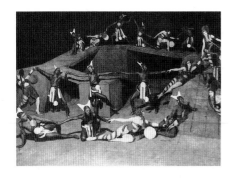

Figs. 1, 2
Joseph the Beautiful, act 1, 1925

overleaf left:
Cat. no. 30
Boris Erdman
Costume design for an Egyptian Dancer,
Joseph the Beautiful, 1925

overleaf right:
Cat. no. 31
Boris Erdman
Costume design for a Jewish Dancer,
Joseph the Beautiful, 1925

have used this kind of uniform and footwear since long ago. Yet even this uniform in different epochs has reflected a specific attitude toward the human being, the human body, and the clothing that covered it. Suffice it to compare the ballet costume of the past—the tutu and pink tights— with the contemporary unisex leotard. Goleizovsky, as an artist of the constructivist epoch, insisted on a costume that fully liberated the body, was next to nudity. For the faun and the surrounding nymphs, Erdman designed costumes made out of cord. The torso of a nymph was bound by rows of cord, a turban of cord served as a cap, and a fringe of cords represented a small skirt. Underneath the cords was the nude body. Goleizovsky situated the entire dance on the scaffold, which the performers never left, moving around the steps and the platforms. The lines of their bodies and of their stretched, lifted, or bent arms and legs, together with the grid formed by vertical and horizontal bands of construction, created a complex, constantly and whimsically changing pattern. Regarding his production, Goleizovsky has said that "the whole thing was like openwork, the way Debussy's music is."[2]

Constructivist design continued to fascinate Goleizovsky. For *The Death of Isolde*, with Richard Wagner's funeral march as its musical score, a construction was commissioned in 1924 from Anatolii Petritsky. A photo of the maquette was published in the journal *Zrelishcha*, but nothing is known about the production.[3] A program for a 12 April 1924 concert at the Great Hall of the Moscow Conservatory has been preserved, which mentions a production by Goleizovsky and "construction and costumes by the artist Petritsky." But even if the ballet was shown then, it was not included in the company's repertory. On the other hand, the second act of the ballet *Joseph the Beautiful* (1925), produced at the Bolshoi Theatre with a musical score by Sergei Vasilenko, undoubtedly was Goleizovsky's most significant work in the 1920s. Erdman designed the construction, which as a result of its exposure to the choreography became aestheticized. Just as in Goleizovsky's previous productions, it was not just an acting platform but a focus of action.

The first act of *Joseph the Beautiful* is set in Canaan, which is represented by several small-scale platforms, some straight and others at an angle, situated at different levels and connected by bridges (figs. 1, 2). A backdrop of black velvet vividly set off the figures of the actors, who Goleizovsky combined in unusual patterns, having them stand, kneel, lie on and hang off the bridges, with arms and legs interlocked at different levels. The small multilevel platforms, which allowed jumping and running up and down, helped dynamize the action at moments of high drama, as for example, in the scene of Joseph's capture (cat. nos. 30, 31).

If in the first act the stage space was fragmented—lacking sharp contrasts but also monolithic form (for the artist and the choreographer had in mind an image of the Canaan hills, the world of Joseph's idyllic youth)—then in the second act the construction assumed a different character. It became monumental and symmetrical by positioning rows of platforms one above the other so that the entire structure was oriented toward its apex, the Pharaoh's throne. This image of the pyramid as a symbol of arrogant, absolute power was the premise for the construction, and the action was structured accordingly through the use of pantomimic episodes, especially the solemn procession of the courtiers, and dances.

The Pharaoh's court was represented by a multifigured composition in which individual groups of dancers repeated over and over the identical poses in profile. The endless repetition of the same image seemed to deny the possibility of inner contradictions, suggesting that a dispassionate, dumb force crushed any expression of individuality, embodied in the figure of the captive Joseph.

The construction served its function by helping the choreographer to structure the action, opening up possibilities for creating diverse compositions of moving bodies and rhythmic combinations of their movements. But even though it initially tended toward utilitarianism, Erdman's stage set helped the choreographer to reveal the ballet's main idea, which was the contrast between spirituality (the world of Joseph) and dumb, senseless tyranny (the world of the Pharaoh).

A construction was supposed to form the basis of Goleizovsky's next but unfortunately unrealized production at the Bolshoi, the ballet *Lola*, which the choreographer worked on in 1925–1926 with the composer Vasilenko and the artist Erdman. For this ballet, whose tragic plot was reminiscent of Lope de Vega's *La Fuente Ovejuna*, Erdman created a set composed of several platforms and a drawbridge.[4] It was assumed that by lowering canvas backdrops representing arches and columns (which, of course, was a move away from constructivist principles) it would be possible to change the place of action—to move from a square, to a palace court, to a dungeon.

There was even less "pure" constructivism in the decorations used by the Leningrad choreographer Fedor Lopukhov, especially in his collaborations with the artist Vladimir Dmitriev, although constructions quite often played a role. In Igor Stravinsky's *Pulcinella* of 1926, which was stylized after commedia dell'arte traditions, the construction was a lightweight, white structure set against a blue sky; two multilevel rotating towers were situated on either side of the stage, with clearly perceptible window outlines, as well as arches and pavilions in between. The design left the scenic space open for dance, yet also allowed the performers to appear at different levels within the towers. Moreover, the construction was easily movable, and the rotating towers seemed to take part in the dance of the crowd. In the finale, the entire stage swirled, both the performers and the set overtaken by the dynamic of the play, its joyful tone.

Lopukhov's production of the ballet *The Nutcracker* in 1929 illustrates a close collaboration between the artist and the choreographer. It was an experiment in which distinct elements of a construction were used; the musical score was rearranged to include conversations and soundless scenes, and the plot after E.T.A. Hoffman was altered through contemporary references. The artist Dmitriev, in an interview with the magazine *Life of Art* (Zhizn iskusstva), said that his decorations, which consisted of moving planes and separate details (a window, a bed, a traffic barrier), served as "an abstract background setting off the dancer's figure and connected in its movement with that of the actors." It also helped to "enrich and expand the possibilities of dance, now emphasizing the location of various groups, now enhancing with its own movement the movement of the actor, or replacing it, as if increasing the corps de ballet."[5] The multicolored, moving flat surfaces built by Dmitriev were incorporated into the action. They formed a corridor for the Nutcracker, the military leader; they were rapidly moved around the stage with dolls and toy soldiers, who were darting to and fro before the battle; and they shaped themselves into symmetrical rows in the episode of the battle with the mice.

In each of these productions, success was achieved when the construction helped the choreographer to convey his idea to the viewer. For this, the artist and the choreographer had to equally understand their tasks and coordinate their efforts. Otherwise, the use of a constructivist set could only discredit the idea. That happened when the Bolshoi Theatre, which in 1922 first began to hire artist-stage designers of the new persuasion, wished to present a ballet with a constructivist decor.

In 1923 the Bolshoi decided to stage *Schéhérazade*, with the score by Nikolai Rimsky-Korsakov; this was to be a new version that would be distinct from the famous 1910 production by Michel Fokine. The decor was commissioned from the artist Mikhail Sapegin. The Bolshoi Ballet at the time was leaderless. Alexander Gorsky had left because of illness and Vasilii Tikhomirov, who had always been extremely conservative, resisting anything new, had not yet succeeded in taking control of the company. Although Goleizovsky had recommended himself on the basis of his innovative productions at the Moscow Chamber Ballet, the Bolshoi's leaders were not sympathetic to his experiments. For these reasons the staging of *Schéhérazade* was undertaken by the dancer Leonid Zhukov.

It appears that Sapegin had never before designed a ballet and he failed to grasp the special character of dance theatre. It would also seem that Zhukov did not convey his ideas to the designer, composing dances in the rehearsal rooms and showing little interest in the sets Sapegin planned to build. Zhukov's banal and unimaginative choreography apparently had no need of constructivist decor.

In the meantime, the artist erected onstage something extraordinary: Almost the entire space was taken over by a structure reminiscent of a ship, whose bow was inclined at a thirty-degree angle. There the main action was supposed to take place. However, according to a critic, "it is guaranteed that any racehorse prancing along such an incline would get a classic case of muscle sprain."[6]

The choreographer tried to situate the majority of the mass dances within the relatively narrow space near the construction. Naturally, congestion and bustle prevailed. Moreover, according to the description given by the well-known art historian Alexei Gvozdev,

> the proscenium is cut from left to right by a scaffold, which obscures the legs of the dancers in the second plane; in their turn, the torsos of these performers cut off the legs of the dancers in the third, elevated plane. . . . The groups scattered on the steps, scaffolds, and platforms (a narrow platform hardly allows space even for a single jump) have no place to dance, and willy-nilly dance became replaced by rotation around its own axis.[7]

Gvozdev concluded that "Something like a negation of the legs occurred in the ballet because of a misunderstood and improperly digested fashion for constructivism."

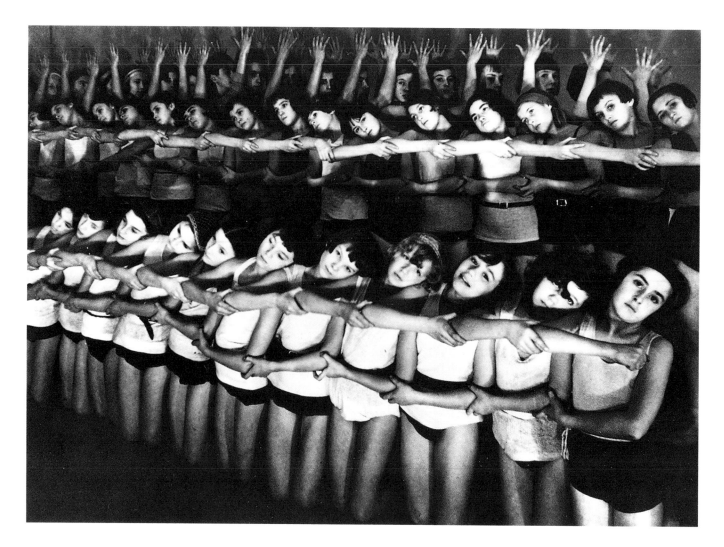

Fig. 3
Margaret Bourke-White
Machine Dance, Moscow Ballet School,
1931
© Roger White, Jane Corkin Gallery,
Toronto

It is important to note that as an ideological doctrine constructivism originated in the worship of the industrial process and technology, and this source accounts for some peculiarities of constructivist influence on dance. From one point of view, human beings were seen as living machines in need of improvement, that is, in need of gaining complete control over their physical abilities. Such a goal was set by the various systems of dance training, including Meyerhold's biomechanics, which prepared the actor's mechanism for fulfilling any task given by the director. First of all, it involved training the physical apparatus; yet it was the kind of training that not only was supposed to strengthen and develop muscles but also was expected to enable dancers to be in charge of their bodies, to live according to a specific rhythm and tempo. It was, to some extent, a system of training the actor's psychic as well as physical apparatus.

Another, more straightforward, means of bringing together dance and constructivism was by direct imitation of the machine. The same principle was also to be found in music where works imitating industrial noises started to appear. Valentin Parnakh, who arrived from abroad and introduced Moscow audiences to jazz, was the first to show a machine-dance in the Soviet Union in 1922. In his concerts, he performed dances that recreated the inner workings of industrial mechanisms to the accompaniment of jazz music. His performances were described as possessing an immediacy and sharpness of jolts, dynamic tension, precision, and persistence of labor processes, intense thumping and pulsing of engines, and rapid movement of levers.[8]

Approximately at the same time, and completely independently from Parnakh, such numbers as *Taylor-jest*, based on movements characteristic of industrial processes, started to be produced at the Foregger Workshop (MASTFOR) and the noise orchestra made its appearance. Nikolai Foregger's first machine-dance also was born in 1922, followed by others. In these dances the performers might imitate a train—by swaying, stamping their feet against the floor, and banging sheets of metal together, even by swinging burning cigarettes in the air so that sparks flew all over as if from a locomotive's smokestack. Or they would imitate the motion of a transmission by a chain of linked girls (fig. 3) circling around two men like a conveyor belt. They also created an image of hammers of various sizes—the smallest, by using their fists, and the largest, by lifting and lowering a dancer held upside down.

The machine-dances of Foregger enjoyed great success and engendered quite a bit of imitation. In a country that had recently embarked upon industrialization, many equated the concept of the mechanistic with that of the contemporary. Machine-like rhythms, constructivist stage sets, the economy of expressive means, and the lack of decoration were all regarded as the most characteristic expressions of contemporaneity. Machine-dances seemed to fit those views (cat. nos. 32, 37).

From what has been stated above, it follows that constructivism influenced dance in two ways: On the one hand, constructivist artists were in demand, and in creating their dances the most talented choreographers knew how to use the possibilities made available by these artists. In this sense, constructivism enhanced dance and yet did not in the least make it constructivist. On the other hand, mechanical dances and machine-dances appeared, engendered to some degree by constructivist ideology. Had these two tendencies ever been united in a production, the result would have been a ballet that could conceivably be regarded as constructivist. Or at least it could have been stated that in such a ballet constructivist principles were embodied in a most consistent manner.

Such a production was never created in Soviet Russia. However *Le Pas d'acier* of 1927 came close to fulfilling these conditions, although it was staged not in Moscow or Leningrad but in Paris by Serge Diaghilev's Ballets Russes. It was however the result of a collaboration between the Soviet composer Sergei Prokofiev and the Soviet artist Georgii Yakulov (who was also one of the ballet's librettists). In addition, the novelist and journalist Ilia Ehrenburg initially took part in the composition of the libretto. Diaghilev intended to invite a Soviet stage director as well, but Meyerhold and Alexander Tairov refused his invitation. Neither did Diaghilev succeed in securing Goleizovsky to work on the production. That is why the ballet was choreographed by Léonide Massine, who had left Russia in 1914 and had only a vague knowledge of Soviet art, not to speak of Soviet daily life. For the most part Massine did what the composer and artist advised him to do. Nonetheless, it is still possible to assume that he was familiar with machine-dances, if not

Cat. no. 32
Boris Erdman
Dance sketch, *Electric Dances*, 1923

Cat. no. 37
Boris Erdman
D'Arto and Kasian Goleizovsky in
Foxtrot Championship, 1923

Fig. 4
Le Pas d'acier, 1927

in Foregger's productions (since Foregger's company did not go to France), then at least with other forms of mechanical dances that appeared during those years.

The construction created for *Le Pas d'acier* by Yakulov defined the choreographic resolution of the production (fig. 4). For the first act he built a set with a platform for the soloists, whereas the mass of the performers was positioned on the ladders and below in front of the platform. A traffic light on one side and a street light on the other pointed to the place of action, which was an image of a railroad station, of sorts. Seven short episodes, some of a strictly mundane character, were played out (for example, "a flea market," where women described in the program as Countesses exchanged clothing for flour with a speculator). Other numbers, "Baba-Yaga and Crocodile" and "Sailor and Three Devils," involved fairytale characters, but even so, as one review noted, "folklore was in the service of modernity."

In the first act the construction was perceived as a symbol of its epoch; "construction" meant the 1920s and Soviet Russia. The eccentricity of the costumes also served as a mark of the times: The Sailor had only one boot and wore a cloak that swerved behind his back, the Countesses wore lampshades on their heads, and the clothing of the mass scenes' participants was characterized by emphatic asymmetry (the sleeves and the pant legs of different lengths and of different colors; one leg was often left bare).

Thus, in the first act the dances seemed to exist independently of the constructivist set. And yet the choreographer had to adjust to the conditions imposed by the stage, which clearly offered little space for broad dance compositions of the traditional kind. "The stage's depth cannot be used for entrances, and thus they take place from the sides, so that the movement is always in profile; there is no movement from the front to the back."[9] In his production Massine failed to establish a rapport with the artist-designer or to find the right means of using stage space to create new choreographic forms. Critics who as a rule reviewed ballet for Paris and London newspapers judged Massine unfavorably.

In many cases, the meaning of what was occurring onstage remained unclear to the audience.

However, the second act was a different matter. It is perhaps the only case in Russian ballet of the 1920s where constructivist stage design and dance of constructivist orientation (i.e. choreography of the machine-dance type) were united in one performance.

Massine himself wrote that in placing the groups on and in front of the platforms, he "built a multilevel composition out of set parts and human figures."[10] The stage image created quite an impression on the viewers, and newspaper reviews offer numerous descriptions:

> At first male and female dancers execute movements that imitate labor: They lift, they rip apart, they carry, they hammer. . . . Then, gradually they themselves become machines. Groups of them move back and forth, like pistons and levers, they circle in and out, engage each other, like gears. The odd and even numbers of women standing in a single row alternately bend and straighten out, as if controlled by a camshaft. Some rows of dancers represent various valves, others—bobbins, others yet—cogwheels. And behind the banner, as if enveloped in clouds of steam and smoke, the silhouettes of the blacksmiths can be discerned. . . . The movements keep accelerating and become more and more energetic. Crescendo, agitato. . . . Cardboard wheels spin, the platform shudders under the blows of hammers.[11]

It was also noted that "L. Massine has created new postures and steps, strange contortions and movements that give the impression of powerful, complicated machinery, pistons working, wheels turning, and intense labor."[12] Others commented that

> the cast is overalled, mackintoshed, or stripped to the buff. And all strain nerve and muscle to keep time with purposeful cacophony, pace with mechanical frenzy. Great hammers clang and boilers let off steam: The soul of man is but a variant of the fuel force with oil and gas.[13]

After reviews of the Paris production appeared in the Soviet press and a suite from the ballet was performed at a 1929 concert, the question of producing the ballet in Soviet Russia was raised. Meyerhold expressed interest in staging *Le Pas d'acier* at the Bolshoi, with Asaf Messerer as the choreographer. However, after listening to Prokofiev's music, many critics surfaced, especially from the Russian Association of Proletarian Musicians. The composer was accused of being unmusical and of resorting to tricks. As Meyerhold wrote in a letter to the director of the Bolshoi, "Proletarian musicians tried to besmirch that remarkable piece of music, and I was simply sneered at. . . ."[14] And even though, according to Boris Guzman, who was in charge of repertory at the Bolshoi, Meyerhold offered to counter Diaghilev's production "with our own solution, to seek new colors, which . . . would completely respond to the demands imposed on the Soviet ballet," the production never took place.[15]

We can only guess at what sort of ballet production it would have been had it been realized. Meyerhold, from all indications, was enthusiastic about producing it—at least Messerer says so in his

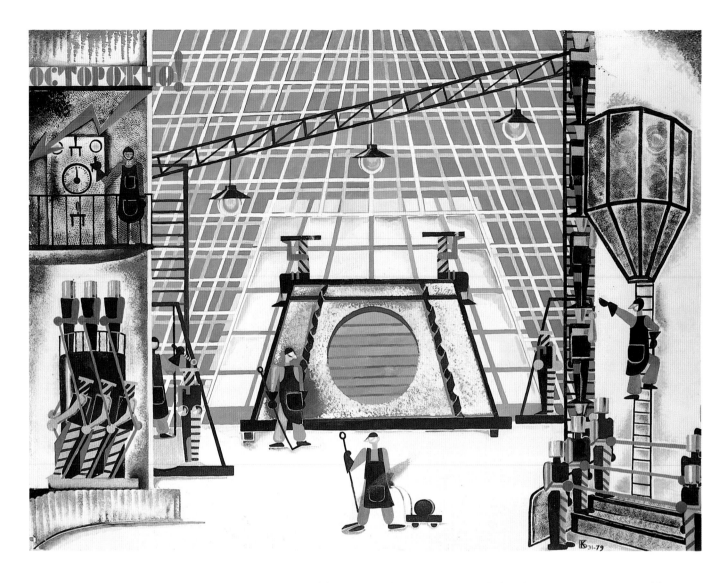

Cat. no. 9

Tatiana Bruni

Set design, *Bolt*, 1979 after 1931 original

opposite:

Cat. no. 11

Tatiana Bruni

Costume design for the Bureaucrat, *Bolt*,
1979 after 1931 original

memoirs.[16] Messerer himself admitted that he was rather shocked by Prokofiev's music, accustomed as he was to the melodies of Peter Ilitch Tchaikovsky and Alexander Glazunov. What could he have possibly choreographed to such a composition? Neither do we know who the director intended to invite as the scenic artist. However, now that we know how Soviet art developed afterward, it is safe to assume that even if *Le Pas d'acier* had become the ideal constructivist ballet one can only dream about, it would have been received with animosity. In 1929 it was already too late to stage such a ballet in Soviet Russia. It is hardly accidental that Lopukhov's eccentric *Nutcracker* was also rejected in the same year—it was born too late. And two years later, in 1931, Dmitrii Shostakovich's and Lopukhov's ballet *Bolt* (cat. nos. 9–11), where, for the last time, machine-dances were shown, was also criticized. There, the actors represented a crane, a tractor, and a mechanical loom (twenty-four female dancers in two rows, moving up and down).

Without a doubt, constructivism exerted a stimulating influence on ballet. It offered choreographers new possibilities for dance construction and mise-en-scène arrangement, and it facilitated the enrichment of the vocabulary of dance. But new tendencies, which dawned at the end of the 1920s and prevailed in the 1930s—specifically, the demands of socialist realism—presented ballet's producers with other problems. In open-plot,

Бюрократ

ТБ
1931—79

Cat. no. 131
Anatolii Petritsky
Costume design for Tennis Players,
The Football Player, 1930

multi-act productions characteristic of the 1930s–1940s, the plot, as it was presented in the libretto, was the principal focus. The composer followed the libretto, and music increasingly became more and more representational. The choreographer also followed the libretto, expounding the ups and downs of the story through dance as well as in pantomimic form. The scenic artist was expected to represent the place of action with maximum veracity, in all its historical and daily concreteness (cat. no. 131). Obviously, a stage construction had no place in such productions, and neither did all the "formalist" experiments, such as machine-dances. Constructivism, just as many other phenomena of the 1920s, was rejected and its achievements forgotten for a long time to come.

Notes

1. Kasian Goleizovsky, "Staroe i novoe: Pisma o tantse" (The Old and the New: Letters about Dance), *Ekran*, 4 May 1922, no. 31:3.

2. Kasian Goleizovsky, interview with the author, 3 May 1966.

3. *Zrelishcha*, 1924, no. 86:7.

4. Based on the description by Pavel Markov in his manuscript "Boris Erdman," at the STD Library, Moscow.

5. Vladimir Dmitriev, quoted in "Shchelkunchik" (The Nutcracker), *Zhizn iskusstva*, 20 October 1922, no. 42:11.

6. Y. Sakhnovsky, "Dve Shekherazady" (The Two Schéhérazades), *Rampa*, 26 October 1923–2 January 1924, no. 13:6.

7. Alexei Gvozdev, "Teatralnaia Moskva" (Theatrical Moscow), *Zhizn iskusstva*, 11 February 1924, no. 7:6.

8. Evgenii Kan, "Moskovskie novatory tantsa" (Moscow Dance Innovators), *Russkoe iskusstvo*, 1923, no. 1:95.

9. S. Volkonsky, "U Diagileva" (At Diaghilev's), *Poslednie novosti*, 14 July 1927.

10. Léonide Massine, *My Life in Ballet*, Phyllis Hartnoll and Robert Rubens, eds. (London: Macmillan, 1960), 172.

11. Robert Dezarnaux, "Théâtre Sarah-Bernhardt," *La Liberté* [Paris], 9 June 1927.

12. Quoted in "The Machine Dance," *Daily Express* [London], 5 July 1927.

13. Quoted in "Le Pas d'acier," *Observer* [London], 10 July 1927.

14. Vsevolod Meyerhold, "Perepiska" (Correspondence) (Moscow: Iskusstvo, 1976), 310.

15. "Boris Guzman o Meyerholde i Diagileve" (Boris Guzman on Meyerhold and Diaghilev), Manuscript, F.648, op. 2, ed. khr. 686, 1.29, TsGALI (Central State Archive of Literature and Art).

16. Asaf Messerer, "Tanets, mysl, vremia" (Dance, Thought, Time) (Moscow: Iskusstvo, 1979), 73–76.

ПРОЗ ОДЕЖ ДА ЗИМ 2 АКТ ЕРА

Л.ПОПОВА 1921

The Constructivist Stage

Georgii Kovalenko

Nothing in Liubov Popova's design for Vsevolod Meyerhold's play *The Magnanimous Cuckold*, which premiered in Moscow on 25 April 1922, would have suggested the familiar and the conventional to a contemporary viewer (cat. nos. 137, 138). Popova did not paint a set, but instead built a construction, an autonomous installation that could function anywhere—on the street or onstage. The wooden structure was composed of two windows and two doors, ladders, platforms, wheels, and the blades of a watermill. The construction seemed to lack semantic value; it harbored no metaphors or veiled signs. Essentially it was a spatial formula whose components, as well as their interactions and correlations, were abstracted and reduced to a minimal level of expression. The functional quality of the construction is said to have resembled a clock whose dial had been removed (cat. no. 139). To some extent, it does suggest the exposed interior workings of a mechanism whose exterior coverings have fallen away, only the most important components remaining. To then remove or change anything would mean the system's collapse.

It was through action that Popova's construction came to life. Energy seemed to pulse through all the crossbeams and planes, stimulating the performances of the actors. A reverse relationship also appeared to exist. The plastic movements of the actors exposed the energetic dynamic of the construction and made it possible to observe its singular graphic purity, the harmony of its linear rhythms. In performance, action and construction were inseparable. Popova's construction was a genuine breakthrough, prophesying unimaginable changes for the theatre, and is generally regarded as the beginning of Russian theatrical constructivism. Despite the sudden appearance of the construction and its amazing novelty, one can detect the inevitability of its emergence, just as for any discovery. Unconsciously, the theatre may have been moving toward it. Certainly, the need for a new approach to stage design had been anticipated. Abram Efros, a perceptive critic, wrote a year before the premiere of *Cuckold* that "what the theatre needs is not an illusion of space, but real space. And not a painterly representation of an object but the very materiality of these objects."[1]

Thus the emergence of the new form of stage design in *Cuckold* was determined by the logical development of ideas pertaining to art and theatre—and not only in Meyerhold's art. In Alexander Tairov's Kamerny Theatre in Moscow the principles of a cubist aesthetic were developed so

Cat. no. 137
Liubov Popova
Work uniform design for Actor No. 3,
the Free Studio of Vsevolod Meyerhold
at the State Higher Theatre Workshop
(GVYTM), Moscow, 1921

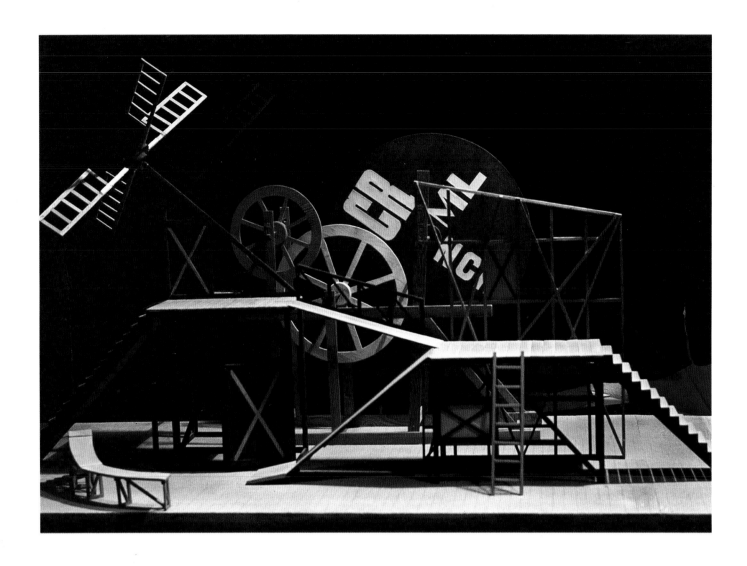

Cat. no. 138
Liubov Popova
Maquette, *The Magnanimous Cuckold*,
reconstruction after 1922 original, n.d.

consistently and purposefully that it seemed as if his artists envisioned where their experiments would lead. In the Russian theatre, constructivist stage design in many respects was nurtured by cubist stage design, appearing as naturally as Russian cubist painting had evolved into non-objective painting. Russian constructivism effortlessly adopted all that had been discovered by cubism. Popova's cubist paintings and the seeming predetermination of her transition to abstraction, which was present even in her orthodox cubist works, foretold her designs for the stage.

A year before *Cuckold*, in 1921, Tairov staged *Romeo and Juliet*, designed by Alexandra Exter, at the Kamerny Theatre. In the words of Efros, "the most cubist cubism in the most baroque baroque" reigned onstage (cat. nos. 62, 64).[2] However, in both Exter's cubism and in her baroque work, one could still detect an unequivocal boundary or limit. Her work probably represented the maximum expression in cubist decor, with no place to go. There was only one way out—toward contructivism.

It is worth focusing attention on the intuitive yet clearly defined ideas of Alexander Tairov. He demanded from Exter the creation onstage of "theatrical obstacles" and "theatrical barriers,"[3] visual aspects of the content of *Romeo and Juliet* that would be inalienably melded with action (cat. no. 56). The actors were obliged to overcome and subordinate the plastic arts, but also to perceive them as something almost inseparable from themselves. Such a directorial conception typifies a constructivist

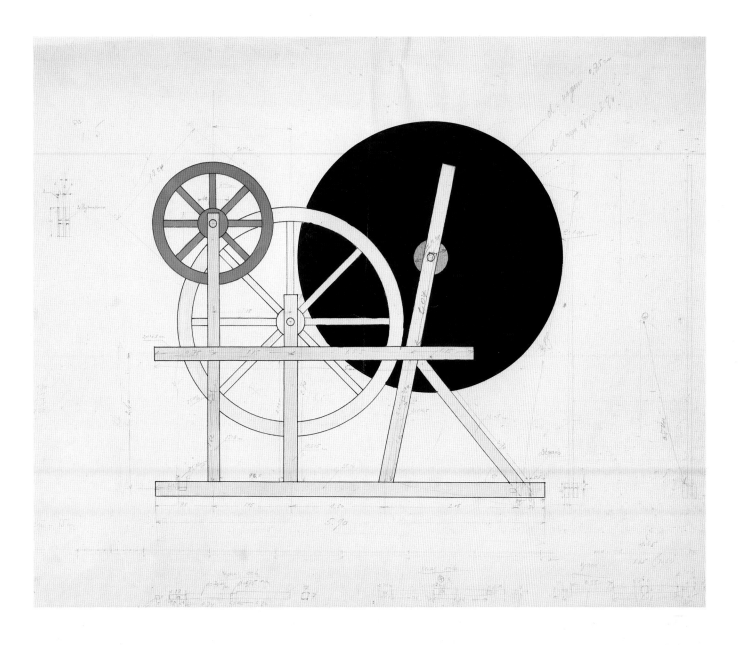

Cat. no. 139
Liubov Popova
Design for construction,
The Magnanimous Cuckold, 1922

play. It was no accident, of course, that literally a few months after
Romeo and Juliet, Exter designed constructions for Kasian Goleizovsky's
Satanic Ballet (not realized). Exter's 1922 design provides one of the
purest, most harmonious expressions of constructivist stage design.

Although anticipated by Exter's work for the Kamerny Theatre,
Cuckold not only announced constructivism as a new era in the theatre,
it did so by presenting sufficiently convincing arguments about
perspectives. Experiments at the Kamerny Theatre in the building of
various systems of separate acting platforms finally led to the effort to
evolve vertically, to experience the volume of the stage not as an
amorphous void but as a substance to be worked with.

By 1921 constructivist ideas were everywhere in the theatre. At the
RSFSR (Russian Soviet Federated Socialist Republic) Theatre No. 1 in
Moscow, Meyerhold staged a new version of *Mystery-Bouffe* (with
the artists Viktor Kiselev, Anton Lavinsky, and Vladimir Khrakovsky)
that abandoned all references to painterly design. The critic Nikolai
Tarabukin observed that *Mystery-Bouffe* visually built "a bridge toward
constructivism." The broken plane of the stage floor, he notes,

Cat. no. 56
Alexandra Exter
Curtain design (damaged),
Romeo and Juliet, 1921

has three horizontal floors, unfolds into the depth and runs upward along a parabola. The ladders, catwalks, and platforms create the moments for the actors' most vivid action. . . . It also includes features of an architectural order. It may be considered the nucleus from which eventually two basic trends in theatre began to develop—constructivism and architecturalism.[4]

By the end of 1920 and the beginning of 1921, most of the artists of the left were completely preoccupied with the problem of truly linking stage design to the social goals of professional artists. The 1917 Revolution had changed everything. Even artistic activity itself was supposed to become completely different. At this time, works of art were discussed in terms usually applied to architecture—to the construction of machines, buildings, or bridges. Concepts of constructivism such as functionalism, the organization of materials, the economy of means, and construction were the badges of the day of artistic identification.

In 1921 it was clear to many artists, including Alexander Rodchenko, Karel Johansson, Konstantin Medunetsky, and the brothers Stenberg, that the construction of a form could and must be one of the most important—if not the most important—premises for its aesthetic design.

It is as if construction transcended its function as the form's technical foundation and literally became the form's aesthetic foundation.

Many artists were convinced that constructivism offered the only way out of the upheavals and disappointments that befell art at the beginning of the century. They rejected all that might pollute a system like constructivism, including any kind of decorativeness, even the feeblest hint at formal decoration. However, a contemporary critic observed that

> the most desirable . . . decorative element is . . . that element which is untouched in its constructiveness, and thus the concept of the "constructive" absorbs the concept of the "decorative," merges with it.[5]

The stage proved to be a highly fertile ground for the constructivists' activities. First, because the art of the theatre is based on physical activity, it was amazingly receptive to the active character of constructivist stage design, reinforcing, enriching, and developing it. Second, and perhaps more important, constructivism onstage proclaimed its ideas with maximum explicitness; it made those ideas visual and finally verified them. That is, the theatre opened up for constructivists those opportunities that they had been denied in industrial art and architecture because of the considerable amount of time needed for their fulfillment.[6]

Constructivism spread throughout the theatre with unimaginable speed. Constructivist installations filled stages everywhere. At times, they appeared where there was no need for them and for reasons that hardly demanded constructivist solutions. But a year and a half after the premiere of *Cuckold*, the poet Vadim Shershenevich wrote that constructivism had become dated. "It has become more irksome than a painted backdrop, woolen cloths, and pavilions."[7]

Of course, the constructivist installations could not have become overused so quickly. But they were often compromised by being erected onstage in the same manner as ordinary sets, i.e., according to purely external considerations. A construction came to be handled practically in the same way as a painted backdrop or an architectural fragment serving as a stage prop.

Following *Cuckold*, only Meyerhold showed mastery of the constructivist method. In his plays of the 1920s, constructivism turned out to be inexhaustible in its possibilities. In *The Death of Tarelkin* (1922), the artist Varvara Stepanova continued and further developed much of what was in Popova's design for *Cuckold*. Unlike Popova's designs, Stepanova's did not claim to organize stage space. They had no connection to the stage frame and could exist anywhere; they were only connected to action. Tarabukin commented that

> if in *The Magnanimous Cuckold* L. Popova created a stationary machine-construction, with which the actor plays in expressing his plastic capabilities, then in *Tarelkin* there is a movable machine-object on hand, which the actor triumphs over by demonstrating his pantomimic wit.[8]

In Meyerhold's *The Earth in Turmoil* (1923), constructivism triumphed over mere decorativeness, painting, stage props, and architecturalism. Nothing could be identified as objects of art; rather, all

overleaf left:
Cat. no. 62
Alexandra Exter
Costume design for the First Woman's Mask, *Romeo and Juliet*, 1921

overleaf right:
Cat. no. 64
Alexandra Exter
Costume design for the Fourth Woman's Mask, *Romeo and Juliet*, 1921

149   The Constructivist Stage

were objects *for* art. This means that the objects existed for the play, for the action, and for the actors. *The Magnanimous Cuckold* (cat. no. 140), *The Death of Tarelkin*, and *The Earth in Turmoil* represented the purest theatrical constructivism.

Constructivist principles would continue to be felt in Meyerhold's art for several years, although they would be invaded by images of another nature and would be swept over by other stylistic currents. Even so, their faint presence would remind of past victories and triumphs.

Tarabukin precisely sensed the breaking point, that moment when constructivism on Meyerhold's stage began to lose its stylistic purity. In the evolution of the theatre, Meyerhold's production of Alexander Ostrovsky's *The Forest* (1924) constituted "a watershed between two periods," just as had Meyerhold's staging of Emile Verhaeren's *Les Aubes* (The Dawns) in 1920 with designs by Vladimir Dmitriev (cat. no. 12):

> *Les Aubes* had marked a turning-away from the painterly illusionism and rich decorativeness that characterized Meyerhold's earlier productions toward nonobjective and utilitarian design. *The Forest*, conversely, designed by Vasilii Fedorov, was perceived as establishing the boundary between nonobjective constructivism, pure utilitarianism, and anti-aestheticism on the one hand, and architecturalist, imagist, and, therefore, painterly tendencies in the principles of stage design, on the other.[9]

The constructivism of the Kamerny Theatre artists for the most part was distinguished by the new decorative meaning that the artists perceived in the construction, which they more or less accentuated. The qualities of function, functionality, and utility were undeniably present in constructivist stage design at the Kamerny Theatre. And they undoubtedly were what was most important. However, the new decorative meaning infused the play with color.

As we have seen, a variant of constructivist stage design was promoted by the Kamerny Theatre. It has been noted that

> Tairov's constructivism meticulously concealed its connection to the world of machines and mechanisms, draped itself in decorative cloths, painted itself with bright and eye-catching tones, illuminated itself by multicolored rays of the projectors, was frankly painterly. . . . Tairov's over-over-aestheticized constructivism in general on many occasions revealed its ability to create images of the past. . . . And even when the play was permeated with contemporary urbanism ([Eugene] O'Neill's *The Negro*, [G.K.] Chesterton's *The Man Who Was Thursday*), in Tairov's interpretation constructivism acquired exquisite beauty, luxurious painterliness.[10]

It would undoubtedly be fascinating to consider all the modifications of constructivism, or rather, all the cases that involved both constructivist vocabulary and plastic expressions of other kinds. The Soviet theatre of the 1920s offers enough examples for such a study, which would allow the discovery of stable constructivist phases, as well as other modes of expression that concealed their constructivist origins.

It must be said that Meyerhold did not consider constructivism as an "ageless" style. Rather, he sensed in constructivism its benevolent and

Cat. no. 140
Liubov Popova
Prop design for a geranium in a pot,
The Magnanimous Cuckold, 1922

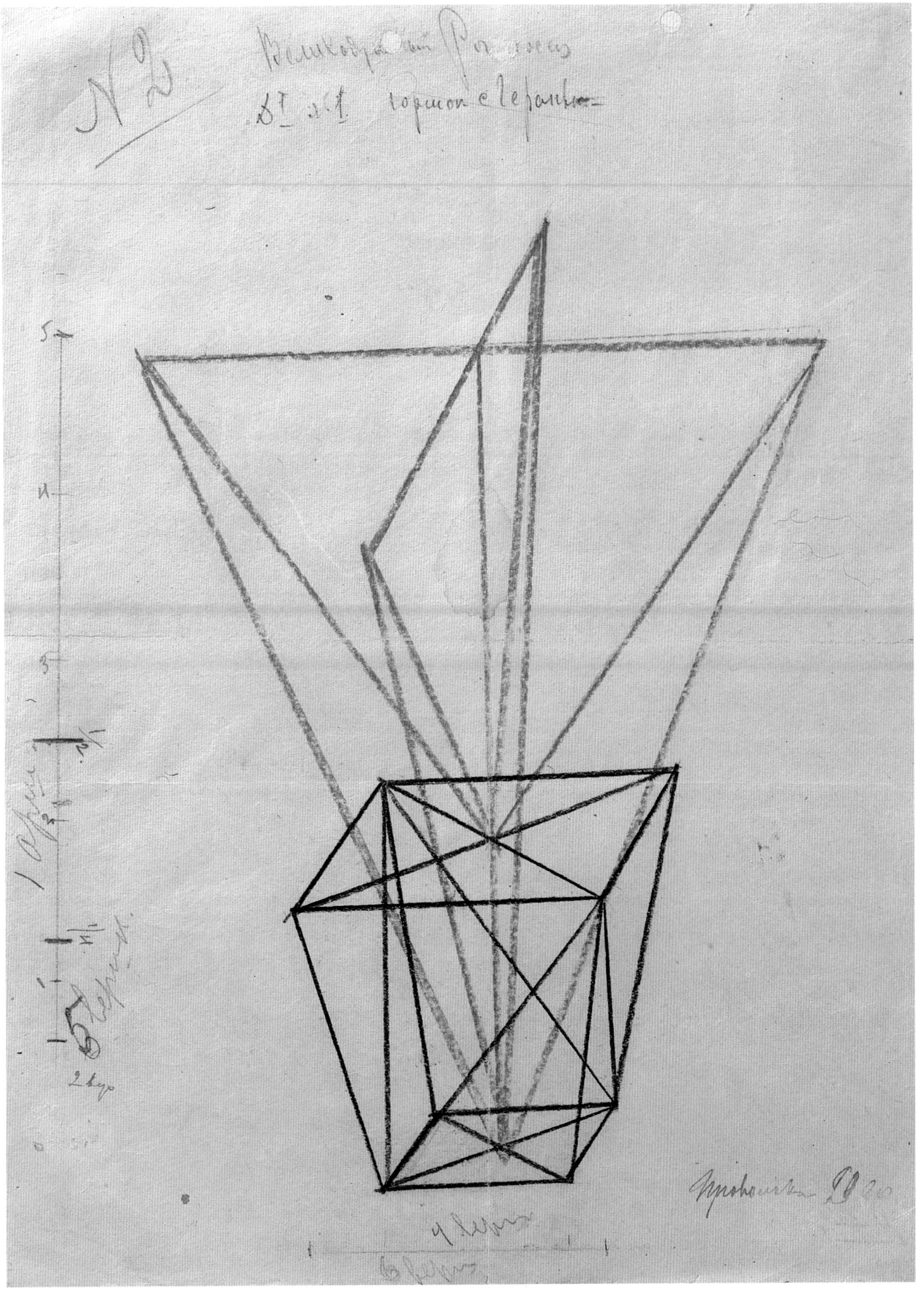
№2
горшок с геранью

Cat. no. 12
Vladimir Dmitriev
Maquette, *Les Aubes*, 1920

revolutionary spirit, its cleansing, invigorating force, and thus he also glimpsed its somewhat transitory nature. For him constructivism was hardly the definitive embodiment of the new theatre, but rather a way out toward the new theatre. Popova was generally of the same opinion:

> I don't think that nonobjective form is the final form. It is a revolutionary state of the form. It is imperative to completely reject object-ness and the related conventions of formal representation. We must begin to feel completely free of all that has already been done in order to listen carefully to the nascent need and then to take a different look at the object's form, which will emerge from this work not only transformed but in fact entirely new.[11]

Notes

1. Abram Efros, "Khudozhniki stsena" (The Artist and the Stage), *Kultura teatra*, 1921, no. 1:11.

2. Abram Efros, *Kamernyi teatr i ego khudozhniki* (The Kamerny Theatre and Its Artists) (Moscow: VTO, 1934), xxxii.

3. Alexander Tairov, *Zapiski rezhissiora: Stati, besedy, rechi, pisma* (A Director's Notes: Essays, Conversations, Speeches, Letters) (Moscow: VTO, 1970), 287.

4. Nikolai Tarabukin, "Zritelnoie oformlenie v GosTIM'e" (Visual Design at the Meyerhold Theatre), *Teatr*, 1990, no. 1:95–96.

5. Moisei Ginzburg, *Stil i epokha* (Style and Epoch) (Moscow, 1924), 122.

6. Christina Lodder, "Constructivist Theatre as a Laboratory for an Architectural Aesthetic," *Architectural Association Quarterly*, 1979, no. 2:24–36.

7. Vadim Shershenevich, "Predlagaiu dlia diskussii [Moi tezisy]" (I Offer for Discussion [My Thesis]), *Zrelishcha* [Moscow], 1924, no. 76:2.

8. Tarabukin, 97.

9. Tarabukin, 98.

10. Konstantin Rudnitsky, "Rezhissior Meyerhold" (Director Meyerhold), in *Nauka* (Science) (Moscow, 1969), 264–265.

11. Liubov Popova, "Zapis nachala 20kh godov" (Notes from the Early 20s), quoted in "Khudozhnik, stsena, ekran" (The Artist, the Stage, and the Screen), in *Sovetskii khudozhnik* (The Soviet Artist) (Moscow, 1975), 159.

"Маски" Арлекины.

18.

Касьян Голейзовский

Designing Gestures
in the Laboratory of Dance

Nicoletta Misler

The history of "modern choreography" in Russia began with
the pioneering cycle of performances that Isadora Duncan made in
St. Petersburg and Moscow in 1905 and 1908 (actually, December 1904
and December 1907, according to the Old Calendar). Both times the
Russian audiences were impressed, and even Léon Bakst and Michel
Fokine were enthusiastic.[1] However, it was not until 1921, under the
new Soviet regime, that "Duncanism," as both apologists and detractors
called it,[2] began to flourish in earnest; for it was in 1921 that Duncan
accepted the Bolsheviks' invitation to establish her school in Moscow.
Duncanism did not necessarily mean just Isadora Duncan, but stood also
for the material, abundant body, like that of a maternal goddess from
classical Greece. Indeed, with her students clothed in Greek tunics,
Duncan did help to emancipate the female body. Additionally, by its
emphasis on freedom from traditional balletic constraints, Duncanism
linked avant-garde dance to proletarian expression. In the 1920s, one
foreign visitor to Russia (the journalist René Fülöp-Miller) even published
a photograph of the Duncan school, or one of the studios inspired by her,
above the caption "Proletarian Training in Dancing."[3]

Parallel to this desire to liberate the body emerged the contrary
effort to justify its gestural quality and to make it serve the efficient
requirements of proletarian labor, even if on a purely theoretical level.
It is to this end that research and experiments were undertaken at the
Central Institute for the Scientific Organization of Labor and the
Mechanization of Man, or, in its abbreviated form, the Central Institute
of Labor (TsIT),[4] which functioned in Moscow in the early 1920s. The
primary aim of the investigations at TsIT was to analyze gestures from a
mechanical and functional standpoint, thus producing "Taylorism with a
human face," adapting to Soviet reality a movement system based on the
work of Frederick Winslow Taylor, a pioneer in time-motion studies. One
result of these two attitudes toward the body—the one "mechanical," the
other giving priority to the individual expression of emotion, which came
to be the focus of a different institution known as the Choreological
Laboratory—was the creation of two opposing trends in research.
Although these trends operated more on a theoretical than a formal
level, both were meant to symbolize the triumphs of socialism.

The ultimate aim of TsIT was to train workers. The institute's
psycho-technical researchers and their colleagues, whose task it was to
study the kinetic faculties of the human organism, tried to quantify the

Cat. no. 95
Kasian Goleizovsky
Costume design for Harlequin,
The Tragedy of the Masks, 1922

energy consumed by each movement when reduced to its essential articulations. TsIT supervised research programs in at least seven specific laboratories, including those dedicated to the use of instruments, bioenergetics, psycho-technics, and biomechanics. The reference to biomechanics is not accidental. The artist Ilia Shlepianov (fig. 1), who was one of Vsevolod Meyerhold's students in the 1920s, also worked at TsIT in the field of movement transcription, and one of the TsIT laboratories (the Studio of Movement Registration) was dedicated precisely to this subject. It was here that Alexei Gastev, director of TsIT, attempted to define superfluous movement and to eliminate the waste of energy using a chronocyclograph (an instrument that can record and analyze a single movement) (fig. 2). The graphic and photographic recording of each movement was then developed into an abstract transcription that became a rudimentary alphabet of movement. The TsIT researchers tried to halt the continuum of the language of movement and therefore to reveal its semantic cadence.

At the same time, investigations being undertaken in another Moscow laboratory pursued quite different aims—antimechanical and aesthetic ones—that became a logical point of reference for all the "Duncan" researches. This was the Choreological Laboratory, organized by a group of art historians and critics, linguists, musicologists, and psychoanalysts within the perimeter of the Russian Academy of Artistic Sciences (RAKhN; later GAKhN).

The aim of the Choreological Laboratory was to study both in theory and from practical observation the activity designated the *art of movement*. What the group meant by this term was a specific artistic activity that subsumed all aspects of movement—not only dance, play, acrobatics, rhythmic gymnastics, creative gymnastics, and "plastic" or artistic movement, but also the movements of labor, physical education, calisthenics, and sports.

Fig. 2
Experiment with a chronocyclograph at
the Central Institute of Labor (TsIT),
Moscow, 1920s

The Choreological Laboratory[5] was established officially in RAKhN
at the beginning of 1923, directed by Alexander I. Larionov and the art
historian Alexei Sidorov.[6] No doubt, the real initiator was Sidorov, who
was just publishing the first Russian book on "free dance" in Europe,[7]
and who, the year before, had requested that RAKhN establish a
Laboratory of Dance Composition directed by Natalia Tian.[8] This had
quickly developed into a Choreological Section at RAKhN that was
renamed the Choreological Laboratory. Basically, choreology also meant
the study of the art of movement, although the laboratory's use of the
word *choreology* indicated the priority afforded to theoretical research,
even though all kinds of practical experiments were conducted there.

In any case, the general wish of the Choreological Laboratory was
to find a comprehensive means of transcription to record the art of
movement and to develop a language of movement and gesture, a focus
that opposed the mechanical process and narrowness of TsIT. To this
end, RAKhN organized at least four exhibitions from 1924–1928
entitled *The Art of Movement*.[9] These exhibitions presented possibilities
for registering and transcribing the various forms of movement via
diverse media, such as cinema, photography, graphics, painting, and
sculpture. It was Choreological Laboratory director Larionov who was
especially active in the realization of these exhibitions, for he was particularly interested in the photographic and cinematographic recording
of gymnastic movements.

Actually, Larionov's interests were a curious mix of interdisciplinary
scholarship, although his real expertise seemed to lie in his ability to iden-
tify the symbolic significance of languages, which he then applied to his
many different pursuits—philately, photography, physical education, and
the graphic form of alphabets (from Cyrillic to Egyptian pictograms).[10]
As was true for the Choreological Laboratory in general, Larionov's
approach to the graphic transcription of movement was based on the

Fig. 3
Studio of Plastic Rhythm (Nikolai
Pozniakov, Director), Moscow, n.d.

study of diagrams used by different choreographers such as Rudolf
von Laban and Olga Desmond.[11]

But Larionov and his colleagues also expanded the very idea of
transcription to a synthesis of all the expressive capacities of gesture,
including both psychological and aesthetic ones. In contrast to TsIT,
the Choreological Laboratory directed its research toward the totality
of gesture. In the thesis of a lecture on the methods of transcribing
movement, the historian Evgenii Yavorsky affirmed that the kind of
notation favored by TsIT, using such instruments as the chronocyclograph, could serve only to "transcribe muscular tension" and record and
analyze elementary movements—and that its instruments "cannot be used
for the dance."[12] Sidorov, the Choreological Laboratory co-director,
while admitting that the chronocyclograph could record a given movement with accuracy, also argued that it could comprehend only the
movement of body parts as mechanical instruments of labor and not
the movement of the body *in toto*.[13]

In its research on body language (an expression that we use today,
but which was also used at RAKhN in the 1920s) and in its practical
endeavors to train the body to express itself through its specific language,
the Choreological Laboratory acted as a pole of attraction, coordinating
all the relevant experiments taking place both in Moscow and in the
provinces. At first, the primary goal of the laboratory was to undertake
"scientific research into the artistic phenomenon of dance."[14] On the one
hand, it pursued this aim by studying the elementary structures of the
body's positions in space, and, on the other, by elaborating experiments
which "might explain the coordination between psychic states and
corresponding plastic poses."[15] Subsequently, the laboratory also studied
systems for recording movement and the connections between musical
and plastic elements and between poetical and plastic forms and images.

Furthermore, the laboratory was in close contact with other
research centers in Moscow. For example, there was Liudmila Alexeeva's
Studio of the Art of Movement, which concentrated on "harmonious
gymnastics," i.e. a gymnastics that not only exercised the body, but also
prompted artistic movement. Alexeeva, incidentally, gave a practical
demonstration of this together with a lecture at the Choreological
Laboratory in October 1924.[16] There was also Nina Alexandrova,[17] a
leading disciple of Emile Jaques-Dalcroze, who founded the Institute of
Rhythm that established direct, formal contact with the laboratory in
April 1924. Nevertheless, the real focus of the laboratory was its interdisciplinary approach to movement both in practice and theory. Alexandrova conducted classes in rhythmic gymnastics and sponsored
discussions on the concept of rhythm in lectures such as that by the
historian Dmitrii Nedovich, who addressed the following subjects:

1. The definition of rhythm is contradictory and inadequate
2. Rhythm as a temporal category of plasticity
3. Manifold artistic rhythm
4. Plasticity is the rhythmization of material
5. Artistic rhythm and natural rhythm are opposite
6. In plasticity the antipode of rhythm is the construction of the body
7. Rhythm cannot be intellectualized[18]

Fig. 4

Members of Studio of Inna Chernetskaia
in *Pan*, Moscow, ca. 1924

However, not all agreed with Nedovich. For example, Nikolai Pozniakov,[19] director of the Studio of Plastic Rhythm, drawing upon his practical experience, argued that if "rhythm and body coincide, then the resistance will be less. Rhythm in one body is not germane to another." Actually, Pozniakov's studio seemed more concerned with gymnastics, something documented by the photographs of outdoor exercises performed in Greek tunics (fig. 3) and also by one of his lectures on the "Role of Mirror Symmetry and Its Combinations in the Organization of Artistic Movement," which he delivered at a meeting of the Physio-Psychological Department of RAKhN.[20]

At the end of 1923 the Studio of Synthetic Dance, directed by Inna Chernetskaia, was added to the Choreological Laboratory. Chernetskaia had started off as a classical dancer with Duncan, but had then left in order to pursue her interest in vaguely expressionist performance in which she tried to integrate the methods of François Delsarte and Konstantin Stanislavsky. In 1924 Chernetskaia gave a lecture on "The Plasticity and Analysis of Gesture,"[21] together with a practical demonstration of her theories to her students at the Studio of Synthetic Dance. The two performances that she presented were *Pan* (fig. 4) and *Danse Macabre*, titles that indicated how far the "synthetic dance" was "still indebted to the symbolist idea of the synthesis between music, painting, and dance."[22] Indeed, this is how Chernetskaia described her method to the presidium of RAKhN:

> Direction (synthetic dance, music, rhythm, etc.) and line (color, design of material) are two organic parts of the dance, and as soon as our instrument (the body) appears against the background of the painterly or musical design, I think that the path of the free dance of the future will occur in an organic fusion of the three arts of painting, music, and dance.[23]

From the practical viewpoint, Chernetskaia and her studio intended to develop the body on all levels by exercising it both at the traditional barre and in acrobatics, mime, plastic movement, gesture analysis, and dramatization:

> Apart from plastic movement [that developed] all parts of the body simultaneously, the studio used a lathe [a measuring instrument] for the legs and the back to ensure accuracy of dance and character.

On the other hand, Chernetskaia insisted on developing the dramatic aspect of dance, i.e. the faculty for expressing individual emotions "justified by the inner experiences and meaning of the totality."[24] Chernetskaia's synthetic dances were also included in the Bal de la Grande Ourse—the annual ball of the Union des Artistes Russes in Paris in 1925.

Among those who collaborated with the Choreological Laboratory was Vera Maia.[25] Like Chernetskaia, Maia had started her career influenced by Duncan's "free dance" before concentrating almost exclusively on the pantomimic aspects of dance and rendering of visual images. Her studio gave particular attention to anatomy and the possibility of using that part of the musculature that was generally disregarded in

traditional dance—consequently, acrobatics were a primary concern (figs. 5, 6). In 1925 she and Tian compiled a program to undertake experiments in "the study of the chromatic components of plastic action."[26]

Another studio that was close to the Choreological Laboratory was the one directed by Lev Lukin, which created semi-erotic compositions to the music of Alexander Scriabin via the contortionist interpretations of Alexandra Rudovich and Alexander Rumnev (fig. 7). One of the most important elements in Lukin's conception was the costume, often reduced to a minimum (as was often the case with Kasian Goleizovsky's parallel productions), reminiscent of a kind of *prozodezhda* (work uniform) which

> is constructed on the contrast of black and silver and deforms the body, breaking the symmetry of both right and left. The contrast of black and white elicits a "displacement" in the parts of the body.[27]

In his memoirs, Sergei Yutkevich speaks of the "non-costumes" that he designed for a cycle of performances presented by Lukin in 1921. In fact, following lessons with Alexandra Exter, Yutkevich abandoned costumes altogether and simply painted the dancer's bodies red, black, and green.[28] Lukin's efforts were often linked to Goleizovsky's studio[29] (cat. no. 95) inasmuch as they both had received their initial training in classical dance. But whereas Goleizovsky's dances moved "even further from dance towards poses, almost exclusively," those of Lukin "[were] always danceable,"[30] In any case, the studios of both Lukin and Goleizovsky are included in the reference list of the Choreological Laboratory as schools of "plastic images and constructive schemes."[31]

At the other end of the spectrum was Nikolai Foregger,[32] whose mechanical dances "aestheticized," so to speak, the researches at TsIT, even though he was not connected with the Choreological Laboratory. True, Foregger did not exclude the emotional element, although he regarded it as something to be "intepreted" and not left to the unconscious, as was the case with Lukin and Chernetskaia. In other words, Foregger supported the idea of emotion controlled rationally in acrobatic exercises.[33] When we think of the contortions of Rudovich (Lukin's favorite ballerina), it is easy to understand how the new experiments availed themselves of the same language, at least from a formal viewpoint. Certainly, what divided Foregger's theories from those of the studios connected with the Choreological Laboratory was his particular attitude toward music. For him, emotional abandonment to music was one of the so-called weaknesses of the plastic dance; according to Foregger, dance should be independent of music. It should form a duet with the music, but not be its illustration.[34]

Fig. 7
Alexander Rumnev, Lev Lukin Studio, Moscow, n.d.

163   The Laboratory of Dance

The fact that the music department at RAKhN was linked to the Choreological Laboratory and that most of the choreographers had received a musical education helped to underscore this interdependence of music and dance. Lukin had graduated from the Gnesin Institute of Music, while Pozniakov, director of the Studio of Plastic Rhythm, had elaborated a method of plastic movement and musical form while studying at the Moscow Conservatory of Music.

Several photographs of Rudovich and Chernetskaia are reproduced in the Sidorov book mentioned above (see note 7), in which he also commented on the dances of Alexander Sakharoff, the Russian dancer who had conducted synesthesia experiments[35] with Vasilii Kandinsky in Munich in the 1910s.[36] Sakharoff would later invent his own method of transcribing movement,[37] something that brings us to the interest in the graphic expression of movement shared by both Kandinsky and the Choreological Laboratory.

It was from Kandinsky's initial proposal to synthesize the arts and sciences that RAKhN evolved, and Kandinsky was one of its founders. In his program for the Section of Monumental Art at the Institute of Artistic Culture in Moscow in 1920 (which he was forced to leave),[38] Kandinsky emphasized how dance, music, and poetry, when viewed in their spatiotemporal form, influenced the human psyche.[39] Moreover, ever since October 1920 he had pushed for pure formal research into artistic languages that would overcome the artificial barriers between the arts, proposing that specific teams of researchers tackle the question of the synthesis of painting, dance, music, literature, and drama. Kandinsky was not just one of the founders of RAKhN, but also one of its most enthusiastic supporters, trying to maintain his contacts there following his emigration to Germany at the end of 1921 and encouraging his colleagues back in Moscow. Sidorov, Kandinsky's close friend, in October 1926 even proposed that RAKhN send its "official" congratulations to Kandinsky on his sixtieth birthday. It was only at the end of 1929 that the RAKhN presidium was forced to exclude Kandinsky from its faculty since he was an émigré,[40] but even though contacts between Soviet Russia and Germany became increasingly more complex during the 1920s–1930s, parallels can still be traced between what the Choreological Laboratory was doing and Kandinsky's own research.

For example, during 1923–1924 one of the principal avenues of inquiry pursued by the Choreological Laboratory was the "coordination of plastic images and poetical, verbal forms."[41] Another parallel between RAKhN and Kandinsky's work at the Bauhaus can be discerned in the artist's attempt to produce graphic schemes of the synthetic dances of Ida Palucca (fig. 8), which he then published in *Das Kunstblatt* in 1926.[42] Conversely, the Laboratory endeavored to "translate" the plastic movements and rhythms of the body, as we see in Larionov's lecture on "Experiment in the Field of Plastic Movement" that he gave at RAKhN in 1923. Larionov indicated with a diagram how space could be filled with gestures. In order to provide an analytical description, he used a graphic transcription and a "score," each line of which represented a different aspect of the movement in question (from its rhythm to its spatial form and time), until the last line, which represented the synthetic total of these elements.[43]

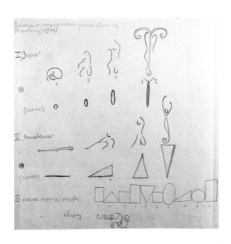

Fig. 8
Ida Palucca, with Vasilii Kandinsky's
graphic rendering of a synthetic-dance
gesture, ca. 1926

Fig. 9
Alexander Larionov
Graphic scheme for the performance *Birth
of a Grain of Wheat*, 1920s

This was the time at RAKhN, incidentally, that Larionov was collaborating with the philosopher and mathematician Pavel Florensky on the compilation of a dictionary of symbols, the so-called *Symbolarium* (unfortunately never published), which was to contain all the ideographic images used by people in different walks of life, including religion, advertising, and philately. In their introduction to this *Symbolarium*, Larionov and Florensky contended that the plastic language of the body could also be expressed by the same symbols, and used the image of the "performance" of the birth of a grain of wheat (fig. 9):

> Given the fact that a dictionary takes account of symbolic and spatial images, problems pertaining to the transference of plastic phenomena to "constructive" categories should be resolved. The plastic representation of the birth of a germ of wheat and of the birth of the plant that it derives from can be achieved by showing the body curled up, which then stands up vertically: Graphically, the correct pose of the germ of wheat can be conveyed by the "point," whereas the position of the plant growing can be translated graphically by the vertical.[44]

According to Larionov, the basis for synthesizing the various components of movement was physical education,[45] even if the term was used in a very specific sense. In fact, Larionov spoke of "plastic construction," which was rather distant from the simple notion of respiratory and muscular exercises. He declared:

> In every aspect, the natural basis of the art of movement is physical education. Consequently, it is essential to work out a system of gymnastics that contains the necessary physiological elements and, at the same time, serves as a vital link between physical culture and the art of movement. In that way the problems of "plastic construction" will be resolved.[46]

The researchers and guests of the Choreological Laboratory were often requested to formalize their own experiments in an appropriate language and to elaborate a graphic equivalent. On a theoretical level Florensky had also delineated the problem of the relationship between gesture and graphic representation in his treatise on spatiality that he was writing just at this time:

> The gesture can be regarded as a line or as a direction. The gesture does not consist of single positions, and the lines that it produces are not composed of points. As gesture, as line or direction, the gesture is an activity wherein unity cannot be fragmented. Thanks to this activity, single points or single states can be presupposed and defined as something secondary and accessory. In its maximum purity, the graphic sign is a system of gestures.[47]

Other members of RAKhN also proposed various forms of graphic transcription of movement, but, unfortunately, their designs have been lost. The historian Yavorsky, for example, underlined the deficiencies of all the different types of transcription, beginning with Larionov's (because Larionov only transcribed movement in two dimensions, as in

a bas-relief, thereby leaving too much space for arbitrary interpretation).
On the other hand Pozniakov's and Sidorov's synthetic transcriptions
registered the movements of a particular practitioner in his or her
individual interpretation and were expressed in a system of linear
impressions. In any case, according to Yavorsky, the major problem
consisted in the poses of so-called "plasticity" being highly individual—
in contrast to those that had been canonized by the classical ballet.[48]

Sad to say, the schemes and diagrams of the Choreological
Laboratory have been lost, but their influence can be detected in more
figural interpretations as, for example, in Grigorii Zimin's illustrations
of Lukin's dances to Scriabin[49] or in Goleizovsky's drawings of his
own choreographies (again to Scriabin's music[50]). Yutkevich also
made drawings of Rumnev's movements in the latter's scandalous
interpretation of Scriabin's *Prélude*, choreographed by Lukin, using a
series of force-lines that were meant to indicate the performer's internal
tension.[51] At that time Rumnev was still an actor and a producer and,
consequently, was well qualified to interpret the elements of pantomime
that Lukin wished to introduce into a new pantomimic ballet—his
interpretation of a detective novel—photographed by Nikolai Svishchev-
Paola, the famous photographer (figs. 10, 11).[52] But perhaps in the case
of Lukin the graphic transcription proved to be easier, because it was
even said that he worked like a "graphic artist. He has rejected color in
costume and impresses only with the play of the lines of the body."[53]

During NEP (New Economic Policy, 1921–1928), the experimental
dance and gymnastic studios, schools, and private clubs multiplied to
such an extent that in September 1924 the government (afraid of losing
control over them) convened a special committee of inquiry, which led to
the closure of many such establishments. The Choreological Laboratory
was also affected, although it was only later that the authorities really
began to scrutinize its activities, owing to its experiments with the nude
body. Actually, the idea of nudity onstage was not especially new. As

early as 1911, the producer Nikolai Evreinov[54] had published a collection of materials on this subject that examined the cult of nudism, soliciting the opinions of painters and sculptors on the question of the aesthetics of the nude body. This fashion returned in 1922 and the choreographers Goleizovsky and Lukin were among the primary supporters. Lukin even called his productions "evenings of free body dance," for which the costumes were often minimal, verging on total nudity. No doubt, this also influenced the experiments of the Choreological Laboratory, which conducted nude body exercises in the name of "scientific sobriety."[55] In any case, the surviving photographs of the Maia and Chernetskaia studios show that the exercise costume consisted basically of underwear (fig. 12). Sometimes the performers wore veils if they wanted to evoke a pantheistic atmosphere (Chernetskaia's *Pan* and Goleizovsky's *Faun*) or strips of dark material to underline the geometric beauty of the athletic body (as in *Joseph the Beautiful* or in Pozniakov's rhythmic-plastic exercises outdoors). Certainly, encouraging the liberation of the unconscious via movement could assume clear sexual connotations when complemented by nudity (we remember the laboratory's interest in psychoanalysis, too), and this did not escape the notice of the public. It is not by chance that a composition whose theme dealt with the liberation of the forces of instinct, i.e. Chernetskaia's *Pan*, showed her topless. Not surprisingly, critics observed that the real content of Goleizovsky's and Lukin's productions was either "an inexorable eroticism or clinical narcoticism. Lukin's *Caresse Dansée* [for example] is the apotheosis of sensuality while his *Prélude* . . . performed by Rumnev conveys the convulsions of an opium user with vivid realism."[56]

Of course, the concept of corporeal expression with all its obvious implications of sexual emancipation was gradually lost from view. By the 1930s, during the Stalin epoch, only the hygienic aspect of nudity and the body beautiful remained—and only in the gymnastic parades and displays. The following appeared in a book on physical education published in 1931:

> In the armies of physical education, nudity can be defined as socially valid. . . . The bodies of the athletes constitute a genuine work of art. In this context nudity in no way carries any sexual character, but has an aesthetic and social value.[57]

Fig. 12
Studio of Vera Maia, Moscow, ca. 1923

Fig. 13
May Day parade, Red Square, Moscow,
1938

Fig. 13
May Day parade, Red Square, Moscow,
1938

The free dance of the 1920s, now rendered ascetic after the elimination of the more turbid and emotional elements, became the real basis for the mass choreographies of the 1930s. It emphasized the hygienic and athletic character of movement and of the trained and healthy body, and served as an excellent basis for the grand Stalin parades. This strange continuity can be observed in certain striking parallels between the experimental solos and the photographs taken by a follower of Alexander Rodchenko during the gymnastic parade on Red Square for May Day 1938 (fig. 13). As we examine these images reproduced in an elegant export album,[58] we can discover how much the body in the gymnastic displays of this parade borrowed from the more experimental choreographies and dances of the 1920s. For example, there are the acrobatic soloists reminiscent of Rumnev and his poses or the human pyramid that brings to mind one of the choreographed groups in Goleizovsky's *Faun* of 1922 (fig. 14).

   The difference between the gymnastic parades of the 1930s and the plastic body expression of the preceding decade (as far as the Choreological Laboratory was concerned) was that the latter's ultimate aim (the "plasticity" of the body) was to express emotions and sensations. Recourse to emotional expression was fundamental to that higher symbolic totality that united the various aspects of the body language. For example, the debate that followed Chernetskaia's synthetic dance demonstration of December 1923 emphasized that

> in some people emotions express themselves in such high relief that one may sense the internal travail of the performer in question. . . . In this case, it is not only a mechanical movement that is being revealed, but also an inner idea.[59]

It is interesting to note that one of the primary apologists of Sigmund Freud's theories in the Soviet Union, Ivan Ermakov,[60] was also a member of the Choreological Laboratory. No doubt his activities also prompted

Fig. 14
Faun, 1922. Illustrated in *Echo*, 1923.

its particular orientation. In fact, the laboratory acted as an intermediary between the practical values of physical education deriving from the purely technical accomplishments of gymnastics and the theoretical research on language. One of the tenets in the laboratory program for 1924–1925 reads almost like a description of the May Day parade mentioned above:

> The study and structural implementation of complex poses that give the illusion of movements similar to static, sculptural phenomena. . . .[61]

But at the same time, another tenet in the program required the implementation of "experiments that clarify the coordinations of psychic states and of the corresponding positions and plastic movements."[62]

In the late 1920s RAKhN became increasingly sociological in its orientation. Some of its sections were closed down, and many of its members were imprisoned and executed. Even the Choreological Laboratory was deprived of its economic subsidy and its members were obliged to apply their theories in much more specific and concrete contexts. For example, Alexandrova, former director of the Institute of Rhythm, sacrificed her time and effort to the publication of booklets on how to organize the growing number of mass parades and demonstrations. The great theoretician Larionov, for his part, was reduced to writing articles for the popular press on the benefits of gymnastics. It is difficult to ascertain what happened to Larionov after the 1930s, although it is reasonable to assume that he shared the fate of most of his RAKhN colleagues—arrested, exiled, shot. No doubt he must have assembled an invaluable archive of photographs pertaining to the Moscow dance studios of the 1920s, as is proven by the rich corpus of such materials now held by the Bakhrushin State Central Theatrical Museum (surely a mere fraction of the original archive). Unfortunately, apart from the provenance index itself (i.e. "acquired from Larionov"), the Museum is not able to provide other evidence that would tell us more about Larionov's later life. Goleizovsky, too, was reduced to designing choreographies for the Stalin parades, such as the banal flower bed for the 1938 May Day celebration (fig. 15).

Fig. 15
Human flower garden choreographed by Kasian Goleizovsky for May Day parade, Red Square, Moscow, 1938

The photographs of this event show us the young, agile, and energetic bodies reminiscent of the bodies of the experimental dancers of the previous years. Nevertheless, they now have very little to do with the "expressive" body to which the Choreological Laboratory used to refer, at least in theory. The body of the Stalin parades is a collective body that can no longer express itself. It is a body that no longer speaks its own language and no longer speaks for itself, but is merely a word or a letter in the discourse of another.

Notes

1. Michel Fokine, *Protiv techeniia* (Against the Current) (Leningrad: Iskusstvo, 1981).

2. See, for example, the criticism by Truvit (pseudonym of Alexander Abramov), "Olimpiada besvkusiia" (The Olympiad of Tastelessness), in *Novyi zritel* 1923, no. 4:4, in which he accuses Sidorov of having put on a disastrous evening of modern dance at the Zimin Theatre, which showed "only the epigones of Duncan." The poster for an evening organized by the Commission for the Amelioration of Student Life at Moscow University also announced an "evening dedicated to all tendencies in the new scenic movement" (presented by Alexei Sidorov on 12 January 1923).

3. René Fülöp-Miller, *The Mind and Face of Bolshevism* (London and New York: Brentano, 1927), illust. opp. 182.

4. Kurt Johansson, *Aleksej Gastev* (Stockholm: Almqvist & Wiksell International, 1983).

5. See "Khoreologicheskaia laboratoriia" (Choreological Laboratory) in *GAKhN-Otchet 1921-1925* (Moscow: GAKhN, 1926), 63-64.

6. Natalia Sidorova, ed., *A.A. Sidorov: O masterakh zarubezhnogo, russkogo i sovetskogo iskusstva* (A.A. Sidorov: On the Masters of Foreign, Russian, and Soviet Art) (Moscow: Sovetskii khudozhnik, 1985).

7. Alexei Sidorov, *Sovremennyi tanets* (Contemporary Dance) (Moscow: Pervina, 1922).

8. Natalia Florovna Tian was born in Moscow in 1892. In 1919–1921 she worked for Proletarian Cultural and Education Organizations (Proletkult) and from 10 November 1922 was a member of the Russian Academy of Artistic Sciences (RAKhN, later GAKhN). In 1922 she was an active member of the Choreological Section there, having access to a large studio where she worked on the problem of movement and to a second studio where she conducted scientific research. See personal file, F.941, op. 10, ed. khr. 612, TsGALI (Central State Archive of Literature and Art, Moscow).

9. The first exhibition was in January 1924 and was not open to the public. See *Biulleteni GAKhN* [Moscow] 1925, no. 1:37–38. The Russian Society of Photography helped with this exhibition, which was only open from 3–10 January. See *Otchet o rabote Russkogo fotograficheskogo obshchestva za 1924–1925 gg.* (Report on the Work of the Russian Society of Photography 1924–1925), F.941, op. 1, ed. khr. 50, 1.188, TsGALI.

10. Until the present no specific research seems to have been done on Alexander Larionov. For some information on his activities at RAKhN, see his curriculum vitae in his personal file, F.941, op 10, ed khr. 344, TsGALI. Larionov asserted that "Apart from verbal and sound language, there exist or existed the languages of signals, of body movements (gestures), of the movement of the face muscles (mimicry). . . . The language of gestures can possess its own distinct system of graphic representation, for example, in the form of a graphic notation of movements having a semantic character," in "Konspekt kursa 'Istoriia pismen' (chitannogo v 1920-1921 uchebnom godu)" (Synopsis of the Lecture Series "The History of Old Writings" [delivered during the 1920–1921 academic year])" in *Vkhutemas* (Moscow, 1921), 8.

11. Rudolf von Laban, *Choreographie* (Jena, 1926); Olga Desmond, *Rhythmographik (Tanznotenschrift), Grundlage zum Selbstudium des Tanzes* (Leipzig, 1919). Larionov gave a lecture on Desmond's rhythmographic system at RAKhN on 11 November 1925.

12. Evgenii Yavorsky, *Analiticheskaia zapis telodvizhenii (Tezisy k dokladu) (13/1/1925)* (Analytical Record of Body Movements [A Thesis for a Paper] [1/13/25]), in F.941, op. 17, ed. khr. 5, 1.46, TsGALI, and *Protokol N. 7 (15) Otkrytogo zasedaniia Khoreologicheskoi laboratorii ot 13/1/1925* (Minutes of Open Session No. 7 [15] of the Choreological Laboratory, 1/13/25), F.941, op. 17, ed. khr. 5, 1.43, TsGALI.

13. *Protokol N.6 (14) Otkrytogo zasedaniia Khoreologicheskoi laboratorii ot 10/1/1925* in F.941, op. 17, ed. khr. 5, 1.57, TsGALI.

14. "Khoreologicheskaia laboratoriia," *GAKhN-Otchet 1921–1925*, 62.

15. "Khoreologicheskaia laboratoriia," *GAKhN-Otchet 1921–1925*, 62.

16. Liudmila Alexeeva, "Tezisy k demonstratsii uprazhnenii garmonicheskoi gimnastiki" (Thesis toward a Demonstration of Harmonic Gymnastic Exercises) *Protokol N. 2 (10) Otkrytogo zasedaniia Khoreologicheskoi laboratorii ot 25/10/1924* (Minutes of Open Session No. 2 [10] of the Choreological Laboratory, 10/25/24), in F.941, op. 17, ed. khr. 5, 1.12–14, TsGALI.

17. Nina Alexandrova finished her course of study with the Jaques-Dalcroze school in Geneva in 1909. Immediately after the October Revolution she organized the Institute of Rhythm within the People's Commissariat for Enlightenment (Narkompros) in Moscow, which she directed for five years before spending another eight years with the Association of Rhythmists. During the early Soviet period she was much involved in educational reforms. For information see Narkompros, ed., *O ritmicheskom vospitanii* (On Rhythmic Education) (Moscow, 1920), and her booklet, *Ritmicheskoe vospitanie: Doklad priniatyi na vsesoiuznom soveshchanii sovetov fizicheskoi kultury* (Rhythmic Education: A Paper Accepted at the All-Union

Conference of the Physical Education Soviets) (Moscow, 1924).

18. *Protokol N. 3 Otkrytogo zasedaniia Khoreologicheskoi laboratorii ot 15/12/1923* (Minutes of Open Session No. 3 of the Choreological Laboratory, 12/1/5/23), in F.941, op. 17, ed. khr. 2, 1.17, TsGALI.

19. Nikolai Semionovich Pozniakov was born in Kursk in 1878. After studying at the Moscow Conservatory he took choreographic lessons with Mikhail Mordkin. Before the Revolution, together with Alexander Larionov, he was a member of the modernist group called the Society of Free Aesthetics. He worked as an associate researcher at the Choreological Laboratory at RAKhN. For information see personal file, F.941, op. 10, ed. khr. 483, TsGALI.

20. *Plenum Fiziko-psikhologicheskogo otdeleniia GAKhN'a ot 16/11/1927* (A Plenary Session of the Physio-Psychological Department of GAKhN, 11/16/27), F.941, op. 12, ed. khr. 27, 1.29, TsGALI.

21. Inna Chernetskaia, "Plastika i analiz zhesta" (Plastique and the Analysis of Gesture), in *Protokol zasedaniia Khoreograficheskoi sektsii ot 10/12/1923* (Minutes of the 12/10/23 Meeting of the Choreographic Section), in F.941, op. 17, ed. khr. 2, 1.14, TsGALI.

22. Chernetskaia's Studio of Synthetic Dance and RAKhN cosigned a kind of contract on 29 November 1923, according to which the Studio was affiliated with the Academy while maintaining its autonomy. The Studio was then allowed to use the premises at RAKhN in return for a nominal fee. See *Polozhenie i plan raboty* (Work Thesis and Goals), F.941, op. 17, ed. khr. 4, 1.1, TsGALI.

23. *Obiazatelnaia zapiska* (Promissory Note), F.941, op. 17, ed. khr. 4, 1.2, TsGALI.

24. *Khudozhestvennyi plan volnoi masterskoi "Sinteticheskogo tantsa" I.S. Chernetskoi* (Artistic Goals of I.S. Chernetskaia's Free Workshop "Synthetic Dance"), F.941, op. 17, ed. khr. 4, 1.3, TsGALI.

25. No detailed research has been made on Inna Chernetskaia or Vera Maia. For some information on their studios see Natalia Sheremetevskaia, *Tanets na estrade* (Dance in Vaudeville) (Moscow: Iskusstvo, 1985), 43-46.

26. *Otchet o rabote Khoreologicheskoi laboratorii GAKhN za 1924–1925 gg.* (Report on the Work of the Choreological Laboratory at GAKhN during 1924–1925), F.941, op. 1, ed. khr. 70, 1.160, TsGALI.

27. Nikolai Lvov, "Goleizovsky i Lukin," *Ermitazh* [Moscow], 1921, no. 11:6.

28. Sergei Yutkevich, *Sobranie sochinienii v trekh tomakh* (Collected Works in Three Volumes), Vol. 1, *Molodost* (Youth) (Moscow: Iskusstvo, 1990), 125–128.

29. Natalia Chernova, ed., *Kasian Goleizovsky: Zhizn i tvorchestvo. Stati, vospominaniia, dokumenty* (Kasian Goleizovsky: His Life and Work. Articles, Reminiscences, and Documents) (Moscow: VTO, 1984).

30. V. Iving [Viktor Ivanov], "Vecher Lukina" (Lukin's Evening), *Teatr i muzyka* [Moscow] 8, no. 21 (1923):717–718.

31. *Shtatnoe raspisanie praktikantov Khoreologicheskoi laboratorii pri RAKhN* (Staff Schedule for Apprentices of the Choreological Laboratory at RAKhN), F.941, op. 17, ed. khr. 1, 1.26, TsGALI.

32. Natalia Sheremetevskaia, "Nikolai Foregger-postanovshchik tantsev" (Nikolai Foregger–Dance Designer), *Teatr* [Moscow], 1972, no. 5:134-142.

33. Nikolai Foregger, "Emotsia i akrobatika" (Emotion and Acrobatics), *Novyi zritel* [Moscow], 1972, no. 40:2.

34. Nikolai Foregger, "Opyty po povodu iskusstva tantsa" (Experiments in the Art of Dance), in P. Romanov, ed., *Ritm i kultura tantsa* (Rhythm and Dance Culture) (Leningrad, 1926), 37–54.

35. See Nicoletta Misler, "Per una liturgia dei sensi: Il concetto di sinestesia da Kandinskij a Florenskij," in *Rassegna Sovietica* [Rome], March-April 1986, 37–44.

36. See Vasilii Kandinksy, untitled statement, *Vestnik rabotnikov iskusstva* [Moscow], 1921, nos. 4-5:4. Also see J. Hahl-Koch, "Kandinsky, Schönberg und der Blaue Reiter," in J. Hahl-Koch, *Vom Klang der Bilder*, exh. cat. Staatsgalerie (Stuttgart, 1985), 354–355.

37. Emile Vuillermoz, *Clotilde et Aleksandre Sakharoff* (Lausanne: Editions Centrales, 1930).

38. Selim Khan-Magomedov, "Sektsiia monumentalnogo iskusstva Inkhuka" (The Monumental Art Section of Inkhuk), *Problemy istorii sovetskoi arkhitektury* [Moscow], 1977, no. 3:18-23.

39. *Institut khudozhestvennoi kultury v Moskve (Inkhuk) programma* (The Moscow Institute of Artistic Culture Program) (Moscow, 1920). Also see Selim Khan-Magomedov, "V. Kandinsky o vospriiatii i vozdeistvii sredstv khudozhestvennoi vyrazitelnosti" (V. Kandinksy on the Perception and Effect of Artistic Means of Expression), *Trudy VNIITE* [Moscow], 1978, no. 17:77–100.

40. Tatiana Pertseva, "V. Kandinsky i GAKhN," *Kandinsky*, exh. cat. State Tretiakov Gallery, Moscow, and The Russian Museum, Leningrad (Leningrad: Aurora, 1989), 56–66.

41. *Otchet o rabote Khoreologicheskoi laboratorii GAKhN za 1924/25 g* (Report on the Work of the Choreological Laboratory at GAKhN during 1924–1925), F.941, op. 1, ed. khr. 50, 1.159, TsGALI.

42. "Tanzcurven: Zu den Tanzen der Palucca," *Kunstblatt* [Potsdam], 10

March 1926. Reprinted in Clark Poling, *Kandinsky: Russian and Bauhaus Years, 1915-1933*, exh. cat. Solomon R. Guggenheim Museum (New York, 1982), 266.

43. F. 941, op. 17, ed. khr. 2, 1.10, TsGALI.

44. Pavel Florensky, "Symbolarium (Slovar simvolov)" (Symbolarium [A Dictionary of Symbols]), *Trudy po znakovym sistemam V* [Tartu], 1971, no. 284:521-527. Ekaterina Nekrasova, "Neosushchestvlennyi zamysel 1920-kh godov sozdaniia Symbolarium'a (Slovar simvolov) i ego pervyi vypusk 'Tochka'" (Unrealized Idea of the 1920s for Creating a "Symbolarium" (a Dictionary of Symbols) and Its First Issue, "The Dot"), in *Pamiatniki kultury: Novye otkrytiia* (Cultural Monuments: New Discoveries), 1982 (Leningrad: Nauka, 1984), 99-115. Also see Yurii Molok, "Slovar simvolov Pavla Florenskogo: Nekotorye marginalii" (Pavel Florensky's "Dictionary of Symbols": Selected Marginalia), *Sovetskoe iskusstvoznanie* [Moscow], 1990, 26:322–343.

45. Alexander Larionov, "Khudozhestvennoe dvizhenie" (Artistic Movement), in Alexander Larionov et al., *Teoriia i praktika fizkultury* (The Theory and Practice of Physical Education) (Moscow: Izdatelstvo Vysshego i Moskovskogo Sovetov fizicheskoi kultury, 1925).

46. From remarks made by Alexander Larionov after Liudmila Alexeeva's lecture "O sisteme garmonicheskoi gimnastiki" (On the System of Harmonious Gymnastics), in *Protokol N. 2 (10)* (see note 16).

47. Pavel Florensky, "Analiz prostranstvennosti i vremennosti v izobrazitelnykh proizvedeniiakh" (Analysis of Spatiality and Temporality in the Visual Arts), unpublished manuscript, to be published in Italian by Nicoletta Misler, 1991.

48. *Protokol N. 7 Otkrytogo zasedaniia Khoreologicheskoi laboratorii ot 13/1/1925* (Minutes of Open Session No. 7 of the Choreological Laboratory, 1/13/25), F. 941, op. 17, ed. khr. 5, 1.43, TsGALI.

49. See Evgenii Kovtun et al., *Avangard, ostanovlennyi na begu* (The Avant-Garde Stopped in Motion) (Leningrad: Aurora, 1989), illust. 451–461.

50. K. [Kasian Goleizovsky?], *Scriabin* (Moscow, 1922).

51. See illust., Yutkevich, *Molodost*, 126.

52. Lvov, 6.

53. A. Fomin, *Svetopis Svishcheva-Paola* (The Photography of Svishchev-Paola) (Moscow: Iskusstvo, 1964).

54. Nikolai Evreinov, *Nagota na stsene* (Stage Nudity) (St. Petersburg: Tipografiia Morskogo Ministerstva, 1911).

55. *Protokol. N. 4 zasedaniia Khoreologicheskoi laboratorii ot 13/7/1923* (Minutes of Session No. 4 of the Choreological Laboratory 7/13/23), F.941, op. 17, ed. khr. 3, 1.23, TsGALI.

56. Lvov, 6.

57. Sergei Mileev, *Iskusstvo i fizicheskaia kultura* (Art and Physical Education) (Moscow-Leningrad: Fizkultura i turizm, 1931), 10.

58. *A Pageant of Youth* (Moscow-Leningrad: State Art Publishers, 1939).

59. Chernetskaia, *Plastika i analiz zhesta*, 1.14.

60. See curriculum vitae in personal file, F.941, op. 10, ed. khr. 20, TsGALI.

61. *Plan raboty Khoreologicheskoi laboratorii GAKhN za 1924/25 g.* (1924–1925 Goals for the Choreological Laboratory at GAKhN), F.941, op. 12, ed. khr. 10, 1.28, TsGALI.

62. *Plan*, 1.28.

**Manifestos of the
Russian Avant-Garde**

Selected Plot Summaries

Exhibition Checklist

Cat. no. 163
Vadim Ryndin
Design for stage construction,
An Optimistic Tragedy, 1933

Manifestos of the Russian Avant-Garde

Erik F. Gollerbakh, from "Teatr kak zrelishche" (Theatre as Spectacle),
in *Teatralno-dekoratsionnoe iskusstvo v SSSR 1917–1927* (Stage Design
in the USSR during the Decade 1917-1927) (Leningrad: Akademia
Khudozhestv, 1927), 32, 36.

Unfortunately, the mass of the theatrical public still remains highly
undiscriminating. I remember one of my conversations with Alexandre Benois
and his sigh, "All it takes is a lamp with a red lampshade and a moon in the
window, and the public is thrilled. . . ." Such is the tragedy of a theatrical artist:
Sophistication and refinement are lost on the viewers.

. . . .

But a wholesale and compulsory introduction of falling, schematic, and
dynamized decorations into ordinary repertory would amount to tastelessness
and insensitivity. The appearance of a dynamo in an antique tragedy, or, let's
say, of a revolving stage (which, by the way, is beginning to be misused) in a
sedate home of merchants—are they not empty trickery, barely disguised as
"a search for style?"

On the borderline between the stasis and the dynamic of the stage is light,
which vascillates between both. Light has traditionally been regarded in easel
painting as a powerful aid to the artist; in theatrical painting, its significance
is even greater: Here light and color represent something inseparable.

Street demonstration, Moscow,
13 October 1930

Vsevolod Samoilov, "Revoliutsionnye prazdnestva" (Revolutionary
Celebrations), in *Teatralno-dekoratsionnoe iskusstvo v SSSR 1917–1927*
(Stage Design in the USSR during the Decade 1917–1927) (Leningrad:
Akademia Khudozhestv, 1927), 189.

In design for an urban setting, two factors can turn out to be problematic:
Either the architecture is killed by the decorations, or the buildings destroy the
decorations. In either case, and first of all, common sense in decorating becomes
lost, which must be prevented by every means.

Temporary stage constructions, which can never create the impression of
monumentality, must not be allowed, unless absolutely necessary, to overwhelm
the grandness and beauty of the already existing monumental architectural
ensemble, which in itself represents the best aspect of urban beauty. A convincing
example is the experience of 1918, when, during the October celebrations,
futurist placards hundreds of feet long covered up huge areas of historical
buildings that are outstanding in their architectural beauty, thus failing to create
the desired effect.

Therefore, in the design of urban settings the primary focus should be
on the strict coordination of temporary installations with the predominant
architecture; with this condition in mind, the artist-decorator must reveal the
revolutionary significance of this or that structure or location.

May Day demonstration, Moscow, 1930

Vsevolod Meyerhold, "Kak byl postavlen 'Velikodushnyi rogonosets'" (How "The Magnanimous Cuckold" Was Staged) (1926), in Alexander Fevralsky, *V.E. Meyerhold*, (Moscow: Iskusstvo, 1968), 52.

II. Material Stage Design (1923)

In material stage design, the constructivist (L.S. Popova) set the goal of making the propaganda aspect of the play the center of the audience's attention. With this goal in mind, the individual who designs the stage, instead of pursuing the aesthetic effect, aims at producing an effect that to the viewers would not be any different from real life phenomena, such as maneuvers, parades, street demonstrations, battles, etc. The costumes and the objects (both large and small) must be just as they are in life, their utility first and foremost, no decorative embellishments, no theatricality. The play develops in a close interpenetration with that which permeates our contemporaneity: technological achievements. The constructivist introduces the cinema screen into his installation system so that the director can use it to enhance the propaganda aspect of the play.

Carnival on the streets of Moscow, 1931

Alexei Gan, "Borba za massovoe deistvo" (The Struggle for Mass Action), in Alexei Gan et al., *O teatre* (On the Theatre) (Tver, 1922), 73.

"Mass action"—not fiction or fantasy but a direct and organic necessity that follows from the very essence of communism.

Proletarian revolution was the product of proletarian culture, which evolves and justifies theoretical postulates of their leaders by the *experience of the masses.*

There is no direct jump from capitalism to communism: There is only the long, hard, and persistent road of rough socialism, in whose crucible communism is born, develops, and matures.

Thus, communism will appear as a streamlined form of mass production and distribution of material benefits. The processes of labor will be cemented by the scientific disciplines of intellectually conscious labor. A different environment is created under the conditions of communist work, in which new systems of creative initiative for both the collective and the individual will arise.

"Mass action" in communism is the action not of civic but of human society, in which the material production will merge with the intellectual production; this intellectual-material culture mobilizes all its power and means in order to subjugate not just nature but the entire cosmos.

Blue Blouse Theatre, 1927

Vsevolod Meyerhold, "Ob antrakte i o vremeni na stsene" (About Intermission and Time Onstage), in L. Vendrovskaia and Alexander Fevralsky, *Tvorcheskoe nasledie V.E. Meierholda* (Creative Legacy of V.E. Meyerhold) (Moscow: VTO, 1978), 46. From a lecture given at the State Higher Directors' Workshop (GVYRM), 19 November 1921.

Yet another "reef" that we must keep in mind in order not to bring the play to a catastrophe is the intermission. Little thought is given to it, and in general the question of the intermission problem has seldom been raised. The point is that intermission is not something separate from the play, it does not exist just so that the decorations can be moved or to give the public an opportunity to rest. We know that in antiquity theatrical plays ran without intermissions, and that was not accidental—after all, the plays could have been structured in a way that could allow the spectator to take a break, to chat with someone sitting next to him. That was never done because the dramatic scenario was designed to capture the audience's attention from beginning to end, so that the attention never strayed from the play, so that all the separate scenes, which in a spiral-like fashion encircle the main axis of the play, entered the viewers' consciousness and were digested during the play, so that after the play the viewers could truly reach their own conclusions, for most dramatic plays are designed in such a way as to leave the conclusion to be decided by the viewer. It is a bad play if it is regurgitated by a preacher; that is, the viewer remains passive, and he cannot contribute anything to the play.

The Magnanimous Cuckold, 1922

Vsevolod Meyerhold, "Kak byl postavlen 'Velikodushnyi rogonosets'" (How "The Magnanimous Cuckold" Was Staged) (1926), in Alexander Fevralsky, *V.E. Meyerhold* (Moscow: Iskusstvo, 1968), 47.

The play was meant to lay a foundation to the new acting technique in a new stage environment, which broke away from stage design centered on the curtain and the portal. In validating the new principle, the play inevitably had to reveal all its construction lines and to schematize that method in the extreme. That principle was successfully realized to the fullest.

The success of the play became the success of the worldview that it was based on; by now it has become an established fact that the entire "left theatre" not only had its origin in this play but also to this day retains the traces of its influence.

The fact that the radical character of the style exhibited in the play was greeted ecstatically by the widest audiences—even though it scared off a segment of the critics—proved that the new public, having acquired the theatre among other cultural achievements of the revolution, persistently felt a need for just that kind of theatrical style. With this play, we wanted to lay a foundation for a new type of theatrical action that demanded neither illusory decorations nor complicated stage props, made do with the simplest handy objects, and gradually evolved from a spectacle by specialists into spontaneous playing by the workers at their leisure.

Blue Blouse Theatre, advertisement for
GUM department store, ca. 1928

Alexander Tairov, "Stsenicheskaia atmosfera" (Stage Ambience) (1921),
in P. Markov, ed., *A. Y. Tairov* (Moscow: VTO, 1970), 160–161.

In order to express his art in a visibile way, the actor uses his material.
That material is the actor's body. The body of an actor is *three dimensional*,
therefore the actor can express himself only volumetrically. Hence it is necessary
to give action space to the actor commensurate with his tasks at hand and to
provide him with an appropriate stage ambience. Such ambience is only possible
within a specific cubic capacity. For such a cubic capacity only the *mock-up*
can serve as a model.

But what should that mock-up be like, what principles should it be
based on?

The actor expresses his art by using his body.

Therefore, the stage should be designed in such a way as to help the actor's
body to assume the necessary shapes, and to respond easily to all the challenges
required by the body's motion and rhythm.

It then follows that the most important part of a stage, which needs to be
planned for each production, is the *stage floor*, the so-called stage area, because
it is there that the actor moves and realizes in a visible form his creative purpose.

Thus, the stage artist must focus his attention on the floor of the stage,
having broken away from his fascination with the backdrop.

Up until now, the artist scorned the stage floor, lavishing the bounty of his
imagination on the backdrop, the curtain, the *paddugy* and the *arlekin* [kinds of
curtains] to which he gave such assiduous and luxurious treatment that it made
one feel as if the stage was not for the actors but for some kind of fantastic birds
hovering in the air.

Therefore it became absolutely necessary to distract the artist from those
parts of the stage that performed only a supporting role and to focus all
his attention on collaborating with the producer on planning/developing
the stage area.

How then should the stage area be developed; what principles should serve
as the foundation for its construction?

First of all, the stage floor should be broken up. It must not represent one
continuous plane, but must be broken up, according to the play's needs, into a
series of multilevel horizontal, or slanting, planes, because a level floor is not
expressive: It provides no opportunities for realizing the play in relief, it provides
no opportunities for the actor to develop his movement to the appropriate
degree, to fully utilize his material.

I assume that this is self-evident. But one could, if one so desired, prove
it to himself any time. Begin by making a series of movements on a level floor.
Then put something like a stool on the floor, using it as a new plane, as a new
area for the development of your movements, and you will see how much richer
your gestures will become, how many new plastic possibilites will open up for
you. And if you had several multilevel areas in front of you, your material would
gain virtually inexhaustible opportunities for gesture and form.

Of course, the naturalist theatre had no need for such development of the
stage area, for in real life all normal people walk on a level floor, and those who
all of a sudden decide to climb over chairs and tables are put in a lunatic asylum.

The Magnanimous Cuckold, act 3, 1922

Ivan Aksionov, "Prostran stvennyi konstruktivizm na stsene" (Spatial Constructivism Onstage), in *Teatralnyi oktiabr* (Leningrad-Moscow, 1926), 33.

In the stage design for *The Magnanimous Cuckold*, the principle of rejection of theatrical flies and suspensions for scenery became canonical for all further works in that style: the play—why and how we have already seen—was assumed to be independent of the stage portal. The fact that all the parts of an installation were necessarily supported by the floor led to a series of consequences that proved to be very convenient for the principal tenets of constructivism as a theory.

The principle of building a stage installation using combinations of standard construction elements had a precedent in the old theatrical technique of combining various "equipment," which were usually disguised under painted canvas. Constructivism, in rejecting "stage decorations," uncovered the machine and began to build an installation out of the various elements of that machine, which were appropriately changed in size. The two vertical elements of the construction in *The Magnanimous Cuckold*—the narrow one and the wide one—provided a scheme for a constructivist installation that remained virtually unchanged since then.

The vertical elements allowed the realization of the following principles: 1) a linear three-dimensional construction; 2) a visual rhythm, conditioned neither by painterly nor by volumetric effects; 3) the use in the design of only those parts relevant to construction and function.

By way of a test, to this was added an attempt to introduce a time-reality element, which provided a time-visual accompaniment to the play, the way music is used to provide a time-audible accompaniment. The different colors of the wheels, which rotated as the play went along, pursued not a decorative but a visual purpose: They enabled the viewer to observe better the variety of rotary movements of the kinetic background.

Since it was constructed of only the functional parts, the installation, which embodied the principle opposite to decoration, demanded a corresponding reinterpretation of the costumes. The costume also had to be suitable for work onstage. Thus the formula for the working (functional) clothes of the actor was born—the notorious *prozodezhda*. The *prozodezhda* was based on the worker's blue blouse-and-pants set, complemented by various accoutrements appropriate to the role or part. Thus, the basic blue shirt-and-pants ensemble could be suitable for both the "persona" of a burgomaster and the "personas" of a count, or a cooper.

Essentially, the play was supposed to serve strictly as a premise and a program: As it evolved, the extra-theatrical play was supposed to result in—since the stage, decorations, and costume were becoming obsolete—leading to the obsolescence of both the actor and the text. A theatrical event would yield to the free play of relaxing workers, who would spend part of their leisure time on a production, improvised perhaps on a spot right next to their workplace, according to a scenario that one of them had invented.

Blue Blouse Theatre, Living Newspaper, ca. 1927

Nikolai Maslennikov. *Khudozhnik v teatre* (The Artist in the Theatre) (Moscow, 1930), 19–20.

Even if it is premature at this point to talk about the existence of proletarian decorative art, it is still possible to state, with sufficient confidence, that in the field of stage design for the revolutionary theatre constructivism is the most contemporary and nearest artistic current. It must be noted that the painterly tradition in the theatre diminishes every year, yielding to the painterly-volumetric decorations and realist constructivism. In this respect, the ongoing process of change in the forms of theatrical decorative art on the provincial stages is particularly indicative. The naturalist-painterly decorations are increasingly being replaced with the realist-constructivist installations. The same process forcefully asserted itself on the amateur stages of major workers' clubs. For example, the Kukhmisterov Club (Moscow), the Morse Club, the Central Moscow Club of Steelworkers, and others widely use realist-constructivist designs and various methods of symbolic decoration in their productions. The majority of clubs in the USSR turn to the so-called symbolic-realist decorations in staging of living newspapers* and vaudeville acts. As a rule, the stage sets of living newspapers are completely portable, convenient for relocation, and permit last-minute changes. In addition, the quick transformation of costumes with the help of wittily designed appliqué work of various kinds is also widely used.

*"The 'living newspaper' as a new form of theatre came into being after the Revolution of 1917 and was a derivative of the 'spoken newspaper.' Because of the high percentage of illiteracy, the newspaper was read loudly to a gathered audience. The animation of 'spoken newspaper' into 'living newspaper' was gradual. The reading of the newspaper developed into the presentation of news by visualization (using posters on stage, staging diagrams and statistics), dramatization (monologue, dialogue, mass declamation and short sketches), and 'musicalization' (news transformed into songs). There were brief international and domestic news items, slogans of the day, decrees, caricatures, editorials, etc." From František Deák, "Blue Blouse," in *The Drama Review* 17, no. 1 (T-57)(March 1973):35–46.

Selected Plot Summaries

This is by no means an inclusive selection of plays. It is meant to provide an overview of thematic material presented on the Russian avant-garde stage. Entries are by Simon Karlinsky unless otherwise noted.

The Bedbug (comedy), 1928, first performed 13 February 1929
Author: Vladimir Mayakovsky

With the coming of the New Economic Policy (NEP), factory worker and party member Ivan Prisypkin ("dusting powder") decides that he has sacrificed enough for the Revolution and now wants rewards. He changes his name to Pierre Skripkin ("violin"), breaks with his communist girlfriend, Zoya (who attempts suicide), and marries the daughter of a rich beautician. The beautician offers a big dowry in exchange for the prestige and safety of Ivan's party card. At the wedding, a fire breaks out and the fireman's spray accidentally freezes Ivan into a solid block of ice.

In 1979 he is defrosted and revived by scientists to a world that has become communist, logical, and antiseptic. Zoya, now an elderly biologist, pronounces him "scum" and his bourgeois outlook a danger to the purity of the new world. But Ivan is saved from being refrozen when a legendary and now-extinct animal—a bedbug—is discovered to have been frozen with him. Ivan is allowed to live in a zoo, nourishing the fabulously valuable bedbug with his blood.

Bolt (ballet), first performed 8 April 1931
Libretto: Viktor Smirnov

A Soviet factory, running at full steam, symbolizes the dynamic tempo of the new life. Certain employees, including a bureaucrat and the hooligan Lenka Gulba and his drinking friends, disrupt work on production. Dismissed from the factory, Gulba in revenge incites the lad Gosha to damage a lathe by inserting a bolt in it. After their conversation is overheard, Gosha is arrested when he returns to the shop. In the end Gosha tells the truth and Gulba is arrested. (Nancy V. N. Baer)

The Death of Tarelkin (satirical comedy), 1869, first performed in 1900
Author: Alexander Sukhovo-Kobylin

This is the third play in the author's great satirical trilogy about the corruption in the Russian judiciary prior to the reforms of the 1860s. Tarelkin, a lowly court clerk, devised the clever scams that enabled his superiors, the investigator Varravin and the police chief Raspliuev, to bilk a wealthy family of its fortune (an event shown in the earlier plays). Since his partners shared none of their loot with him, Tarelkin fakes his own death and assumes the identity of his deceased neighbor Kopylov. He plans to go into hiding and blackmail his partners with legal documents he has stolen.

But Varravin figures out Tarelkin's scheme. He intimidates numerous witnesses, convincing them that Tarelkin, who now has the identities of two men, both officially dead, has returned from the grave and is thus a werewolf, dangerous to society. Tarelkin confesses under torture, and returns the stolen documents in order to save his life. He promises to devote his days to illegal vodka distilling and never again to meddle in judiciary matters.

The Dybbuk (melodrama), first performed 1922
Author: S. An-sky [Solomon Rappoport]

Khanan, a poor but brilliant talmudic scholar, falls in love with Leah, the daughter of a rich merchant at whose house he has been a guest. Although their love is mutual, Leah's father opposes the marriage. Half-crazed by his love for Leah, Khanan begins to study Hebrew mysticism. When Leah's father announces that he has found a suitable husband for his daughter, Khanan becomes despondent and dies.

In act 2, the soul of Khanan enters the body of Leah as a *dybbuk*, a migrant soul in eastern European Jewish folklore. At her wedding, Leah rejects the bridegroom. She is brought to a godly man, a *zaddik*, to be exorcised. The *zaddik* successfully expels the ghost, or *dybbuk*, from the girl, but her soul disappears with it and her body dies, thus uniting the lovers. (Nancy V. N. Baer)

Famira Kifared (Thamyris Kitharodos) (classicistic tragedy), 1906, published 1913, first performed 1916
Author: Innokentii Annensky

Famira's mother, the nymph Argiope, was loved by Zeus. But Argiope preferred a mortal, King Philammon of Thrace. Soon after the birth of their son, Famira, Zeus punished Argiope with twenty years of insanity. Famira was raised by a peasant nurse.

As the play opens, Famira is the most admired cythara player in Greece. (The cythara is analogous to the modern Indian cythar, not the zither.) Argiope, released from her punishment, wants the return of her son, but he no longer needs her. To entice him, the mother promises Famira he will understand mysteries about the art of music if he challenges Euterpe, the muse of music, to a competition. She knows that this kind of pride (hubris) is always punished by the gods.

Famira, who dreamed of besting Euterpe and becoming her lover, is defeated and condemned to the loss of his musical ability. In despair he blinds himself. The gods punish the mother by turning her into a seeing-eye bird, to be perched on her son's shoulder as his guide. Argiope is content, now having her son to herself.

The Forest (comedy), 1870, first performed 1871
Author: Alexander Ostrovsky

Two down-and-out actors, the tragedian Neshchaslivtsev ("Unlucky") and the comedian Shchaslivtsev ("Lucky"), travel by foot to the estate of the former's rich aunt, Raisa. Raisa is gradually selling the family-owned forest to support her hobby, keeping young men. Now in her mid-fifties, she likes the men increasingly younger; her current beau is a high-school dropout. To preserve appearances, she intends to marry the boy to Neshchaslivtsev's young cousin, Aksiusha.

Neshchaslivtsev is at first well received by his aunt Raisa, who thinks he is a military man on leave. But then they discover each other's secrets: Raisa learns he is only a provincial actor and he discovers her affair with the teenager.

Raisa now wants her disgraceful nephew to leave, so she bribes him with 1,000 rubles (less than what she owes him for his share in her sales of woodland). Aksiusha is in love with a merchant's son, but his father won't have her unless she brings 1,000 rubles for her dowry. Everyone begs rich Raisa to provide the dowry.

Raisa cannot; her lover will marry her only if she gives him her entire fortune. So that Aksiusha can marry the one she loves, Neshchaslivtsev gives his bribe to her. As the preparations begin for the two weddings—one promising, the other ominous—the two actors leave the estate as broke as they came.

Good Treatment for Horses (theatrical revue), 1921, first performed January 1922
Author: Vladimir Mass, after a poem by Vladimir Mayakovsky

In Mayakovsky's poem, in the center of Moscow a diverse group of characters mocks a fallen, overworked horse. But then a poet addresses the horse with words of encouragement, telling it that all poets and artists are overworked horses. The horse takes heart, gets up, and heads for its stable.

In the play, the crowd reacts first to the horse and then to the challenge of creating a restaurant that is a "fancy, disgusting, schmancy, cheap, profitable place." An American impresario arrives and urges the restaurant owner to turn her place into a cafe with entertainment. In the last act the cabaret comes alive with satires and dances. (Nancy V. N. Baer)

The Inspector General (comedy), 1836, first performed 19 April 1836
Author: Nikolai Gogol

The elders of a provincial town, led by the governor, hear that an inspector general from St. Petersburg is coming to examine their various institutions. In a case of mistaken identity, they assume that the young fop Khlestakov, a visitor to their town, is the inspector general, and they proceed to flatter and bribe him in order to conceal the state of civic affairs. Khlestakov is delighted at this unexpected attention and goes on his way greatly contented with their bounty.

To the horror of the elders, the real inspector general suddenly arrives, an event that culminates in the famous "mute" scene in which the actors strike poses of astonishment and remain silent for several minutes before the curtain descends. (John E. Bowlt)

The Locksmith and the Chancellor (drama), 1921, first performed 1921
Author: Anatolii Lunacharsky

Based on recent political events in Germany, this play was an allegory of two opposing worlds—the vulgar, pseudodemocratic world of the bourgeoisie, and the world of the underprivileged workers. The Chancellor, von Turau, is the class enemy; the Locksmith, Stark, is the protagonist; Frei is the compromising socialist. Although not unequivocal, the play ends with the condemnation of the Chancellor and the advocation of the Locksmith. (John E. Bowlt)

The Magnanimous Cuckold (comedy), 1920, first performed 1920
Author: Fernand Crommelynck

Bruno, the village scribe, is passionately in love with his devoted and obedient young wife, Stella. He is so infatuated by the possession of such an attractive woman that he boasts of her charms everywhere, even forcing his friend Petrus to admire her bare breasts.

Once his jealously has been aroused, Bruno, pursuing an insane logic of his own, cannot rest until he has put all doubts to an end by absolute certainty. He therefore compels the suffering Stella to sleep first with Petrus and then with all the men in the village as he pursues the phantom of an unknown and non-existent lover. Stella abandons her husband only at the very end, running off with the cowherd. (Alma H. Law)

Mystery-Bouffe (parody of a medieval mystery play), 1918, second version 1921, first performed 1 May 1921
Author: Vladimir Mayakovsky

A flood, similar to Noah's, has inundated the earth, except for the North Pole, which is also about to go under. Escaping to the last dry spot and building an ark in which to survive are "seven pairs of the clean" (members of the ruling classes, all distinguished by nationality, such as the Abyssinian negus, an Indian rajah, an Orthodox priest, an American,) and "seven pairs of the unclean" (members of the proletariat, none of whom have nationality, such as a blacksmith, a baker, a laundress).

Safe in the ark, the passengers try out various forms of government: first, a monarchy, under which the negus gets all the food; then, a bourgeois republic, during which only the clean are permitted to eat. The unclean are visited by a man who can walk on water (a parody of Christ, a role that was played by Mayakovsky). Reversing the message of the Sermon on the Mount, he tells the unclean to throw the clean overboard and then to storm heaven and hell.

The unclean are not fearful of the devils in hell; compared to their lives before the Revolution, hell seems a vacation. In heaven, the unclean intimidate the angels, among whom are Tolstoy and Jean-Jacques Rousseau, and confiscate God's thunderbolts to use for electrical power. Back on earth the flood has receded but earth is now ruled by the Queen of Devastation. However, the unclean unite with anthropomorphized machines and utensils, the group jointly defeating Devastation to create a communist paradise on earth.

One-Sixth of the World (theatrical revue), first performed
22 February 1931
Authors: Alexander Yarkov and Nikolai Ravich

An American millionaire comes to the Soviet Union to try and persuade his brother to emigrate. But the brother refuses, making a long speech in which he denounces American imperialism. The political theme is supplemented by singing, ballet numbers, and declamations; the cast numbers about two hundred. (John E. Bowlt)

An Optimistic Tragedy (heroic tragedy), 1932, first performed
18 December 1933
Author: Vsevolod Vishnevsky

During the postrevolutionary civil war a modest and very feminine woman commissar is sent by the bolshevik headquarters to bring order to an unstable situation on one of the Red Navy ships. She establishes her authority by calmly shooting two sailors who attempt to rape her. The sailors are split into three factions: anarchists, former czarist officers, and a small group of communists. Winning over the czarist group by appealing to their patriotism, and setting the anarchist leaders against each other, the commissar engineers the triumph of the bolshevik faction on the ship. She herself is accidentally killed at the end, which turns the optimistic outcome into a tragedy. Two one-man choruses comment periodically on the action, in the manner of classical Greek tragedy.

The Red Poppy (ballet), first performed 14 June 1927
Libretto: Mikhail Kurilko and Vasilii Tikhomirov

Tao-Hoa, a Chinese dancer, meets a Soviet captain whose ship has brought grain as a present from the Soviet trade unions. Tao-Hoa's manager plots with his European bosses against the Soviet captain, attempting to make Tao-Hoa hand him a cup of poisoned tea, which she refuses to do. The Manager shoots at the captain while trying to escape during an uprising of the people and Tao-Hoa, shielding the captain with her body, dies with the red poppy in her hands, a symbol of his love. (From Anatole Chujoy and P.W. Manchester, *The Dance Encyclopedia* [New York: Simon & Schuster, 1967], 757.)

Stenka Razin (drama), 1919, first performed 6 February 1924
Author: Vasilii Kamensky

Stenka Razin, who was a historical seventeenth-century rebel and river pirate, routs government troops in Central Russia. Attracting increasing popular support, he equips a fleet and sails the Caspian Sea as far as Persia, where he captures a princess who falls in love with him. When her presence causes discord among his men, he throws her into the water as a gift to the river Volga. He then sails up the river as far as Astrakhan, pirating, killing nobles, and looting churches and stores. But after bloody encounters, he is caught by the Ataman of the Don Cossacks and is sent to Moscow and executed. (Nancy V. N. Baer)

The Storm (or *Thunderstorm*) (drama), 1870, first performed
1 November 1871
Author: Alexander Ostrovsky

Trapped in a loveless marriage in a provincial town, the merchant's wife
Katerina is tyrannized by her brutal mother-in-law, Kabanikha ("Mrs. Wild
Boar"). During her husband's absence, she has a brief love affair with a
neighbor's nephew, Boris, a more cultivated man than the others in her milieu.
After the husband's return, a thunderstorm so terrifies Katerina that she
confesses her infidelity to Kabanikha. The cruel treatment she receives drives
Katerina to drown herself in the river Volga. The weak husband then accuses
his mother of murdering his wife.

Victory over the Sun (opera), first performed 5 December 1913
Libretto: Alexei Kruchenykh, with a prologue by Velimir Khlebnikov

The libretto of this "cubofuturist opera" is written in a neologistic
"transrational" or trans-sense language, its many invented words built on
existing Russian word stems. Influenced by Italian futurism, the text glorifies
speed, technology, and male strength. It is strongly misogynist; all references
to women are invariably hostile.

Propelled by their energy and the need to exercise their power, the
"Strongmen of the Futurity" capture and subjugate the sun. This causes an
airplane to fall out of the sky. The pilot lives, the only casualties being a bridge
and a woman, both of them crushed by the plane. The opera ends on a jubilant
note, with a paraphrase from Shakespeare that was cited in the beginning:
"All's Well that Begins Well and Has No End."

We (theatrical revue), 1920–1921, not produced
Author: Alexei Gan, after Evgenii Zamiatin

(Note: Zamiatin's anti-utopian novel, which inspired Aldous Huxley's *Brave
New World* and George Orwell's *1984*, was banned by the Soviet government.
It was translated into English and other languages in the 1920s and published
in the Soviet Union during *glasnost*.)

In the twenty-ninth century, people live in a utopian society, the Single State,
ruled by a dictator, the Benefactor. All aspects of everyone's life are regulated by
the ubiquitous police, the Guardians, who control work, leisure, and sex. Sex is
promiscuous but requires government-issued coupons to perform.

Names are replaced by four-digit numbers, a vowel followed by three
figures for women, a consonant plus the same for men. The mathematician
D-503, a docile citizen, falls in love with a rebellious woman, I-330. I-330 takes
D-503 beyond the Single State boundary, where people live in the open instead
of in transparent buildings and go naked instead of wearing identical, state-
issued uniforms. I-330 and her free-thinking friends are caught by the Guardians
and sent to the Machine of the Benefactor, an updated guillotine. D-503
voluntarily undergoes brain surgery, which restores his confidence in the
Benefactor and makes him revert to his old conformist ways.

Cat. no. 1
Nina Aizenberg
Costume design for a Cafe Girl,
Pianka-Durman, 1926

Exhibition Checklist

Objects have been organized by production
and are listed alphabetically by artist and
then chronologically by date. Dates of
objects are assumed to be the year of production except where noted. Dimensions
are given in centimeters, height preceding
width. Page numbers are given in brackets
for works illustrated. If not otherwise
indicated, works have been lent by the
Bakhrushin State Central Theatrical
Museum, Moscow. As in the catalogue
text, transliteration follows a modified
Library of Congress system except where
English-language usage dictates otherwise.
Examples are Vladimir Mayakovsky (not
Maiakovsky) and Vsevolod Meyerhold
(not Meierkhold). The city founded in
1703 as St. Petersburg was renamed
Petrograd in 1914, and Leningrad in 1924.
In the checklist, it is referred to by the
name it had at the time in question.

Nina Aizenberg
Moscow 1902–1974 Moscow

Pianka-Durman (Drunken Stupor)
(theatrical revue)
Premiere: 1926, Blue Blouse Theatre,
Moscow

1   Costume design for a Cafe Girl
Pencil and watercolor on paper,
36.1 × 25.2 cm [p. 191]

*A performance cycle based on the life
of Communist Youth Organization
Member Spichkin*
Authors: Vladimir Mass
and Ivan Verkhovtsev
Premiere: 1929, Blue Blouse Theatre,
Moscow

2   Costume design for a Woman
Pencil and gouache on paper,
33.2 × 23.2 cm

3   Costume design for Spichkin
Pencil and gouache on paper affixed to
wood veneer, 36.2 × 24.9 cm

Natan Altman
Vinnitsa 1889–1970 Leningrad

Uriel Acosta (drama)
Author: Karl Gutzkow
Director: Alexei Granovsky
Premiere: 1922, State Jewish Theatre
(GOSET), Moscow

4   Set design
Pencil, gouache, collage, and lacquer on
cardboard, 34.5 × 48 cm

5   Set design
Brush and india ink, collage, and lacquer
on cardboard, 45.6 × 51 cm

The Dybbuk (melodrama)
Author: S. An-sky [Solomon Rappoport],
translated by Haim Bialik
Director: Evgenii Vakhtangov
Premiere: 1922, Habimah Theatre,
Moscow

6   Costume design for the Hunchback
Pencil, watercolor, and white lead paint on
paper, 35.2 × 23 cm

7   Costume design for an Old Woman
Pencil, watercolor, and white lead paint on
paper, 36 × 22.6 cm

Yurii (Georges) Annenkov
Petropavlovst-on-Kamchatka
1889–1974 Paris

The Storming of the Winter Palace
(mass action)
Director: Nikolai Evreinov, with
Alexander Kugel, Konstantin Derzhavin,
Dmitrii Temkin, and Nikolai Petrov
Producer: Dmitrii Tenin
Music: Hugo Wahrlich
Premiere: 7 November 1920, Winter
Palace (formerly Uritsky) Square,
Petrograd

8   Set design
Watercolor, gouache, and pen and india
ink on paper, 24.9 × 27.5 cm

Tatiana Bruni
Born St. Petersburg 1902

Bolt (ballet)
Music: Dmitrii Shostakovich
Choreography: Fedor Lopukhov
Libretto: Viktor Smirnov
Premiere: 8 April 1931, State Academic
Theatre for Opera and Ballet, Leningrad
Note: The set designs for this ballet were
a collaborative effort of Tatiana Bruni
and her husband Georgii Korshikov
(1899–1944). *Bolt* was reconstructed in
Leningrad in 1979 with costumes and sets
remade after the original under Bruni's
supervision.

9   Set design, 1979 after 1931 original
Watercolor, pencil, white lead paint, and
gouache on paper affixed to plywood
veneer, 60.3 × 80.4 cm [p. 140]

10 Costume design for the Japanese Fleet, 1979 after 1931 original
Pencil, watercolor, foil, fabric, and collage on paper, 51.6 × 42.9 cm

11 Costume design for the Bureaucrat, 1979 after 1931 original
Pencil, watercolor, gouache, and collage on paper, 56.2 × 40.7 cm [p. 141]

Vladimir Dmitriev
Moscow 1900–1948 Moscow

Les Aubes (The Dawns) (tragedy)
Author: Emile Verhaeren,
translated by Georgii Chulkov
Directors: Vsevolod Meyerhold
and Valerii Bebutov
Premiere: 7 November 1920, RSFSR
(Russian Soviet Federated Socialist
Republic) Theatre No. 1, Moscow

12 Maquette
Wood, metal, fabric, thread,
cardboard, gouache, and silver paint,
35 × 51.5 × 40 cm [p. 154]

Sergei Eisenstein
Riga 1898–1948 Moscow

The Mexican (drama)
Author: Boris Arvatov,
adapted from Jack London
Directors: Valentin Smyshliaev
and Sergei Eisenstein
Premiere: 1921, First Workers' Theatre
of the Proletkult, Moscow

13 Set design
Pencil, watercolor, pen and india ink,
and brush and india ink on paper,
20.9 × 29.3 cm [p. 118]

Macbeth (tragedy)
Author: William Shakespeare
Director: Valentin Tikhonovich
Premiere: 1921, V. Polenov Theatre,
Moscow

14 Set design
Pencil, pen and india ink, and brush
and india ink on paper, 26 × 32.7 cm
Note: This design was a collaborative
effort of Sergei Eisenstein and
Sergei Yutkevich.

15 Costume design for Lady Macbeth
Pencil and watercolor on cardboard,
23.5 × 16.7 cm

16 Costume design for Duncan,
King of Scotland
Pencil, watercolor, and bronze and silver
paint on paper, 24.6 × 16.7 cm

17 Costume design for a Gatekeeper
Pencil, watercolor, silver paint, and white
lead paint on paper, 25.7 × 18.9 cm

Good Treatment for Horses
(theatrical revue)
Author: Vladimir Mass,
after a poem by Vladimir Mayakovsky
Director: Nikolai Foregger
Choreography: Nikolai Foregger
Premiere: January 1922, the Foregger
Workshop (MASTFOR), Moscow
Note: Sergei Yutkevich also designed
costumes for this production (see no. 210).

18 Costume design for Etoile
Pencil, watercolor, pen and india ink, and
brush and india ink on paper, 26.6 × 17 cm
[p. 119]

19 Costume design for a Woman
in the scene "Hands Up"
Pencil and watercolor on paper,
26.5 × 13.5 cm [p. 119]

20 Costume design for
the First Coquette
Pencil and watercolor on paper,
27.5 × 14.3 cm [p. 50]

21 Costume design for Gipsy-Pipsy
Pencil, watercolor, pen and india ink, and
brush and india ink on paper, 30 × 20 cm
[p. 51]

King Hunger (play)
Author: Leonid Andreyev
Director: Valentin Tikhonovich
Premiere: 1921, First Workers' Theatre
of the Proletkult, Moscow

22 Costume design for the Thief in act 2
Pencil and watercolor on paper,
24.2 × 13.4 cm

23 Costume design
for the Professor in act 3
Pencil, watercolor, and brush and india ink
on paper, 24 × 13.3 cm

24 Costume design
for the Chairman's Mistress
Pencil and watercolor on paper,
24 × 13.4 cm

25 Costume design for an Ex-Lawyer
Pencil, watercolor, and pen and india ink
on paper, 24 × 13.4 cm

Heartbreak House (fantasy)
Author: after George Bernard Shaw
Director: Vsevolod Meyerhold (?)
Premiere: 1922, Actor's Theatre, Moscow

26 Set design
Cloth, string, and collage on paper,
35 × 48.8 cm [p. 122]

Boris Erdman
Moscow 1899–1960 Moscow

Money Box (comedy)
Author: Eugène Labiche
Director: Boris Ferdinandov
Premiere: 1922, Experimental-Heroic
Theatre, Moscow

27 Costume design for three characters
Pencil, gouache, foil, and collage on paper,
59.7 × 46.3 cm

28 Costume design for three characters
Pencil, gouache, white lead paint, and
collage on paper affixed to cardboard,
66 × 50 cm

29 Costume design for two characters
Pencil, gouache, and collage on paper
affixed to cardboard, 66.4 × 51.5 cm

Joseph the Beautiful (ballet)
Music: Sergei Vasilenko
Choreography: Kasian Goleizovsky
Premiere: 3 March 1925, Experimental
Theatre (a Bolshoi affiliate), Moscow

30 Costume design
for an Egyptian dancer
Pencil, watercolor, and gouache on paper,
70 × 44.5 cm [p. 132]

31 Costume design for a Jewish dancer
Pencil, gouache, and brush and india ink
on paper, 70 × 44.5 cm [p. 133]

Electric Dances
Choreography: Nikolai Foregger
Premiere: 1923, the Foregger Workshop
(MASTFOR), Moscow

32 Dance sketch
Pencil, pen, and brush and india ink on
paper, 19.3 × 16.2 cm [p. 137]

Famira Kifared (Thamyris Kitharodos)
(classicistic tragedy)
Author: Innokentii Annensky
Music: Henri Fortier
Director: Alexander Tairov
Premiere: 2 November 1916,
Kamerny Theatre, Moscow

33 Dance sketch
Pencil, pen and india ink, and brush and
india ink on paper, 22 × 10.1 cm [p. 175]

Machine Dances
Choreography: Nikolai Foregger
Premiere: 1923, The Foregger Workshop
(MASTFOR), Moscow

34   Dance sketch
Pencil, pen and india ink, and brush and
india ink on paper, 22 × 18.4 cm [p. 208]

Unidentified production

35   Dance sketch, ca. 1923
Pencil, pen and india ink, and brush and
india ink on paper, 26.7 × 19 cm [p. 3]

Foxtrot Championship (dance)
Music: Yurii Yurgenson
Choreography: Kasian Goleizovsky
Premiere: 1923, Crooked Jimmy Theatre,
Moscow

36   Costume sketch
Pencil and brush and india ink on paper,
19.4 × 19.8 cm [p. 62]

37   D'Arto and Kasian Goleizovsky
Pencil and brush and india ink on paper,
18.3 × 17.4 cm [p. 137]

Eccentric Dances: Foxtrot
Music: Yurii Milutin
Choreography: Kasian Goleizovsky
Producing organization: Chamber Ballet
Premiere: 1923, Moscow

38   Costume sketch, 1922
Pencil and pen and india ink on paper,
23.2 × 20.6 cm

Spanish Dances
Music: Isaac Albéniz
and Enrique Granados
Choreography: Kasian Goleizovsky
Producing organization: Chamber Ballet
Premiere: 1923, Moscow

39   Costume design for a female dancer
Pencil and brush and india ink on paper,
28.3 × 21 cm

40   Costume sketch
Pencil, pen and india ink, and brush and
india ink on paper, 21.8 × 19.7 cm [p. 23]

Alexandra Exter
Belostok, near Kiev 1882–1949
Fontenay-aux-Roses, near Paris

41   Curtain and portal design for
the Kamerny Theatre, Moscow, 1916
Pencil, watercolor, ink, white lead paint,
and bronze and silver paint on paper,
52.7 × 74.2 cm [p. 88]

Famira Kifared (Thamyris Kitharodos)
(classicistic tragedy)
Author: Innokentii Annensky
Music: Henri Fortier
Director: Alexander Tairov
Premiere: 2 November 1916,
Kamerny Theatre, Moscow

42   Poster design
Pencil and gouache on cardboard,
99.5 × 69.3 cm [p. 30]

43   Maquette, 1987 reconstruction
after 1916 original
Wood, cardboard, fabric, and gouache,
58.7 × 85 × 49.3 cm [p. 42]

44   Frieze composition
Pencil, watercolor, gouache, brush and
india ink, and bronze and silver paint on
paper, 360 × 78 cm [p. 32]

45   Costume design for a Bacchante
Pencil, gouache, brush and india ink, and
bronze paint on paper, 44.5 × 31.3 cm
[p. 31]

46   Costume design for a Satyr
Gouache and brush and india ink on paper
affixed to cardboard, 50.3 × 42.5 cm

Salomé (tragedy)
Author: Oscar Wilde,
translated by Konstantin Balmont
Director: Alexander Tairov
Music: Josef Hüttel
Choreography: Mikhail Mordkin
Premiere: 9 October 1917,
Kamerny Theatre, Moscow

47   Set design for opening scene
with Jokanaan and Salomé
Pencil, brush and india ink, gouache, and
silver paint on paper, 26.6 × 35.2 cm
[p. 43]

48   Set design for death scene and finale
Pencil and gouache on paper,
22.8 × 30.8 cm [p. 89]

49   Costume design for Three Slaves
Pencil, gouache, and bronze paint on
cardboard, 68.1 × 52 cm [p. 107]

50   Costume design for Salomé
Gouache and bronze paint on cardboard,
67 × 52.3 cm [p. 108]

51   Costume design
for a Girl with a Vase
Gouache and bronze paint on cardboard,
67 × 52.3 cm

52   Costume design for Two Jews
Pencil and gouache on cardboard,
68 × 52.4 cm [p. 109]

53   Costume design for Herodias
Gouache and bronze paint on cardboard,
71.5 × 55.5 cm [p. 60]

54   Costume design for Herod
Gouache and silver paint on cardboard,
67.5 × 43.4 cm

55   Maquette, 1987 reconstruction
after 1917 original
Wood, cardboard, fabric, Plexiglas, metal,
and gouache, 51 × 64 × 34 cm

Romeo and Juliet (tragedy)
Author: William Shakespeare
Director: Alexander Tairov
Premiere: 17 May 1921, Kamerny Theatre,
Moscow

56   Curtain design
Pencil, gouache, and silver paint on
cardboard, 43.5 × 58 cm [p. 148]

57   Curtain design for act 1
Pencil, gouache, and silver paint on paper
affixed to cardboard, 43.5 × 58 cm

58   Detail of set design
Gouache, pencil, and silver paint on
cardboard, 46.6 × 32 cm

59   Set design for a square in Verona
Pencil, gouache, and bronze paint on
paper, 26 × 36.2 cm

60   Set design for a square in Verona
Pencil and gouache on paper, 23 × 36.7 cm
[p. 45]

61   Costume design
for the Second Musician
Gouache and bronze and silver paint on
cardboard, 50.2 × 35.6 cm

62   Costume design
for the First Woman's Mask
Pencil, gouache, and bronze paint
on cardboard, 54.5 × 35.1 cm [p. 150]

63   Costume design
for the Second Woman's Mask
Gouache and bronze paint on cardboard,
51.6 × 35.7 cm

64   Costume design
for the Fourth Woman's Mask
Gouache on cardboard, 49.9 × 32.4 cm
[p. 151]

65   Costume design
for a Woman at the Ball
Gouache, bronze paint, and collage on
cardboard, 50.9 × 36.3 cm

66   Costume design for Tybalt
Pencil, gouache, and bronze and silver
paint on cardboard, 54.8 × 34.8 cm
Verso: Abstract composition, 1920–1921
Pencil and gouache on cardboard

67   Costume design
for the Servant Gregory
Gouache and silver paint on cardboard,
55 × 35.8 cm

Satanic Ballet
Music: Alexander Scriabin
Choreography: Kasian Goleizovsky
Note: This production was not realized.

68   Sketch of stage construction, 1922
Pencil and gouache on paper,
48.7 × 55.1 cm [p. 128]

Unidentified production

69   Costume design for a man, 1920
Gouache on cardboard, 48.2 × 35.7 cm
[p. 4]

Spanish Dance
Choreography: Mikhail Mordkin
Premiere: 1920, Kiev

70   Costume design for a female dancer
Gouache and lacquer on cardboard,
49.2 × 34.7 cm

Vasilii Fedorov
Moscow 1891–1917 Moscow

The Forest (comedy)
Author: Alexander Ostrovsky
Director: Vsevolod Meyerhold
Premiere: 19 January 1924,
Meyerhold Theatre (GosTIM), Moscow

71   Costume design for
Madame Gurmyzhsky, 1923
Pencil on paper, 35.7 × 22.5 cm

72   Costume design for
Madame Gurmyzhsky, 1923
Gouache and lacquer on paper,
35.1 × 24.6 cm

73   Costume design for Bulanov, 1923
Pencil on paper, 35.8 × 22.3 cm

Boris Ferdinandov
1889–1959

The Storm (drama)
Author: Alexander Ostrovsky
Director: Boris Ferdinandov
Premiere: 1922, Experimental-Heroic
Theatre, Moscow

74   Costume design for Katerina
Gouache, cardboard, collage, and lacquer
relief on cardboard affixed to plywood,
37.5 × 24 cm

75   Costume design
for Madame Kabanova
Gouache, collage, and lacquer relief
on cardboard affixed to plywood,
36.5 × 23.2 cm

76   Costume design for a Noblewoman
Gouache, collage, and lacquer relief
on cardboard affixed to plywood,
38.5 × 24.7 cm

King Harlequin (pantomime)
Author: after Rudolf Lothar's
Fool on the Throne
Director: Alexander Tairov
Music: Henri Fortier
Premiere: 29 November 1917,
Kamerny Theatre, Moscow

77   Set design
Tempera on plywood, 28.9 × 39.5 cm

78   Costume design for a Clergyman
Pencil and gouache on cardboard,
35.5 × 27 cm

79   Costume design
for a Man with an Oar
Pencil and gouache on cardboard,
34 × 26.2 cm

Filonov School
(Collective of Masters of Analytic Art)

Rebekka Leviton
Kharkov 1906–1987 Leningrad

The Inspector General (comedy)
Author: Nikolai Gogol
Director: Igor Terentiev
Music: Vladimir Kashnitsky
Premiere: 9 April 1927,
Theatre of the Press House, Leningrad

80   Set design for act 3
Pencil, watercolor, and gouache on paper,
31 × 37.3 cm [p. 24]

81   Costume design for the Mayor's Wife
Pencil and gouache on paper,
41.4 × 26.3 cm

82   Costume design for the Servant Osip
Pencil and watercolor on paper,
46.5 × 29 cm

Filonov School
(Collective of Masters of Analytic Art)

Artur Liandsberg
Velikie Luki 1905–1963 Leningrad

The Inspector General (comedy)
Author: Nikolai Gogol
Director: Igor Terentiev
Music: Vladimir Kashnitsky
Premiere: 9 April 1927,
Theatre of the Press House, Leningrad

83   Set design
Watercolor and gouache on cardboard,
51 × 68.5 cm
Leningrad Museum of Theatrical
and Musical Arts

Nikolai Foregger
(b. Nikolai Greifenturn)
Moscow 1892–1939 Kuibyshev

84   Costume design for
a Man in a Tatar Dance, early 1920s
Pencil, watercolor, pen and india ink,
brush and india ink, and lacquer on paper,
21.2 × 25.5 cm

85   Costume design for the dance
number "Hesitation," early 1924
Pencil on tracing paper with gauze
backing, 27.5 × 20.5 cm

86   Uniform and logo design for
the Foregger Workshop (MASTFOR),
1922–1923
Color pencil and gouache on paper,
34 × 40.5 cm [p. 119]

Pyotr Galadzhev
Staryi Krym 1900–1971 Moscow

Fantasy (dance)
Music: Alexander Scriabin
Choreography: Kasian Goleizovsky
Producing organization: Chamber Ballet
Premiere: 1922, Moscow

87   Costume design for Riki-Bak
Pencil and watercolor on paper,
20 × 12.5 cm
Central Cinema Museum, Moscow

Sketches for Lukin Ballet Studio, Moscow,
1921–1922

88   Costume design for a female dancer
Pencil, gouache, and collage on paper,
21.6 × 15.3 cm
Central Cinema Museum, Moscow

89   Costume design for a female dancer
Pencil and watercolor on paper,
21.1 × 11.7 cm
Central Cinema Museum, Moscow

90   Costume design for a female dancer
Pencil, gouache, and collage on paper,
21.5 × 14.9 cm
Central Cinema Museum, Moscow

91   Costume design for a male dancer
Pencil and watercolor on cardboard,
24 × 14.1 cm
Central Cinema Museum, Moscow

92 Costume design for a male dancer
Pencil and watercolor on paper,
20 × 13.4 cm
Central Cinema Museum, Moscow

93 Costume design for a female dancer
Pencil, watercolor, and pen and india ink
on paper, 20.1 × 12.2 cm
Central Cinema Museum, Moscow

94 Costume design for
a female dancer in a mazurka
Pencil and watercolor on paper,
20.6 × 13.7 cm
Central Cinema Museum, Moscow

Kasian Goleizovsky
Moscow 1892–1970 Moscow

The Tragedy of the Masks (ballet)
Music: Boris Beer
Choreography: Kasian Goleizovsky
Producing organization: Chamber Ballet
Premiere: 1922, Moscow
Note: Nikolai Musatov (b. 1895) also
created designs for this production.

95 Costume design for Harlequin
Pencil, watercolor, white lead paint, and
gouache on paper, 47.5 × 35.6 cm [p. 156]

Valentina Khodasevich
Moscow 1894–1970 Moscow

Archangel Michael (play)
Author: Nadezhda Bromlei
Directors: Boris Sushkevich
and Nadezhda Bromlei
Premiere: 1922, First Studio of the
Moscow Art Theatre, Moscow

96 Design for stage construction, 1922
Pencil, watercolor, gouache, bronze and
silver paint, and collage on paper affixed
to cardboard, 24.4 × 36.6 cm [p. 69]

97 Detail of set design, 1922
Pencil, gouache, silver paint, collage, and
lacquer on cardboard, 22.7 × 30.7 cm

98 Costume design for Lucille, 1922
Pencil, watercolor, brush and india ink,
bronze paint, and collage on tracing paper,
68.6 × 43.3 cm [p. 71]

99 Costume design for a Man, 1922
Pencil, brush and india ink, white lead
paint, bronze paint, and collage on paper,
63.5 × 45 cm [p. 70]

Alexander Khostenko-Khostov
(also known as Alexander Khostov-
Khostenko)
Borisovka, Ukraine 1895–1968 Kiev

Mystery-Bouffe (parody of
a medieval mystery play)
Author: Vladimir Mayakovsky
Director: Grigory Avlov
Premiere: 1921, Heroic Theatre, Kharkov

100 Curtain design
Pencil, watercolor, gouache, and collage
on cardboard, 57.7 × 78.5 cm [p. 20]

The Love for Three Oranges (opera)
Libretto: Sergei Prokofiev,
after Carlo Gozzi
Music: Sergei Prokofiev
Director: Ivan Lapitsky
Note: This production was prepared,
but not produced, by the State Opera
Company, Kharkov, for the 1926–1927
season of the Berezil Theatre.

101 Costume design for
the Magician Celio, 1926
Pencil, gouache, watercolor, brush and
india ink, and collage on paper affixed
to cardboard, 40.8 × 34.6 cm
State Museum of Theatre, Music,
and Film Art of the Ukraine, Kiev

Jonny spielt auf (Johnny Strikes Up)
(opera)
Libretto: Ernst Křenek
Music: Ernst Křenek
Director: Mikhail Diskovsky
Premiere: 1929, State Opera, Kiev

102 Set design for a Hotel
Pen and india ink, brush and india ink,
and collage on graph paper, 77.7 × 54 cm
Central State Archive of Literature and Art
(TsGALI), Moscow

Die Walküre (opera)
Libretto: Richard Wagner
Music: Richard Wagner
Director: Feodor Lopatinsky
Note: This production, planned for a 1929
premiere at the State Opera, Kiev, was
not realized.

103 Crescendo of movable
colored constructions, 1929
Pencil, color pencil, gouache, and collage
on paper, 50 × 60 cm
Collection Igor Dychenko, Kiev

The Red Poppy (ballet)
Music: Reinhold Gliere
Choreography: Mikhail Dyskovsky
Libretto: Mikhail Kurilko
and Vasilii Tikhomirov
Premiere: 1929, State Opera, Kiev

104 Costume design for Tao-Hoa, 1928
Pencil, watercolor, gouache, and bronze
paint on paper, 34 × 34.5 cm
State Museum of Theatre, Music,
and Film Art of the Ukraine, Kiev

Viktor Kiselev
Moscow 1895–1984 Moscow

Mystery-Bouffe (parody of
a medieval mystery play)
Author: Vladimir Mayakovsky
Director: Vsevolod Meyerhold
Music: compiled by Alexander Orlov
Premiere: 1 May 1921, RSFSR (Russian
Soviet Federated Socialist Republic)
Theatre No. 1, Moscow
Note: *Mystery-Bouffe* was first staged by
Meyerhold on 7 November 1918 at the
Communal Theatre of Musical Drama
in Petrograd. The play was rewritten by
Mayakovsky in 1921 to make it relevant
to events that had taken place in the
intervening three years. The 1921
production was designed by Viktor
Kiselev, Vladimir Khrakovsky, and Anton
Lavinsky (see nos. 106–107).

105 Costume design for Clemenceau
Pencil, watercolor, brush and india ink,
white lead paint, and collage on paper,
29.4 × 22.3 cm

Anton Lavinsky
Sochi 1893–1968 Moscow

Mystery-Bouffe (parody of
a medieval mystery play)
Author: Vladimir Mayakovsky
Director: Vsevolod Meyerhold
Premiere: 1 May 1921, RSFSR (Russian
Soviet Federated Socialist Republic)
Theatre No. 1, Moscow
Note: See note for previous entry.

106 Set design
Pencil, water[c]olor, and white lead paint
on pape[r,] 75 cm [p. 46]

107 [Co]stume design for an Angel, 1921
P[encil a]nd watercolor on paper,
[...] × 19.7 cm [p. 46]

Aristarkh Lentulov
Vorona, near Penza, 1882–1943 Moscow

The Demon (opera)
Libretto: after Mikhail Lermontov
Music: Anton Rubinstein
Director: Alexander Tairov
Premiere: 1919, Theatre of Moscow Union
of Workers and Peasant Deputies, Moscow

108 Maquette
Wood, cardboard, paper, fabric,
and bronze and silver paint,
60.5 × 106.5 × 36.4 cm

109 Costume design for the Demon
Gouache, charcoal, and bronze paint on
paper, 53.5 × 37 cm [p. 19]

110 Costume design for Gudal
Pencil, gouache, and bronze and silver
paint on paper affixed to paper,
55.5 × 37.5 cm

111 Costume design for Tamara
Gouache and silver paint on paper affixed
to cardboard, 54 × 40 cm

El Lissitzky
(Lazar Lisitsky)
Polshchinok, near Smolensk
1890–1941 Moscow

I Want a Child (play)
Author: Sergei Tretiakov
Director: Vsevolod Meyerhold
Note: This production, planned for a
1928 premiere at the Meyerhold Theatre
(GosTIM), Moscow, was not realized.
Lissitzky worked on his designs from 1928
to 1930.

112 Maquette of stage and auditorium
(reconstructed by N. Kustov), n.d.
Wood, fabric, and metal,
68 × 147 × 72.5 cm [p. 75]

Kazimir Malevich
Kiev 1878–1935 Leningrad

Victory over the Sun (opera)
Libretto: Alexei Kruchenykh, with a
prologue by Velimir Khlebnikov
Music: Mikhail Matiushin
Premiere: 5 December 1913,
Luna Park Theatre, St. Petersburg

113 Costume design for
the Attentive Worker
Pencil, brush and india ink, and gouache
on paper, 27.2 × 21.2 cm [p. 39]
Leningrad State Museum of Theatrical
and Musical Arts

114 Costume design for the Enemy
Pencil, watercolor, and brush and india ink
on paper, 27.1 × 21.3 cm [p. 96]
Leningrad State Museum of Theatrical
and Musical Arts

115 Set design for act 2, scene 5
Pencil on paper, 21 × 27 cm [p. 40]
Leningrad State Museum of Theatrical
and Musical Arts

Ivan Maliutin
Tultchino Village, Tula Province
1889–1932 Moscow

116 Maquette for car of agitprop
train, reconstructed (n.d.) after early
1920s original
Wood, fabric, glass, cardboard, and metal,
20.5 × 66.5 × 61.5 cm

Vadim Meller
St. Petersburg 1884–1962 Kiev

Assyrian Dances
Music: Anton Arensky (?)
Choreography: Bronislava Nijinska
Producing organization: Bronislava
Nijinska Choreographic Studio
Premiere: 1919, State Opera, Kiev

117 Costume design
Gouache on cardboard, 59.5 × 32 cm
Collection Igor Dychenko, Kiev

Mephisto (dance)
Music: Franz Liszt, arranged
by Karl Müller-Berghaus
Choreography: Bronislava Nijinska
Producing organization: Bronislava
Nijinska Choreographic Studio
Premiere: 1920, State Opera, Kiev
Note: *Mephisto* was an expanded version
of *Mephisto Valse*, a solo dance
choreographed and performed by
Nijinska in 1919.

118 Costume design for the Blue Dancer
Watercolor and gouache on paper affixed
to cardboard, 54 × 40 cm [p. 34]
Collection Brigitta Vetrova, Kiev

The City (dance)
Music: Sergei Prokofiev
Choreography: Bronislava Nijinska
Producing organization: Bronislava
Nijinska Choreographic Studio
Premiere: 1921, State Opera, Kiev

Costume design for a Male Dancer
watercolor, and gouache on
card, 55.9 × 41 cm [p. 53]

Gas (drama)
Author: Georg Kaiser
Director: Les Kurbas
Premiere: 1923, Berezil Theatre, Kiev

120 Costume design for an Engineer
Pencil, watercolor, gouache, pen and india
ink, and brush and india ink on paper
affixed to cardboard, 49.6 × 24.4 cm

Ignatii Nivinsky
Moscow 1881–1933 Moscow

Princess Turandot (comedy)
Author: after Carlo Gozzi
Director: Evgenii Vakhtangov
Premiere: 28 February 1922, Third Studio
of the Moscow Art Theatre (also called
Vakhtangov Studio), Moscow

121 Maquette, 1921
Wood, cardboard, fabric, thread,
watercolor, and gouache,
45 × 70 × 42.5 cm

122 Set design, 1921
Watercolor, gouache, silver paint, and
collage on cardboard, 37 × 50 cm [p. 81]

123 Costume design for Brighella, 1921
Pencil, watercolor, and gouache on paper,
44 × 34.8 cm [p. 80]

124 Costume design for
Prince Calaf, 1921
Pencil, watercolor, gouache, bronze paint,
and collage on paper, 44 × 35.4 cm [p. 80]

Anatolii Petritsky
Kiev 1895–1964 Kiev

Eccentric Dances: Jazz Band
Music: Matvei Blanter, Yurii Milutin,
Dmitrii Pokrass, and Isaak Dunaevsky
Choreography: Kasian Goleizovsky
Premiere: 1923, State Choreographic
School, Moscow

125 Costume design
Gouache and brush and india ink
on paper, 61.5 × 49.5 cm
Collection Anatolii A. Petritsky, Moscow

126 Costume design
Gouache, and brush and india ink
on paper, 61.5 × 49.5 cm
Collection Anatolii A. Petritsky, Moscow

Nur and Anitra (ballet)
Music: Alexander Ilyinsky
Choreography: Mikhail Mordkin
Note: This version of the ballet was
rehearsed but not produced.

127   Costume design for
a female dancer, 1923
Pencil, gouache, and collage on paper
affixed to paper, 53.5 × 35 cm

128   Costume design for a Warrior, 1923
Pencil, gouache, and watercolor on paper
affixed to cardboard, 56.3 × 40.5 cm
Collection Igor Dychenko, Kiev

William Tell (opera)
Libretto: after Friedrich Schiller
Music: Gioacchino Rossini
Director: Vladimir Manzyi
Choreography: Igor Moiseyev
Premiere: 1927, Theatre of Opera
and Ballet, Kharkov

129   Costume design for a Woman
Pencil, watercolor, and collage on paper,
66.1 × 49.2 cm [p. 55]

130   Costume design for a Knight
Gouache, watercolor, brush and india ink,
and collage on paper, 64.8 × 49 cm

The Football Player (ballet)
Music: Viktor Oransky
Choreography: Nikolai Foregger
Libretto: V. N. Kurdiumov (?)
Premiere: 1930, Theatre of Opera
and Ballet, Kharkov

131   Costume design for Tennis Players
Pencil, color pencil, brush and india
ink, and white lead paint on paper,
71.1 × 66 cm [p. 142]

132   Costume design for Runners
Pencil and gouache on paper,
71.3 × 55.8 cm

Liubov Popova
Ivanovskoe, near Moscow
1889–1924 Moscow

Romeo and Juliet (tragedy)
Author: William Shakespeare
Director: Alexander Tairov
Note: This production, scheduled for a
1920 premiere at the Kamerny Theatre,
Moscow, was not realized. It was produced the following year with sets and
costumes designed by Alexandra Exter
(see nos. 56–67).

133   Design for the garden
in front of the house, 1920
Pencil and gouache on cardboard,
23.2 × 35 cm [p. 44]
Private collection, Moscow

134   Costume design for
a Servant with a Tray, 1920
Pencil, gouache, and brush and india ink
on paper, 35.5 × 27 cm
Private collection, Moscow

The Locksmith and the Chancellor
(drama)
Author: Anatolii Lunacharsky
Director: Andrei Petrovsky
Premiere: 1921, Comedy Theatre
(formerly the Korsh Theatre), Moscow

135   Set design for the study, 1920
Gouache and brush and india ink
on paper, 46 × 37.2 cm [p. 77]
Private collection, Moscow

The Struggle and Victory of the Soviets
(mass festival)
Author: Ivan Aksionov
Director: Vsevolod Meyerhold
Note: This project, scheduled to coincide
with the Congress of the Third International in spring 1921, was not realized.

136   Set design for the mass festival
The Struggle and Victory of the Soviets
on the occasion of the Congress of the
Third International, Khodinskoe Field,
Moscow, 1921
Pen, drafting instruments, and india ink
on paper, 46.7 × 62.5 cm [p. 74]
State Tretiakov Gallery, Moscow
Note: This design was a collaborative
effort of Liubov Popova and
Alexander Vesnin.

137   Work uniform (*prozodezhda*)
design for Actor No. 3, the Free Studio
of Vsevolod Meyerhold at the State Higher
Theatre Workshop (GVYTM), Moscow,
1921
Gouache, brush and india ink, pen and
india ink, collage, and lacquer on paper,
33 × 25.3 cm [p. 144]
State Tretiakov Gallery, Moscow
Note: Popova's work uniform was worn
for rehearsals and demonstrations at
GVYTM.

The Magnanimous Cuckold (comedy)
Author: Fernand Crommelynck
Director: Vsevolod Meyerhold
Premiere: 25 April 1922, Actor's Theatre,
Moscow

138   Maquette (n.d.), reconstruction
after 1922 original
Wood, metal, and gouache,
75 × 135 × 61.5 cm [p. 146]

139   Design for construction
Pencil, watercolor, and pen and ink on
paper, 54.7 × 45.4 cm [p. 147]

140   Prop design for a geranium in a pot
Pencil and colored pencil on paper,
35.5 × 29.6 cm [p. 153]

141   Work uniform
(*prozodezhda*) design
Pencil on paper, 32.5 × 24.1 cm [p. 92]
Note: The concept of an actor's work
uniform was conceived by Popova prior to
The Magnanimous Cuckold (see no. 137).

142   Work uniform
(*prozodezhda*) design
Pencil and colored pencil on paper,
37.2 × 22.4 cm [p. 92]

143   Engineering schematic
after original construction, 1930
Pen and ink on tracing paper with gauze
backing, 53.7 × 72.3 cm

Earth in Turmoil (also called
Earth on End) (agit-play)
Author: Sergei Tretiakov, after *La Nuit*
(The Night) by Marcel Martinet
Director: Vsevolod Meyerhold
Premiere: 4 March 1923, Meyerhold
Theatre (GosTIM), Moscow
Note: This production was originally to
have marked the fifth anniversary in 1922
of the October Revolution.

144   Schematic for
stage construction, 1923
Pencil on paper, 22.7 × 26.8 cm

Isaak Rabinovich
Kiev 1894–1961 Moscow

Salomé (tragedy)
Author: Oscar Wilde
Director: Konstantin Mardzhanov
Premiere: 1919, Lenin First State Dramatic
Theatre of the Ukrainian Soviet Socialist
Republic (formerly the Solovtsov Theatre),
Kiev

145   Costume design for Salomé
Pencil, watercolor, gouache, bronze paint,
and tempera on paper affixed to paper,
68.1 × 50 cm

146   Costume design for a Sadducee
Pencil, gouache, watercolor, and tempera
on paper affixed to paper, 68.1 × 49.7 cm

The Inspector General (comedy)
Author: Nikolai Gogol
Note: This production, scheduled for a 1920 premiere at the Korsh Theatre, Moscow, was not realized.

147 Costume designs for the Police Chief and a Policeman, 1920
Pencil, gouache, and silver paint on paper, 50 × 67.5 cm [p. 26]

148 Costume design for the Mayor, 1920
Pencil, gouache, and silver paint on paper affixed to cardboard, 50 × 68.1 cm [p. 26

Don Carlos (drama)
Author: Friedrich Schiller
Director: V. Sokhnovsky
Premiere: 1922, Comedy Theatre (formerly the Korsh Theatre), Moscow

149 Set design, 1922
Tempera and lacquer on cardboard, 23.7 × 19.8 cm

Lysistrata
Author: Aristophanes
Director: Vladimir Nemirovich-Danchenko
Premiere: 1923, Music Studio of the Moscow Art Theatre, Moscow

150 Maquette (n.d.), reconstruction after 1923 original
Wood and white lead paint, 53 × 53 × 26.5 cm

Alexander Rodchenko
St. Petersburg 1891–1956 Moscow

We (theatrical revue)
Author: Alexei Gan, after Evgenii Zamiatin
Director: Sergei Eisenstein
Note: This play, scheduled for a 1920 premiere at the Proletkult Studio, Moscow, was not produced. Evgenii Zamiatin's anti-utopian novel (which inspired both Aldous Huxley's *Brave New World* and George Orwell's *1984*) was banned by the Soviet government.

151 Costume design for a Soldier, 1919
Tempera and pen and india ink on cardboard, 52.7 × 36.6 cm

152 Costume design for a Worker, 1919
Tempera and white lead paint on cardboard, 52.3 × 36.5 cm [p. 12]

153 Costume design for a Peasant, 1919
Tempera, white lead paint, and pen and india ink on cardboard, 53 × 36.5 cm

154 Costume design for a Clown, 1920
Pencil and gouache on paper, 53.2 × 36.6 cm [p. 17]

The Bedbug (comedy)
Author: Vladimir Mayakovsky
Director: Vsevolod Meyerhold
Music: Dmitrii Shostakovich
Premiere: 13 February 1929, Meyerhold Theatre (GosTIM), Moscow
Note: The Bedbug was divided into two parts: "Part One: The Present," was designed by the Kukryniksy (collective name for the artists Mikhail *Ku*priianov, Porfirii *Kry*lov, *Ni*kolai Fokolov). Alexander Rodchenko created the designs for "Part Two: The Future," set in 1979.

155 Set design for "Part Two: The Future"
Watercolor, pen and india ink, brush and india ink, white lead paint, and lacquer on paper affixed to cardboard, 25.8 × 21.6 cm

156 Costume design
White lead paint, collage, pencil, colored pencil, pen and india ink, and brush and india ink on black paper affixed to cardboard, 41.8 × 29.7 cm [p. 57]

157 Costume design
Pastel, pencil, colored pencil, pen and india ink, and brush and india ink on black paper affixed to cardboard, 42 × 29.8 cm [p. 57]

One-Sixth of the World (theatrical revue)
Authors: Alexander Yarkov and Nikolai Ravich
Director: Nikolai Gorchakov
Music: Viktor Oransky
Choreography: Kasian Goleizovsky
Premiere: 22 February 1931, Music Hall, Moscow

158 Costume design for a Telephone Operator
Pencil, colored pencil, pen and india ink, and collage on paper, 31 × 21.5 cm
Rodchenko-Stepanova Archives, Moscow

159 Costume design for a Newspaper Girl
Pencil, gouache, and pen and india ink on paper affixed to cardboard, 30.5 × 22.3 cm
Rodchenko-Stepanova Archives, Moscow

160 Advertisement for a Vocalist Workshop
Pencil, gouache, and pen and india ink on paper, 31 × 22.8 cm
Rodchenko-Stepanova Archives, Moscow

161 Costume design for Uncle Sam on Stilts
Pencil, gouache, and pen and india ink on paper, 32 × 22.5 cm
Rodchenko-Stepanova Archives, Moscow

162 Costume design for an American Girl advertising coil springs
Pencil, gouache, and brush and india ink on paper, 32 × 22.3 cm
Rodchenko-Stepanova Archives, Moscow

Vadim Ryndin
Moscow 1902–1974 Moscow

An Optimistic Tragedy (drama)
Author: Vsevolod Vishnevsky
Director: Alexander Tairov
Premiere: 18 December 1933, Kamerny Theatre, Moscow

163 Design for stage construction
Pastel on paper, 68.3 × 92 cm [p. 176]

Georgii Stenberg
Moscow 1900–1933 Moscow

Phèdre (tragedy)
Author: Jean Racine, translated into Russian by Valerii Briusov
Director: Alexander Tairov
Premiere: 8 February 1922, Kamerny Theatre, Moscow
Note: This production, with designs by Alexander Vesnin (see nos. 194–197), was presented in Berlin (Deutsches Theatre) and Paris (Théâtre des Champs-Elysées) in February and March 1923.

164 Alisa Koonen as Phèdre, 1923
Pencil on paper, 47.4 × 32 cm

165 Nikolai Tseretelli as Hippolytus, 1923
Pencil on paper, 45.5 × 30 cm

Vladimir Stenberg
Moscow 1899–1982 Moscow

Georgii Stenberg
Moscow 1900–1933 Moscow

Day and Night (operetta)
Music: Charles Lecocq
Director: Alexander Tairov
Choreographer: Natalia Glan
Premiere: 18 December 1926, Kamerny Theatre, Moscow

166 Costume design for a Newspaper Man
Pencil and collage on paper, 36.7 × 14.5 cm

167 Costume design for a Girl
Pencil, colored pencil, and gouache on paper, 34.8 × 19.5 cm

168 Costume design for a Man
Pencil, colored pencil, and gouache
on paper, 34.8 × 18.7 cm [p. 121]

169 Costume design for a Man
Pencil, colored pencil, watercolor,
gouache, brush and india ink, and collage
on paper, 34.8 × 18.8 cm [p. 114]

The Hairy Ape (drama)
Author: Eugene O'Neill
Director: Alexander Tairov
Premiere: 14 January 1926,
Kamerny Theatre, Moscow

170 Set design
Gouache and silver paint on paper affixed
to cardboard, 58.2 × 78.2 cm [p. 126]

The Beggar's Opera (ballad opera)
Author: Bertolt Brecht, after John Gay
Music: Kurt Weill
Director: Alexander Tairov
Premiere: 24 January 1930,
Kamerny Theatre, Moscow
Note: In 1930, Tairov saw the Brecht-Weill
Die Dreigroschenoper (The Three-Penny
Opera) in Berlin. That same year he staged
The Beggar's Opera, his version of the play
named after the eighteenth-century
original by John Gay.

171 Set design
Pencil and gouache on cardboard,
58.5 × 78.5 cm [p. 125]

Varvara Stepanova
Kovno [Kaunas], Lithuania
1894–1958 Moscow

The Death of Tarelkin (satirical comedy)
Author: Alexander Sukhovo-Kobylin
Director: Vsevolod Meyerhold
Premiere: 24 November 1922, Meyerhold
Studio, State Institute of Theatrical Art
(GITIS), Moscow

172 Costume design for a Doctor
Watercolor, pen and colored ink, and brush
and colored ink on paper, 34.6 × 35.6 cm
[p. 94]

173 Costume design for Tarelkin
Watercolor, pen and colored ink, and brush
and colored ink on paper, 34.5 × 35.4 cm
[p. 79]

174 Costume design for Varravin
Watercolor, pen and india ink, and brush
and india ink on paper, 34.8 × 35.6 cm
[p. 94]

175 Costume design for
Raspliuev, Chief of Police
Watercolor, white lead paint, and pen and
india ink on paper, 34.6 × 35.5 cm [p. 79]

176 Costume design for Polutatarinov
Watercolor, pen and india ink, and brush
and india ink on paper, 34.9 × 35.8 cm
[p. 94]

Vladimir Tatlin
Moscow 1885–1953 Moscow

The Flying Dutchman (opera)
Music: Richard Wagner,
after Heinrich Heine
Libretto: Richard Wagner
Note: This production was not realized.
Tatlin worked on his designs from
1915 to 1918.

177 Design for a Ship, 1915–1918
Oil on canvas, 87 × 156 cm [p. 86]

178 Design for a Mast, 1915–1918
Colored pencil on tracing paper, 73 × 51 cm
[p. 86]

179 Costume design for
a Helmsman, 1915–1918
Pencil, watercolor, and gouache on
cardboard, 63.8 × 47.9 cm

180 Costume design for
a Helmsman, 1915–1918
Pencil on paper, 76 × 50.8 cm

181 Costume design for
a Woman, 1915–1918
Pencil and watercolor on paper,
70 × 50 cm

Zangezi
Author: after a poem by Velimir
Khlebnikov, adapted and realized
by Vladimir Tatlin
Premiere: 1923, Experimental Theatre of
the Museum of Artistic Culture, Petrograd
Note: Tatlin also played the principal role
in this production.

182 Set design
Charcoal on paper, 72.2 × 106.8 cm

183 Costume design for Grief
Charcoal on paper affixed to cardboard,
54.6 × 37.6 cm [p. 87]

184 Costume design for Laughter
Charcoal on paper affixed to cardboard,
54.6 × 37.6 cm [p. 87]

A Comic Actor of the 17th Century (play)
Author: Alexander Ostrovsky
Directors: A. Gurov and P. D. Ermilov
Premiere: 1935, Second Studio of the
Moscow Art Theatre, Moscow

185 Set design
Pencil on graph paper, 30 × 22 cm

186 Costume design
for Drunken Klushin
Pencil and watercolor on graph paper,
43.9 × 29.4 cm [p. 27]

187 Costume design for the Devil
Pencil on paper, 41.6 × 28.3 cm [p. 28]

188 Costume design for Yakov at Home
Pencil on paper, 41.6 × 28.3 cm [p. 28]

189 Costume design for an Angel
Pencil and watercolor on paper,
44 × 32 cm

Alexander Vesnin
Yurevets, Volga Province
1883–1959 Moscow

L'Annonce faite à Marie (The Tidings
Brought to Mary) (mystery)
Author: Paul Claudel
Director: Alexander Tairov
Premiere: 16 November 1920,
Kamerny Theatre, Moscow

190 Costume design for an Old Man
Pencil, gouache, white lead paint, and
bronze paint on cardboard, 39.3 × 24.4 cm

191 Costume design for Violaine
Pencil, gouache, white lead paint, and
bronze paint on cardboard, 40 × 25.2 cm
[p. 91]

192 Costume design for Pierre de Craon
Pencil, gouache, and bronze paint on
cardboard, 39.9 × 24.8 cm

193 Costume design for the Mother
Pencil, gouache, and white lead paint on
cardboard, 39 × 25 cm

Phèdre (tragedy)
Author: Jean Racine, translated
by Valerii Briusov
Director: Alexander Tairov
Premiere: 8 February 1922,
Kamerny Theatre, Moscow
Note: This production was presented on
tour in Berlin (Deutsches Theatre) and
Paris (Théâtre des Champs-Elysées) in
February and March 1923.

194 Program cover design
Gouache, bronze paint, and pen and ink
on paper, 48 × 31.5 cm [p. 84]

195 Set design
Charcoal and tempera on cardboard,
43 × 63 cm

196 Costume design for Hippolytus
Pencil, gouache, and bronze and silver
paint on paper, 52.3 × 32.9 cm

197 Costume design for Phèdre
Pencil, gouache, and bronze paint on paper
affixed to cardboard, 58 × 38 cm [p. 123]

The Man Who Was Thursday (drama)
Author: adapted from G. K. Chesterson
by Gleb Krzhizhanovsky
Director: Alexander Tairov
Premiere: 6 December 1923,
Kamerny Theatre, Moscow

198 Costume design for Wednesday
Pencil and watercolor on paper,
39.3 × 27.2 cm [p. 124]

199 Costume design for Thursday
Pencil and paper collage on plywood,
43.8 × 29.1 cm

200 Costume design for a Woman
Pencil, tempera, white lead paint, brush
and india ink, and collage on paper,
39.5 × 27.5 cm [p. 124]

201 Costume design for a Woman
Tempera, charcoal, white lead paint, and
brush and india ink on paper,
39.9 × 27.4 cm

The Struggle and Victory of the Soviets
(see no. 136)

Konstantin Vialov
Moscow 1900–1976 Moscow

Unidentified production

202 Sketch of a maquette for
an unrealized Heroic Revolutionary
play, 1922
Pencil, pen and india ink, and brush and
india ink on paper affixed to cardboard,
22.8 × 17.8 cm

The Camorra of Seville
Director: Evgenii Prosvetov
Premiere: 1923, Theatre of the
Revolutionary Military Soviet, Moscow
Note: Although the Soviet critic Vladimir
Kostin refers to a production of *The
Camorra of Seville* in a "studio from which
would later grow the Central Theatre of
the Red Army," the standard reference
books on the history of Soviet theatre
make no mention of this production or
of a play of this name.

203 Costume design for a Bandit
Pencil, watercolor, and collage on paper,
33.5 × 23.8 cm [front cover]

204 Costume design for a Tobacconist
Pencil, watercolor, pen and india ink,
brush and india ink, and collage on paper,
33.7 × 23.6 cm

Stenka Razin (play)
Author: Vasilii Kamensky
Director: Valerii Bebutov
Premiere: 6 February 1924,
Theatre of Revolution, Moscow

205 Costume design for Stenka Razin
Watercolor, pen and india ink, brush and
india ink, and collage on paper,
32.7 × 23 cm [p. 81]

Georgii Yakulov
Tiflis (Tbilisi) 1882–1928 Erevan

Princess Brambilla (capriccio)
Author: after E. T. A. Hoffmann
Director: Alexander Tairov
Music: Henri Fortier
Premiere: 4 May 1920,
Kamerny Theatre, Moscow
Note: Georgii Yakulov also performed
in this production.

206 Set design
Pencil, watercolor, gouache, and white
lead paint on tracing paper affixed to
cardboard, 43.5 × 62.2 cm [p. 67]

207 Set design for act 4
Pencil and watercolor on paper,
31 × 47.1 cm

Mystery-Bouffe (parody of
a medieval mystery play)
Author: Vladimir Mayakovsky
Directors: Vsevolod Meyerhold
and Valerii Bebutov
Note: This production, scheduled for a
1920 premiere at the RSFSR (Russian
Soviet Federated Socialist Republic)
Theatre No. 1, Moscow, was not realized.
Meyerhold staged the play in 1921 with
designs by Viktor Kiselev, Vladimir
Khrakovsky, and Anton Lavinsky
(see nos. 105–107).

208 Set design, 1920
Pencil, watercolor, and bronze and silver
paint on tracing paper, 36.2 × 41.2 cm

Sergei Yutkevich
St. Petersburg 1904–1985 Moscow

Carnaval (ballet)
Music: Robert Schumann
Choreography: Kasian Goleizovsky
Producing organization: Chamber Ballet
Premiere: 1921, Moscow

209 Set design
Pencil, watercolor, and collage on paper,
30 × 37.8 cm
Collection Goleizovsky Family, Moscow

Good Treatment for Horses
(theatrical revue)
Author: Vladimir Mass, after
a poem by Vladimir Mayakovsky
Director: Nikolai Foregger
Music: Matvei Blanter
Choreography: Nikolai Foregger
Premiere: January 1922,
the Foregger Workshop (MASTFOR)
Note: Sergei Eisenstein also designed
costumes for this production
(see nos. 18–21).

210 Costume design for
the dancer Ludmilla Semenova
Pencil, watercolor, pen and india ink,
and brush and india ink on paper,
32.8 × 22.5 cm [p. 63]

Index

Italicized numbers represent illustrated works.

Photo Credits

Photographs of works illustrated in the catalogue courtesy of the Bakhrushin State Central Theatrical Museum, Moscow, with the following exceptions: cat nos. 113–115—Leningrad State Museum of Theatrical and Musical Arts; cat. nos. 133, 136, 137—State Tretiakov Gallery, Moscow; cat. nos. 112, 138, 139, 145, 178, 183, 184, 194, Kolesnikov figs. 3–4—Henry Art Gallery, Seattle; Baer fig. 7—Tate Gallery, London; Bowlt fig. 1—Institute of Modern Russian Culture, Los Angeles; Bowlt fig. 6—T. Strizhenova, *Iz istroii sovetskogo kostiuma* (Moscow, 1972), 96; Nash fig. 1—J. Flam, *Matisse: The Man and His Art 1869–1918* (Ithaca: Cornell, 1986), 239, fig. 237; Nash fig. 2 —M. Chamot, *Goncharova: Stage Design and Paintings* (London: Oresko, 1979), 30, pl. 5; Nash fig. 4—J. Milner, *Vladimir Tatlin and the Russian Avant-Garde* (New Haven: Yale, 1984), 82, pl. 84; Nash fig. 5 —P. Hulten, *Futurismo & Futurismi* (Milan: Bompiani, 1986), 482; Nash fig. 7 —A. d'Harnoncourt, *Futurism and the International Avant-Garde* (Philadelphia Museum of Art, 1980), 16, fig. 6; Nash fig. 8—D. Robbins, *Albert Gleizes 1881–1953* (New York: The Solomon R. Guggenheim Museum, 1964), 18, fig. 3, cat. no. 46; Nash fig. 9—*Kazimir Malevich 1878–1935* (Los Angeles: The Armand Hammer Museum of Art and Cultural Center, 1990), 8, fig. 9; Nash fig. 10—Hulten, 453; Nash fig. 11—M.W. Martin, *Futurist Art and Theory 1909–1915* (Oxford: Clarendon Press, 1968), pl. 216; Souritz fig. 3—Jane Corkin Gallery, Toronto, and Fotofolio, New York; Souritz fig. 4—W.A. Propert, *The Russian Ballet 1921–1929* (London: John Lane, The Bodley Head Ltd, 1931); Misler fig. 1—R. Fülöp-Miller, *The Mind and Face of Bolshevism* (New York: Brentano, 1926); Misler fig. 2—Fülöp-Miller; Misler fig. 7—TsGALI; Misler fig. 8—W. Kandinsky, "Tanzcurven zu der tanzen der Palucca," *Kunstblatt*, 1926, no. 10; Misler fig. 9—TsGALI; Misler fig. 13—A. Rodchenko and V. Stepanova, *A Pageant of Youth* (Moscow: State Art Publishers, 1939); Misler fig. 14—E. Souritz, *Soviet Choreographers in the 1920s* (Durham: Duke, 1990), fig. 27.

Theatre in Revolution: Russian Avant-Garde Stage Design 1913–1935 was produced by the Publications Department of The Fine Arts Museums of San Francisco: Ann Heath Karlstrom, Director of Publications, and Karen Kevorkian, Editor.

The book was designed by Desne Border, San Francisco. Display type is Helvetica Black Condensed and text type is Sabon. Photocomposed by Mackenzie-Harris Corporation, San Francisco. Printed on 128 gsm matte paper by C&C Offset Printing Co. Ltd., Hong Kong, through Overseas Printing Corp., San Francisco.